Praise for *How I Got Into Sex...Ed*

"One of my favorite conversations with anyone who is even closely related to the field of sexuality education is to hear their story on how they actually got into 'sex ed.' We each have our own story, and there are very few repetitions because it is such a personal journey. This tome is that personal voyage reminding the reader of the passions, joys, and challenges of why we are in the exciting field of sex ed."

Konnie McCaffree
President
American Association of Sexuality
Educators, Counselors and Therapists

"What a pleasure it was to read these moving and sometimes funny essays. I am hard-pressed to pick a favorite since there are essays from people who've been in the field for decades (their insights were moving) and the freshness of those who are 'new' to the field. This is a great place to start a number of conversations such as 'Should I get into the field?' and 'Can I really make a difference?' I think anyone who reads this book will be able to answer both with a resounding yes. Congratulations!"

Lynn Barclay
President/CEO
American Sexual Health Association

*"**How I Got Into Sex...Ed** is a treasure! If you've ever wondered if this path was right for you or what it feels like to be a sex educator or how to get the right kinds of education, training, or opportunities to work as a sexuality education professional, this book is for you!"*

Debby Herbenick, PhD, MPH
Director, The Center for Sexual Health Promotion
Indiana University

D1475758

"What an entertaining and informative way to learn about the role of sexuality education in our lives. Each of these authors presents their unique entrée into this field in a brief, easy-to-read essay, and collectively they provide a tapestry of professional pathways and the role sex can play in our lives—professional lives, that is! A fun read."

Pat Paluzzi, CNM, DrPH
President/CEO
Healthy Teen Network

*"Sexuality educators are highly devoted to their profession, and they have individual paths to their career. **How I Got Into Sex...Ed** is an excellent and fascinating book that includes an impressive collection of stories about how a large number of sexuality educators initially got their inspiration to their favorite mission. This path has been full of surprises, fortunate coincidences, and excellent colleagues who inspired them to select a career that they have not regretted. They all seem to be grateful for this turning point in their lives, and they enjoy and love what they have been able to do since then. I persuade you to become acquainted with these stimulating stories."*

Osmo Kontula
Chair of Sexuality Education Committee
World Association for Sexual Health

How I Got Into Sex...Ed

Karen Rayne
Editor-in-Chief

Catherine Dukes and Bill Taverner
Associate Editors

This book was produced with generous support from contributors to The Center for Sex Education, the national education division of Planned Parenthood of Central and Greater Northern New Jersey, Inc.

Acknowledgements

From Karen
Thanks to each of you who contributed to this book. I feel blessed to have read each of your stories and to know a piece of you.

Thanks to my daughters.

And thank you to my co-editors, Bill Taverner and Cat Dukes, and to Jeffrey Anthony and the Executive Planning Team for the 2013 National Sex Ed Conference. Each of you is fantastic, and I'm grateful to call you friends.

From Cat
It has been such an honor to be part of this project. I'm so very grateful to have had the opportunity to work with sex ed giants Bill Taverner and Karen Rayne during the planning of the 2013 National Sex Ed Conference and now this extraordinary e-book. I also want to thank Jeffrey Anthony, the 2013 Conference Planning Team, and all the incredible sex educators who contributed their powerful stories to this book. Thanks to my husband, Tim, and our three children for your love and support. I'd also like to thank the extraordinarily talented team at Planned Parenthood of Delaware's Sexuality Education Training Institute — Sandra Greenfield, Bryce Komaroff, Kate Randall, and Rebecca Roberts. Working with such an incredible team and seeing the work you do in sex education with youth, adults, parents, and professionals inspires me every day.

From Bill
I'm grateful to have had the opportunity to work with Karen and Cat on this book. How fortunate we are to have had so many colleagues share their stories with us! Many thanks to major supporters of The Center for Sex Education who made this book — and all our work — possible: Barbara E. Bunting, Alexandra and Eric J. Schoenberg, Pat Stover, Naida S. Wharton, and Raymond and Nora Wong.

Table of Contents

Preface

Eric J. Schoenberg

MBA, MSE, PhD

Franklin Lakes, NJ

PROFESSIONAL LIFE
Current workplace: Adjunct Associate Professor, New York University/Stern School of Business
Favorite workplace: Board of Directors, Planned Parenthood of Central and Greater Northern New Jersey

How I Got Into Sex...Ed

I am not a sex educator myself, but I have become a passionate supporter of sex education for a simple reason: While many of the vast problems facing humans have no easy solutions, and perhaps no hard solutions either, I believe we could make enormous progress if we could simply ensure that every child born is a wanted child. Sure, sex education *also* enhances people's lives, prevents disease, and promotes the formation of stable and happy families, but providing everybody with the knowledge necessary to choose for themselves the right time to procreate would be a great advancement for humanity, and I salute those educators who have devoted their careers to help making that happen.

Introduction

This book was born out of the excitement among Bill Taverner, Cat Dukes, and myself when we saw the outstanding roster of speakers coming to the 2013 National Sex Ed Conference. We wanted to hear from each of them about the many and varied experiences that brought them into the field of sexuality education.

The themes that emerged from this collection of stories are as familiar to me as my own path. Sexuality educators seem to stumble onto their profession, but once there, they become passionately devoted. Many sex educators consider their job their calling — something deeper than just a job they do for 40 hours a week in order to afford the rest of their lives.

The stories that were submitted to us are so fabulous, so deep and personal. Some of the authors are well-known, others are just starting out in the field. What they all have in common is passion for this line of work.

I hope that the deep dedication and enthusiasm of sexuality educators is what you get from reading this collection of personal essays. Whatever led these educators to their path, whether it was a history of trauma, self-exploration, family conversations, exceptionally high- or low-quality sexuality education, or some other experience, we want to share their professional excitement and insights with you.

The stories are arranged in alphabetical order by last name. You may approach the book in alphabetical order — from Carole Adamsbaum to Mara Yacobi — to be sure that you catch every story. Some of the authors may surprise you! Or perhaps you might seek out the educators you know and then read back through the ones who are new to you. Or you may open at random and let your reading flow by chance!

Regardless of how you approach these wonderful stories, we're glad you're here to share them!

Karen Rayne, PhD
Editor-in-Chief

Carole Adamsbaum

RN, MA
NJ Mental Health Screener, Teacher Certification,
AASECT Sexuality Educator

Denville, NJ

PROFESSIONAL LIFE
Current workplace: St. Clare's Hospital, Denville, NJ
First workplace: Parsippany Hills High School, Parsippany, NJ
Favorite workplace: Parsippany Hills High School, Parsippany, NJ

EDUCATIONAL LIFE
Favorite course: Not a formal academic course, but the ASET retreats
Least favorite course: General teacher certification courses

TEACHING LIFE
Favorite topic to teach: Talking to teens about being better sexuality educators for their children
Most challenging topic to teach: Sexuality and religion

INSPIRATIONS
Sex educator: Peggy Brick (and many others)
Book: *Guide to Getting It On* by Paul Joannides

How I Got Into Sex...Ed

My earliest memories all contain thoughts of being a nurse. My vision came complete with crisp, white uniforms and lifesaving heroics. These dreams all started with the arrival of the visiting nurse when my sister contracted polio. I swear I heard superhero theme music whenever she walked through the door! My nursing goal was cemented by reading the entire Cherry Ames series (twice). So, in 1975, how did I end up in front of a classroom filled with bored-faced teens???

To my mind, I had secured a plum position. I was a health teacher in my own school district. At last, my kids and I would have the same days off. I was making a decent salary, and I had a pension and some job security. WOW! I knew enough about nutrition, first aid, and drug and alcohol use to write lesson plans and lecture at students. Sadly, weeks later, I was still in front of a classroom full of disinterested, fidgety teens.

It was at this juncture that serendipity interceded with a series of events that changed my entire career. Because I was a nurse, my students assumed I was a good source of information about sexuality. Little did they know that in four years of nursing school, the word *sex* had never been uttered, even when we studied obstetrics and gynecology! I knew how to deliver a baby but next to nothing about the emotional and physical gymnastics that came beforehand. I knew after that first question that I had to find a book, a class, some help.

(Sound the drums!) Planned Parenthood to the rescue! I visited their education department in Morristown, NJ, and honestly confessed to my lack of knowledge. I knew even then that it was not just for my students. It was for me. I realized that this was a subject about which I wanted to feel educated and confident. The agency was (and is) wonderful. They never made me feel stupid, and they were able to point me in the right direction.

My luck continued. I found a Unitarian Universalist program called "About Your Sexuality," held in Belle Mead, NJ, with a retreat at a monastery on the Hudson River. It certainly took me outside of my comfort zone! The sessions were life changing. I definitely learned about sexuality, but I also learned about teaching, real teaching. Lecture was only one facet of education, and not a very interesting one. I now had role-playing, brainstorming, slang, music, question boxes, journals, advertising, and room for my own ideas. From that point on, I not only had a better knowledge base in sexuality, but I was also a better teacher and I knew so much more about myself. I was hooked on sex!

However, the revelation was not instantaneous. I vividly remember feeling so alone and uneasy at that monastery. We were brainstorming slang terms for the words at the top of a posted sheet of newsprint. I looked them over and smiled because I knew there was someone else in the room who came from Brooklyn. On the sheet titled "Condom" someone had written "Coney Island Whitefish." Talk about an ice-breaker!

Like Hansel and Gretel, I discovered a path of breadcrumbs. Each day led to more critical knowledge and the inner circles of sexuality education. I discovered the Sex Information and Education Council of the United States (SIECUS). [1] I researched, I called, I listened, and I joined. AASECT came into my purview with meetings, conventions, and workshops. (Join AASECT and see the USA!) There is a way to become a Certified Sexuality Educator, they said, and I did.

I met people. Networking is what really inspired me. I had finally found a career; I was on the right path. I continue to marvel at my fellow sex educators' level of talent, imagination, knowledge, and willingness to share.

I know now that sexuality education is a process. You are always evolving. There are always new things to learn, new methods of presenting material, new educators to meet. The truth is, I have not *become* a sexuality educator; I am still in the process. There have been a few indicators along the way that have bolstered my confidence. For example, there was the day a main-office school secretary told me that any mail with the word "sex" on it was placed in my mailbox. I am not sure she realized how good that felt to me. There was the day the superintendent of schools came to me with a copy of my recent purchase order in hand. She was questioning the appropriateness of my requisition for a vibrator. I assured her that the dental vibrator was going to be used for pouring dental molds. Just the fact that she was willing to discuss it before I clarified was her way of saying she respected my knowledge and judgment.

I instituted weekly journals for my seniors. I spent many hours reading, commenting, and answering questions, and I was rewarded with great feedback. One particularly memorable young man offered this insight during class discussion: "Mrs. A, your name comes up more often in the back seat of my car than my penis." OMG, I've made it!

Jeffrey W. Anthony

Certified Health Educator

Morristown, NJ

PROFESSIONAL LIFE
Current workplace: The Center for Sex Education (CSE, Morristown, NJ
First workplace: Rutgers, The State University of New Jersey, New Brunswick, NJ
Favorite workplace: I plead the Fifth.

EDUCATIONAL LIFE
Favorite course: Health and Social Justice
Least favorite course: Health and Social Justice

TEACHING LIFE
Favorite topic to teach: Anything where questions are asked and it is a dialogue, not bloviating and didactic lecturing
Most challenging topic to teach: Identity and privilege

INSPIRATIONS
Sex educator: Dr. Francesca Maresca

NATIONAL SEX ED CONFERENCE
Title of presentation: *I'm the Registrar. Did you register?*

How I Got Into Sex...Ed

Once upon a time, there was a boy who needed to know everything. And he thought he did. And then things happened, and he didn't have the answers as to why.

I think we all realize that the boy I'm talking about is Harry Potter.

Okay. It's me. But I do look like him.

From an early age, circa 3rd grade, I was labeled as "gay" without having any context of that meaning. Naturally, I felt shunned and different, and befriended the teachers, who were generally much kinder individuals. Not always.

Skip ahead a few years to high school, though keeping with the general concept of feeling like an outcast. We had health class. I grew up in Jersey, so we had a great program, right? Right....

My health ed teachers were not bad people; they were just phys ed teachers who had taken anatomy, so naturally they were assigned to teach sex ed. I can still remember my teacher blushing when saying the word "penis." Naturally, because I was... am... a know-it-all, I knew anatomy inside and out (ha!), and so I ended up teaching a few lessons to my classmates.

But the real lesson I learned was fear. It wasn't fear of STIs or pregnancy, but of dying alone.

We had a guest speaker who spoke of the late 80s with great fondness and remorse. I can still remember the sadness in his eyes. We'll call him Jack. Jack survived "GRID"[2] and was living with AIDS. I remember hearing the pain in his voice. I remember that all the other students made sure to give him a clear and wide berth when leaving the classroom.

I gave him a hug. And I was shunned for several days or maybe weeks. I really have no idea know long it was, since being shunned was pretty much the norm for me.

I became afraid of dying alone. I was coming to terms with the fact that I was gay.

A little later in high school, I had my trust violated in a rather serious way, leaving me feeling all the more alone.

I buried my emotions, came out to friends, and learned everything I could, about anything that held my interest long enough. A productive coping mechanism, at least. I went to Rutgers University to become a genetic engineer, and then I took a Rutgers chemistry class...let's just say that having a PhD in chemistry should be a prerequisite for that class. I floundered and ended up being academically expelled from Rutgers, which was both the greatest failure of my life and the best thing that ever happened to me. As part of the process of facilitating my return, I shifted my focus to public health.

My wandering mind seized on the topic. I found public health to be absolutely fascinating and amazing. I took every class I could as a nonmatriculated public health major. Then I took Health Program Evaluation, followed by yet another health-related class. Finally, I found myself in Sexual Health Advocacy. That was a jump into my own reflecting pool, and I didn't like what I saw.

Among other things, I had to confront my emotional repression and protective barriers. I was clinically depressed. My personal growth and healing had stagnated. (Well, it had actually never really happened.)

That summer I went to a retreat for peer educators. It was like a demolition crew brought down all my industrial-strength walls. It made me ripe to learn, grow, and heal.

Then I took Health and Social Justice with Dr. Francesca Maresca, who had been my professor for all the previously mentioned public health classes. That was my best and worst class. That's where I learned about my privilege — what my white cis-gendered male identity affords me — both in spite of my own suffering and in the context of my suffering. All the lessons learned were hard ones. I experienced cognitive dissonance over and over again. It's hard to make the distinction between hearing "you are not persecuted because of your identity" and "your experiences don't matter because of your identity"; the latter, of course, is not the point of understanding privilege.

However, learning from Francesca and her colleague Liz Amaya-Fernandez, I was able to put myself in an environment of support, growth, and, most importantly, healing.

So, given this long preamble and backstory, how *did* I get into sex ed? In taking the sexual health advocacy class, I was trained to be a peer educator. I was trained to go into residence halls and to Greek Life organizations and provide sexuality programs. It was always so much fun listening to the questions. I also trained to be part of the educational theater peer education group, greatly expanding how I taught sex education.

During the remainder of my undergraduate career at Rutgers, I pursued my Health Education Certificate, and eventually I will become a Certified Health Education Specialist.

Working with Liz, I had the opportunity to volunteer with the CFLE. I worked with Bill Taverner on social media projects, and then the National Sex Ed Conference. And then the CFLE was hiring, so I applied, and I was hired.

And that's how I got into sex ed...a series of unfortunate events that were extremely fortunate for me. I don't know how much of the "how" is important. What's more critical is the "why." Why do I do it? Growing up, I didn't always have a hand out to pull me up. In fact, I can think of only a few individuals who gave me their hands. Now I strive to be a person who is there to help others up when they are looking for a hand.

Lauren Barineau

MPH, CHES

Atlanta, GA

PROFESSIONAL LIFE

Current workplace: Georgia Campaign for Adolescent Power and Potential (GCAPP), Atlanta, GA

First workplace: As an Emory graduate student, I volunteered with the Pipeline Program run by Emory's Center for Science Education in Atlanta, GA. This innovative program connected medical students, pre-med undergraduates, and high school students through teaching and mentorship. The high school students had an opportunity to learn about all aspects of health and the human body from Emory-based mentors and build relationships with these mentors to support them throughout their college and medical school admissions process. My role was to coordinate a health fair with the high school seniors, which served as a culminating experience through which they could share their knowledge with others. It was refreshing and inspiring to watch teens identify and explore public health concepts around which to design health fair booths, and to see them excitedly create interactive ways to disseminate health information to their peers.

Favorite workplace: I'm a current member of the 2013 class of the Georgia Women's Policy Institute (GWPI), an initiative of the nonpartisan advocacy group, Georgia Women for a Change in Atlanta, GA. I've had the opportunity to learn about the legislative process, identify a policy gap that would improve the lives of women and children, and then draft and advocate for the policy change. The GWPI has given me an appreciation of how systemic social change can be more successfully achieved through the creation of supportive policies and the ways in which women can play a unique role in shaping the health and well-being of Georgia's citizens through advocacy.

EDUCATIONAL LIFE

Favorite course: In my first year of graduate school, I took History of Public Health at the Rollins School of Public Health. This survey course for public health students traced the history of our field through some of its most critical and defining moments including germ theory, smallpox eradication, the vaccination debate, and breast cancer screening. It left me with a deep appreciation for the rapid development of our field, the unique constraints related to ensuring the health of the public, and the importance of context and community in our work.

Least favorite course: Biostatistics. Need I say anything else?

TEACHING LIFE

Favorite topic to teach: As a training and technical assistance coordinator, my work primarily focuses on training teachers and other facilitators in the core elements of effective sex education, one of which is answering difficult questions from students. I find some sex educators feel nervous about the types of questions teens will ask and how to answer them appropriately. Training teachers to identify various question types, providing a formula for responding to questions in a values-neutral and respectful way, and practicing this skill through role-play is one of the most rewarding elements of training. I also enjoy watching and hearing the reactions from teachers when we introduce this topic by sharing some of the most outrageous questions we've ever been asked!

Most challenging topic to teach: In my role as a 7th- and 8th-grade sexual health educator, I was surprised to realize how often the topic of pornography comes up in class. Whether it's a question about porn or a student refers to it as a response to a discussion question, I sometimes struggle to come up with an age-appropriate and honest answer. As pornography becomes increasingly accessible and extreme, I am hoping for additional resources and strategies to effectively address pornography and its relationship to healthy sexuality in the sex ed classroom.

<u>**INSPIRATIONS**</u>

Sex educator: I first met Nora Gelperin by attending Training Institute in Sexual Health (TISHE) and through my work on the Working to Institutionalize Sex Education (WISE) project in Georgia. Nora is exceptionally warm and friendly in her professional relationships, and she is an experienced, exemplary trainer. I am continually impressed by her creative ideas for introducing and engaging trainees in new material and her ability to skillfully add meaning to an activity through excellent group processing. I aspire to one day be as confident and knowledgeable as Nora in my role as a trainer.

Book: As a teen, I loved reading and rereading *Girltalk* by Carol Weston and *The Period Book* by Karen Gravelle, both of which have continued to be revised and republished. Using a book as a tool can be a great way to introduce or elaborate on certain topics when engaging young people in conversations about sex and relationships.

NATIONAL SEX ED CONFERENCE

Title of presentation: *They Said What?!: Exploring Self-Disclosure as Sexuality Educators*

Presentation description: Being faced with a choice to share personal information is something we encounter every day as sexuality educators. This workshop explores the pros and cons of self-disclosure in the sexuality classroom, highlights guidelines for sharing in ways that enhance learning, and helps you determine how much is too much to say.

How I Got Into Sex...Ed

Growing up, my family dynamic was one of open dialogue, which sometimes included typically taboo subjects such as sex. One specific discussion that I believe directly shaped my understanding of sexuality comes to mind as having led me to the field of sexual health.

My adolescent brother and I were trapped in the car on a family road trip, and my mom sensed an opportunity. She said,

"You know, your dad and I really hope that when you're older and in a healthy relationship, you have good sex." We both groaned and rolled our eyes; this wasn't the first time my parents had initiated conversations to ask our opinions and answer questions about sex. But this time, the message was clearly different. This conversation wasn't just about puberty or the meaning of slang words, but a suggestion, an expectation even, that sex was supposed to be *good*. Knowing we couldn't escape the car, my mom went on to explain that she hoped my brother and I would choose to wait until after high school to have sex because she felt that would give us the time to discover who we were as individuals, and as a result, find partners with whom we could develop strong relationships. It was important to my parents that we were educated about sex and that we considered all sexual health risks and were thoughtful about physical and emotional consequences. She emphasized that we should seek relationships in which we were able to make choices about sex without being pressured. "When you find those relationships," she continued, "I hope you feel comfortable and safe enough to communicate with your partner about sex, which will eventually lead to good sex. Sex is a really important and fun part of a relationship." Although we were a bit embarrassed at the time, my brother and I listened quietly and nodded along in the backseat. As I grew into adulthood, it became a conversation that has stayed with me.

It wasn't until I was in college that I realized my experience with my parents was unique. I just assumed that everyone grew up in a family like mine that openly discussed body parts and changes, talked about healthy relationships and what I should expect from a partner, and asked and answered questions about sex and sexuality. I was genuinely surprised to learn that many of my peers never, ever talked with their parents about sex, and if they did, their parents wouldn't have acknowledged that sex was, dare I say, *enjoyable*! I began to realize how our cultural nervousness about sex was preventing children and teens from hearing any positive messages about sex and sexuality from some of the most trusted adults in their lives.

My choice to enter the field of sexual health education was a direct result of my parents' honesty and their message that sex is a healthy part of mutually respectful and caring relationships and that with the right partner, sex could and should feel good. My parents purposefully shared their values around sexual activity and their expectations of healthy relationships so that I could develop an understanding of the context around sexuality, not just the mechanics of anatomy. I can see the impact of my parents' choice to communicate using a sex-positive approach reflected in my comfort when talking about healthy sexual decision making both professionally and personally. At a sexual health curriculum training, I was once asked how I became so comfortable talking about "this stuff" with strangers. When I gave the question some thought, I realized that my ease came from talking about sex early, often, and openly with trusted adults in my life.

I'm committed to promoting the value of using a sex-positive approach in family communication about sexuality. If children and teens begin to hear messages about sex and relationships in a way that acknowledges that they are healthy parts of personhood, they will be more comfortable talking about sex and can better avoid the consequences of risky sexual behavior. It is essential that these messages not only come from families, but also from schools, houses of worship, and other youth-serving agencies so that healthy and age-appropriate messages about sex are reinforced in every aspect of our communities. I'll continue to work in the field of sexual health to train parents, families, teachers, and other trusted adults in ways to effectively initiate conversations so that all young people have opportunities to receive healthy, positive messages about sex. My hope is that this work will spark families and teens to ask one question, begin one conversation, or share one value about sex with each other as the start of a journey toward open communication about sexuality.

Brandy Barnett
MS

Atlanta, GA

PROFESSIONAL LIFE
Current workplace: Georgia Campaign for Adolescent Power & Potential (GCAPP) — Atlanta, GA
First workplace: Boys & Girls Clubs of Northwest Georgia, Rome, Georgia (Abstinence Grant Coordinator/Project Director)
Favorite workplace: GCAPP

EDUCATIONAL LIFE
Favorite course: Introduction to Health Promotion
Least favorite course: Accounting

TEACHING LIFE
Favorite topic to teach: Reproductive Anatomy
Most challenging topic to teach: Effective communication using "I" statements

INSPIRATIONS
Sex educator: My mother (not by profession, but she was my first and most influential sex educator)

NATIONAL SEX ED CONFERENCE
Title of presentation: *STDs? Keeping It "100" and Less Einstein!*
Presentation description: Working with adolescents in STD education and prevention can be extremely rewarding, but it is not without its challenges. Sexuality educators typically focus on presenting medically accurate information, but simplifying the message helps youth grasp the key concepts. Learn practical strategies for thinking more like an adolescent and less like an educator to deliver your message effectively. Keep it "100"...that means keep it real (real simple)!

How I Got Into Sex...Ed

I am a trainer and technical assistance coordinator, and I also teach sex education to adolescents and provide workshops for parents of adolescents on effective communication about sexuality. I work in the state of Georgia with the Georgia Campaign for Adolescent Power & Potential (GCAPP). If someone had asked me 10 years ago if this was the path my career would take, I either would have laughed or had a slight heart attack (nothing too severe, I was too young and fabulous to perish so early).

The "Talk"

I suppose my introduction to sex education officially started when I was in middle school. The first real conversations about growing up, love, dating, and sex that I remember having occurred with my mom. Of course, friends and older relatives were talking, but this talk was different. My mother sat my twin sister and me down on her bed for "the puberty talk." I was initially freaked out about what to expect during puberty, but then she went on to discuss sex. Now, I had some idea about the topic, but boy, oh boy, she threw us a curve ball! She told us things the pastor never told us, information other parents weren't telling their kids, and definitely it wasn't what our friends were saying about sex. This discussion consisted of everything from puberty, to sex, to responsibility, but ultimately culminated with my mother saying, "I won't be mad if you decide to have sex. I prefer that you wait until you're married or at least until you're an adult, but if you decide to have sex before then PLEASE come and talk to me before you do. I won't pretend it will never happen. Just knowing we can talk through it together will mean the world to me." Just to know my mother loved me enough to increase my awareness, discuss the realities of getting involved in a sexual relationship, how to be protected, and ultimately to know I had her support spoke volumes! After this conversation, I knew I had a true advocate who would be honest with me for my safety. It was the type of support and advocacy I needed to make the best choices for me and my future, not the choices others were making or trying to pressure me into making. I honestly believe my mother's transparency is the reason I chose responsibility over doing what I thought everyone else was doing. It kept me from having to experience the consequences of getting involved in unhealthy behaviors and allowed me to turn my attention to focusing on my future goals and enjoying my youth.

My mommy (that is how I address her) did not have all the answers, and she never claimed she did. Although straightforward and outspoken, she still had very strict and clear expectations regarding when to engage in sex. More importantly, she was *honest* and very transparent about the realities of peer and partner pressure and the likelihood that I would one day want a connection with a partner, and she expressed that teens and young adults are more than capable of making healthy choices if given the tools. She even took my sister and me to the "town clinic" (a town in rural Georgia reminiscent of *The Little House on the Prairie,* "90s edition") to discuss birth control options with the physician if ever we wanted it. She wasn't encouraging sex at all; she made her expectations and desires very clear — she preferred that we delay having sex, but she knew that the clinic was a resource we needed to know about and have access to. This was in no way typical of a small-town, spiritually minded parent! She was extraordinary!

My mother, a single parent, provided love and support regardless of our choices, which made the possibility of being healthy and responsible more realistic to me. Most importantly, her openness helped me realize that parental expectations should be made clear and sex is not something to be covered up by lies or silence, but brought to light in love. These conversations helped me to learn how to value myself as a young woman and to expect to be respected. I also realized over the years that not every young person was as fortunate as me to have such conversations with a loving and trusted adult.

The "Purpose with a Passion"

Ultimately, my professional introduction into sexuality education did not begin until my final year of my Master of Health Promotion program. I had always envisioned myself becoming a professional in sports medicine/athletic training, a collegiate track and field coach, or even owning a chain of fitness centers, or perhaps working in a university health center, but destiny had other plans. I was assigned a presentation for a health promotion course, and decided to focus on STD and HIV/AIDS education and prevention for women of color. My goal was to empower women to take charge of their own sexual health through correct and consistent use of condoms and negotiating condom use or abstinence with a partner. I cannot even remember how well I performed on the presentation, but the process sparked a keen interest in behavioral change in communities of color.

Even after gaining this new experience, I envisioned my career would be working with college-aged students or adults, and at first I vehemently resisted working directly with adolescents. After having worked with pre-teens and teens in camps and as a coach, I was ready for something different. However, I kept being drawn back into work with adolescents, primarily because I saw opportunities to provide information to help them make healthy choices beyond "Don't drink and drive" and "Just say No" to whatever it is *no* is supposed to stop. I was aware youth needed more information; information like what my mom and other trusted adults gave me. Young people are impressionable and eager to learn, but are often confused about how to deal with their changing bodies, emotions, and relationships. Yet, no one would dare take them by the hand and give them honest and medically accurate information that could potentially save their lives. Parents did not know what to say except "Don't bring a baby home"; schools were ignoring the issues, and communities pretended that only a certain type of kid has sex or gets pregnant! I knew the reality: Those who were uninformed were most at risk.

I would like to think I am honoring my mother's legacy when I teach sex education. I want to convey that youth can enjoy being young, vibrant, and full of potential, but they deserve accurate information and guidance so that they can be responsible as well. I would also like to think that I am helping young people to understand they are more than just a statistic in a database or a product of their environment — they are unique and worthy of every opportunity afforded to them to let their individual light shine. I teach sex education, not because I believe I am brilliant or someone who is particularly spectacular in this field, but because I was once in a young person's shoes; had my mother not taken ownership of her responsibility as a caring parent and included sexuality in our ongoing conversations, it is frightening to imagine what my life could have been. It does not take an academic scholar, a PhD, or a physician to teach sex education. It takes a willingness to step outside the box, to eschew being comfortable, to get real, and to give adolescents the tools they need to succeed. My mom, with no degree or professional certification in health or sexuality education, taught me more than any professor, college course, research findings, or cohort in the field could have. She taught me empathy, understanding, and the impact of good information.

Even today my mom will say she is proud of what I am doing. She is pleased to know that someone is trying to help young people think through their choices and take ownership of their actions. Though I have thanked her for her support over the years on numerous occasions, I doubt she understands just how influential she has been and how that has created a trickle-down effect. She educated me, I educate others, and maybe those I reach will continue imparting knowledge down the line. Thanks, Mommy!

Rachel Billowitz

MPH

Flagstaff, AZ

PROFESSIONAL LIFE
Current workplace: Northern Arizona University and North Country HealthCare, Flagstaff, AZ
First workplace: Intern, Planned Parenthood, St. Paul, MN
Favorite workplace: Sexual Health Education Consultant, North Country HealthCare, Flagstaff, AZ

EDUCATIONAL LIFE
Favorite course: Women, Health, and Reproduction at Macalester College, St. Paul, MN

TEACHING LIFE
Favorite topic to teach: Sexual Decision-Making
Most challenging topic to teach: Sexual Assault Prevention

INSPIRATIONS
Sex educator: Heather Corinna
Book: Robie Harris's books

NATIONAL SEX ED CONFERENCE
Title of presentation: *Developing Parent-Child Communication Programs to Support Sexual Health*
Presentation description: Research indicates that open communication about sexuality between parents/guardians and their children can increase self-esteem and help young people better protect their sexual health. Because parents/guardians are often unsure of how to begin the conversation or what to say, professional sexuality educators can offer Parent-Child Communication (PCC) programs in their communities to encourage dialogue. Educators who wish to offer such programs often face challenges when planning and offering them, such as reaching diverse audiences, encouraging attendance, and selecting appropriate

methodologies. This workshop is designed to empower educators to feel confident in their ability to plan and facilitate PCC programs.

How I Got Into Sex...Ed

I grew up in a liberal, progressive family, where we talked openly about current events and politics. My parents were both medical providers, and I was comfortable talking to them about bodies, sex, and health. I had friends in high school who experienced unplanned pregnancies, sexual assault, and unhealthy relationships, and I was acutely aware of issues of gender, sexism, and women's rights.

When I arrived at college, I knew enough about patriarchy to know that I wanted to find a way to kick its ass. I went to Macalester College in Minnesota, a liberal arts school where social activism was the norm. I found a student group called People for Reproductive Rights Organized (PRRO). These women and men weren't just sitting around drinking coffee and deconstructing the dominant paradigm; no, they were shakin' it up. Together we worked on behalf of pro-choice candidates, we offered peer education about sexual health on campus, and we did clinic defense and patient escort work.

I attended college at a time when Operation Rescue was very active around the country. (They're now called Operation Save America.) This anti-choice group is very militant in preventing women from accessing legal medical services, namely, abortion services. In the early to mid-90s, they led mass protests at clinics that offered abortions, and harassed and intimated women as they tried to enter the clinics. They also blocked clinic entrances by chaining or gluing themselves to the clinic doors, and they would lay down across the entrances of parking lots, making it impossible for patients to enter the clinic property. PRRO would go to clinics around the Twin Cities and escort patients from their cars into the clinics. One

30

day we heard about a clinic in rural Wisconsin that was being targeted for a big protest by Operation Rescue, so we piled into a van and drove there to offer support to the clinic staff and the patients. There were about 400 people assembled, roughly 200 people on each side. The pro-choicers got there first, at 5:30 am, so we made two concentric circles, two layers of a human chain, all the way around the perimeter of the building. We only broke the circle to let patients and escorts in. There was a preacher there, yelling at us, literally thumping his Bible, and he was so close to me that when he shouted, little bits of spit flew out of his mouth and landed on my check. I couldn't move. I couldn't let get go and break the chain to wipe it off. So I had to stand there, and I kept chanting, "This clinic stays open! This clinic stays open!"

In that moment something clicked for me: I thought, "This is important stuff. Women should have access to legal medical services. This is worth getting spit on. I'm gonna fight for this for a long time."

After college, I worked as a healthcare assistant and abortion counselor in three different clinics. It was emotionally draining work, and there was always the threat of risk to my personal safety. I did the work because of the women who I had the privilege of meeting there. I met some amazingly strong women, and it was an honor to be involved in such a pivotal day in their lives. I counseled women about informed consent, educated them about birth control for the future, and held their hands during the procedure. In talking with them, I heard recurrent themes: a lack of understanding about physiology and fertility, a lack of understanding about how birth control works or how to use it correctly, a lack of money to pay for birth control, as well as tales of failed birth control, domestic violence, and coerced sex. I heard the range of emotions that women experienced: guilt, shame, embarrassment, grief, numbness, relief. I saw a lot of relief on women's faces when it was done. Despite the common threads, their stories were unique, and there were always nuances to the story that I would never be privy to.

My experiences working in abortion clinics confirmed my belief that abortion will always need to be safe and legal. I began to wonder, "How can I help to reduce the number of women who are facing unplanned pregnancies in the first place?" I went to graduate school and earned a Master of Public Health degree, with an emphasis in health education. I had volunteered with Planned Parenthood throughout graduate school, and four months after completing my program, a health educator position opened. I applied for it, was hired, and began my career in sexual health education.

At first I naively thought that this work would be easier to do. Clearly, both sides of the abortion debate could agree on prevention, right? WRONG! I have faced numerous barriers in this work, including lack of funding. This is what is most frustrating to me: The very people who want to restrict access to abortion are the same people who want to restrict access to medically accurate education and family planning services.

Despite frustrations and challenges, I have stayed with the job because I believe in the power of embracing sexuality as part of our humanity. I believe teaching sex ed is a way of promoting social justice. As an educator in northern Arizona for the past 12 years, I've had the joy of teaching thousands of students. I have taught in a variety of settings, including schools, community groups, churches, detention centers, group homes, and shelters. I love my job. I love being the one who talks about topics that most people want to avoid. I love helping people understand that they deserve to be healthy and happy, and providing a place for them to explore how to do that. Someone at a conference last year asked me why I teach sex ed, and that got me thinking, so I wrote this piece:

Why I Teach Sex Ed

For many reasons...

For many people...

For Katie, who visibly relaxed in a puberty education class when I explained that menstrual blood can be brown and not red, and that one breast is often slightly larger than the other.

For Julia, who became pregnant at 14, then miscarried after her "boyfriend" beat her up when she told him the news.

For Caleb, who sat silently during the class on homophobia and how to be an ally, then whispered a quiet "thank you" on his way out the door at the end of class.

For Kevin, who asked if it was okay NOT to masturbate.

For Juanita, who was upset that "vaginal fluids" didn't have a more special name, and suggested we call them "super fun vagina juices."

For Matt, who shared with me his idea for a brainstorm activity that asked boys to think of how they can use their strength in nonviolent ways, and for all the boys who gave examples such as "shovel snow for your neighbor" and "help your mom carry in the groceries" when I later led the activity in class.

For Melissa, who prepared her peer education mock presentation on how to perform breast self-exams in honor of her grandmother, who died of breast cancer.

For the person who asked, via the anonymous question box, if putting Skittles inside the vagina after intercourse would work as contraception.

For Rebecca, who realized through our discussions on healthy relationships that she was not being treated as well as she deserved, and needed to end her relationship, and actually did.

For my sister, and for all parents, who are striving to raise sexually healthy kids in a society filled with unhealthy and unrealistic messages about body image, gender stereotypes, and relationships.

For my mother, who served as a nurse in an abortion clinic and an educator in a college health center, who taught me that it is not just a job when it is one's calling, who taught me that reproductive healthcare is a fundamental human right that is worth fighting for, and who died before she had a chance to see me fight.

For my father, who taught me that working for social justice is our opportunity as well as our imperative, who is still around today to see me fight, and who tells me he is proud of me.

And for myself, because there is nothing more important to me than figuring how I can help to make the world a more peaceful and just place for ALL!

Peggy Brick
MEd

Kennett Square, PA

PROFESSIONAL LIFE
Current workplace: Retired. Most recent workplaces include Instructor, Osher Lifelong Learning Institute; Kendal Continuing Care Retirement Community; Founder/Past President, Sexuality and Aging Consortium, and Sexuality Education Consultant.
First workplace: Clifton Park Junior High School, Baltimore, MD
Favorite workplace: I've loved every place I've worked! No way I could choose one.

EDUCATIONAL LIFE
Favorite course: Introduction to Sociology at Ohio Wesleyan University, which opened my eyes. Also, graduate courses at Columbia University, which laid the groundwork for my sexuality education work.
Least favorite course: Why should I bother to remember?

TEACHING LIFE
Favorite topic to teach: Whatever I'm currently teaching, recently "Older, Wiser, Sexually Smarter"
Most challenging topic to teach: I'm currently teaching about Alzheimer's disease, and student concerns are profound.

INSPIRATIONS
Sex educator: Sol Gordon inspired me to become a sexuality educator. And I could name 100 others!
Book: Many have been essential for me, but one I wish all sexuality educators would read is *Intimate Matters: A History of Sexuality in America*, by John D'Emilio and Estelle B. Freedman.

How I Got Into Sex…Ed

At 85 years of age, I'm challenged to tell "how I got into sex… education." I wonder, did it begin at Camp TeAta where, for 13 summers, we girls tried to figure it all out, particularly the "old bags shack" where our favorite counselors lived and who (we whispered) were lesbians? Or was it at home where Mother frequently warned that her bridge club friends were talking about "those girls who necked in the back of the movie theater and had a bad reputation?" Or was it at college, where rumors about who was "doing it" were spread with awe and fascination? Possibly the most important reason for my becoming a sex educator was my foundation in sociology and psychology at Ohio Wesleyan University and as a graduate student at Columbia University, 1946–1951.

Of course, hundreds of experiences had prepared me for the fall of 1969 when peripatetic psychologist and sex educator Sol Gordon arrived at Dwight Morrow High School (DMHS) in Englewood, NJ. Sol was hired to help me develop full-year courses in psychology and sociology that would, Sol being Sol, include sexuality. Thus began my 40-year journey as a sex educator.

But first, I had to become a teacher. This began in 1964 when our three children were all in school and Allan, my unfailingly supportive husband, reported a radio announcement about a program called Project Mission, created by the Ford Foundation, which would prepare teachers for work in the inner city. What a great opportunity! A year later, I'd watched 12 "master teachers" demonstrate a variety of approaches to connecting successfully with 12- to 14-year-old children in an all-Black school in Baltimore, MD. For the next two years, encouraged to create and experiment, I developed my interactive approach to teaching that was enhanced by the theory of Paulo Friere's *Pedagogy of the Oppressed*. Twenty years later, I gave a keynote, "Toward a Pedagogy of

Sexuality: Education for Critical Consciousness" at the World Association of Sexuality in Hong Kong.

But back to DMHS, where I "got into" sex education. For the year, Sol Gordon and I taught seven classes, five sociology and two psychology, and — here's the key to my future life — at the end of the year, we brought all those students to the auditorium for a "Sex Week." We showed provocative sex ed films from Canada, and Sol waved his arms as he gave his inimitable responses to anonymous student questions. The dedication to Sol Gordon in *Older, Wiser, Sexually Smarter: 30 Sex Ed Lessons for Adults Only* includes one of his oft repeated aphorisms:

> *"Authorities say masturbation is ok...*
> [Then he'd pause and continue slowly.]
> *...if you don't do it...*
> [Then he'd pause again.]
> *...too much!*
> [He'd give a little laugh.]
> *...but nobody knows...*
> [He'd pause again and say faster and louder,]
> *...how much is too much!*
> [And, after the laughter subsided, he would say,]
> *...and <u>once</u> is too much if you don't like it."*

Sol was an inspiration; think of the wisdom in that silly "joke."

Sol left, and during the next 15 years I created a 10-week unit, "Human Sexual Behavior," a popular finale to the full-year, elective courses. Using a multidisciplinary approach, we examined, for example, the history of contraceptives and condoms, the differences between sexually repressive and sexually permissive societies, new research on adolescent sexual behavior in the United States, and contemporary theories on the role of parents in sex education. Most lessons began with a values clarification exercise designed to challenge students to think about each topic in terms of their personal beliefs. Frequently, students worked in small groups, discussing scenarios they had suggested anonymously. Role-playing difficult situations was especially popular with students who were unsuccessful when doing traditional academic work, but highly successful when acting out their real-life problems. My only poor evaluation came from one supervisor who, while watching students acting and role-playing, complained that "I wasn't teaching." I requested a re-evaluation and gave a traditional stand-up lecture, which was graded "excellent." When will they ever learn?

One of my favorite lessons was "Silent Day." Students entered silently and for the full period read whatever they chose from *Changing Bodies, Changing Lives.* I remember one timid 15-year-old boy telling me as he left that he'd chosen to read about rape because an old woman in his apartment building had been raped that week. I learned, once again, how varied and how profound are people's needs for sexuality education that is sensitive to their particular concerns. A "Sex Questions" box on my desk always invited anonymous questions, and every course I've taught since, including those on Sexuality and Aging, has begun with anonymous questions. Questions reveal the inadequacy of rigid curricula and help teachers understand the concerns that must be addressed if sex education is to have a significant impact on students' lives.

But I was a very atypical sexuality educator. I was teaching in a liberal, supportive community where, when I described the sex unit on parents' night, the common response was, "I wish I could take that course!" While other sex educators were attacked as the Far Right targeted sex education, the only question I ever had was from a board member who disapproved of a single question on a 70-item "Sex Knowledge Pre-Test" I had distributed in advance of the Sexual Behavior Unit. For a week students could search for answers from parents, teachers, or anyone they chose. The board member asked, "Why did students need to know that '25% of people over 75 years of age still had intercourse?'" I explained my belief that we are sexual from birth to death and that students needed to understand that older people were still sexual. We agreed to disagree. Ironically, I retired at age 70, and the topic of sexuality and aging has been my passion ever since.

I was atypical in other ways. The majority of sex education teachers were coaches or health educators. Their focus was pregnancy and STD prevention, which emphasized the dangers of sex. Most had no professional development in sex education, were ill-prepared to teach this sensitive subject, and surely didn't think of themselves as "sexuality educators." I did. I attended AASECT conferences, gave "State of Sexuality Education" presentations at Eastern Region SSSS meetings, and became devoted to SIECUS, writing for the *SIECUS Report* and eventually becoming chair of the board of directors.

Over the years, I continued to discover wondrous new ways to "get into sex ed." In 1984, I left DMHS and soon became director of education at Planned Parenthood of Bergen County, NJ (now the amazing CFLE at Planned Parenthood of Central and Greater Northern New Jersey [PPCGNNJ]). There, an enthusiastic board and supportive CEOs understood the many benefits to the agency of a strong education department and encouraged our creative approach to providing sex education across the lifespan. Suddenly, being a sex educator meant developing grants, creating teaching manuals, providing graduate courses for teachers, facilitating professional development workshops across the nation, and writing articles that articulated my theory and practice of sexuality education. Now more than 30 years old, my first article, "Sex and Society: Teaching the Connection" in the *Journal of School Health,* expressed my conviction that meaningful sex education helps students examine the "mixed messages" they receive from a "sexually confused and confusing society."

To really "get into sex ed," I had to be a student of that society. Always, I was guided by books, including *Sexual Conduct: The Social Sources of Human Sexuality* by John Gagnon and William Simon; *Intimate Matters: A History of Sexuality in America* by John D'Emilio and Estelle B. Freedman; and *Sex is Not a Natural Act* by my provocative mentor, Leonore Tiefer. While many sex educators felt they were relegated to a low status among researchers and therapists, I was privileged to meet monthly in New York City with a group of feminist sexologists who respected me as an educator and challenged me to think and rethink my pedagogy. My feminist perspective was articulated in an article entitled "Sex Education is a Feminist Issue" in the groundbreaking journal, *New Directions for Women,* and for nine years, its editor, Phyllis Kriegal, and I provided professional development workshops through our agency, Affirmative Teaching Associates.

It was this stimulating background that enabled me to work with an enthusiastic staff at the CFLE to target deficits in current sex education curricula. Together we created exciting teaching manuals that featured interactive activities that examined feelings, attitudes, values, and beliefs and developed the skills needed for helping students to integrate information into their lives. Thus, *Positive Images: A New Approach to Contraceptive Education* replaced boring lectures on contraceptive devices; *Teaching Safer Sex* replaced HIV films focused on T-cells; and *Unequal Partners* challenged students to think about the quality of their relationships. *Bodies, Birth, and Babies* and *Healthy Foundations* taught early childhood teachers and parents about young children's sexual behaviors.

In a rapidly changing society, getting into sex ed is a continuing adventure. Creative educators will always be seeking new ways to reach students with various needs at various stages of life. For example, right now there's a profound need for resources to prepare staff to understand and respect the sexual rights of old people, especially residents in long-term care facilities, many with dementia. Oh! I do wish I were just "getting into sex...ed."

Steve Brown

PsyD

New Britain, CT

PROFESSIONAL LIFE
Current workplace: Director, Traumatic Stress Institute, Klingberg Family Centers; Coordinator, Risking Connection Training Program, New Britain, CT
First workplace: Planned Parenthood of Washington, D.C.
Favorite workplace: CFLE

EDUCATIONAL LIFE
Favorite course: Topics in Human Sexuality, Swarthmore College, Swarthmore, PA (1982)
Least favorite course: Mr. Cordray's health class in 8th grade, Walnut Hills High School, Cincinnati, OH

TEACHING LIFE
Favorite topic to teach: Dating and Courtship Skills
Most challenging topic to teach: Acquaintance and Date Rape

INSPIRATIONS
Sex educator: Mary Jo Podgurski
Book: *Sex and Sensibility* by Deborah Roffman

NATIONAL SEX ED CONFERENCE
Title of presentation: *Being a Trauma-Informed Sex Educator*
Presentation description: By most estimates, one in four girls and one in six boys will experience sexual abuse by the time they are 18. When you include other forms of trauma, the statistics are even more alarming. Sex educators can assume that, in any group, there is a significant number of youth that are trauma survivors, especially when serving at-risk youth. Trauma-informed care describes services aimed at ameliorating the pervasive impact of trauma and minimizing the risk of re-traumatization. This workshop will address what sex educators need to know about trauma's effects, gain

sensitivity to how youth may experience sex ed groups, and learn to adapt their teaching and educational messages to serve these vulnerable youth.

How I Got Into Sex...Ed

Like many members of my generation (and subsequent generations), my teen years were filled with angst, anxiety, awkwardness, mystery, and shame about my developing sexuality. While fortunate to come from a family with adequate resources and loving parents, I received little formal information about sexuality. I did receive a great many informal messages — that sexuality was not something you talked about, it's a topic shrouded in shame, and that you could only learn by picking up information from the media and tidbits from friends' stories. Then, during my sophomore year at Swarthmore College, I took an evening elective course called "Topics in Human Sexuality"; this was around the same time I had my first serious relationship. I was simply stunned by how comfortable the leaders were when talking about sexuality and the transformative power of creating a space where young people could talk openly about the topic. Far beyond any information that I learned, what struck me most was the feel of the room, how empowered I felt, and how different the experience was from any I'd had before. I remember some small voice somewhere in my soul saying, "I'd like to do this kind of work someday." The combination of this course and a loving, fun, sexually healthy new partner made my foray into the world of romantic and sexual relationships a positive and memorable one — in stark contrast to my adolescent angst.

As I was prone to do back then, I ignored that small voice and instead went into the world of politics and grassroots organizing for several years. But the voice never died; it only got stronger. In 1987, I began looking for jobs in the field of sexuality education and reproductive rights, and in 1988, I was lucky enough to be hired by Peggy Brick to be a sexuality educator at the CFLE. In 1991, I published the first edition of *Streetwise to Sex-Wise: Sexuality Education for High Risk Youth,* which is now used internationally by schools and agencies serving high-risk youth.

Although I eventually became a clinical psychologist, sexuality and sexuality education have always been themes in my work. I specialize in the area of psychological trauma, where I've had the privilege of working with both sexual abuse survivors and youth with sexual behavior problems. I worked in a long-term treatment program for sexually abusive youth. I train public mental health staff to provide sexuality education to youth in their care. I do psychosexual evaluations of children with sexual behavior problems. Part of my current work explores the nexus between sexual violence and healthy sexuality by looking at themes such as: how sexual violence prevention can embrace the goal of defining and promoting healthy sexuality; how prevention can move beyond a problem avoidance perspective to one of health promotion; how sex education is connected to sexual health and sexual safety; how adults can help sexually violent youth shift from a sexual abuse paradigm to one rooted in healthy sexuality.

As has been true since 1983 when I first entered my "Topics in Human Sexuality Class," I have been continually struck with the transformative power of quality sexuality education. When people model the ability to talk about sexuality comfortably, educationally, and with appropriate boundaries, others are often moved, enlightened, and grateful. Nothing is more gratifying that seeing a group of learners "get it" on a deep level, understand the impact of their own sexual learning or their current behavior, connect with other learners about the larger goal of open communication about sexuality, and move toward new skills and behavior. I've had that experience many times as a learner, and I love to facilitate that experience in others.

Barbara Bunting

Summit, NJ

PROFESSIONAL LIFE
Favorite workplace: Board of Directors, Planned Parenthood of Central and Greater Northern New Jersey (PPCGNNJ)

EDUCATIONAL LIFE
Favorite course: Joyce, Yeats, & Eliot
Least favorite course: Basic Motor Skills (required physical education course in college)

How I Got Into Sex...Ed

In November of my junior year in college, my best friend, "Susan," discovered she was pregnant after a summer romance in Colorado. There was no way she was going to tell her mother, and there was no way she was going to carry the baby to term. After checking with her OB/GYN and confirming the news, she (we) had to figure out exactly what to do. It seemed that an abortion was the only solution.

This was over 50 years ago, long before *Roe v. Wade* finally legalized the procedure. Through very careful research — you couldn't talk about it to just anyone — we got the name of a doctor in Baltimore who would perform the abortion. Actually, it was the name of a middleman who would meet her in Baltimore and take her to the doctor's office in the suburbs. It would cost $500. (That was a helluva lot of money in those days!)

Susan and I were both on financial aid and had to raise the money from friends — again, it wasn't an easy subject to broach, so we had to be extremely circumspect about whom to ask. Once the $500 was raised, we then had to consider the cost of bus fare to Baltimore. About a week after her "rabbit test" (that's what we called a pregnancy test in those days) came back positive, we had the money and a bus ticket. She was to be met at the Baltimore bus terminal by the middleman.

We walked to our local Peter Pan bus terminal, Susan with $500 pinned inside her bra. After I put her on the bus, I sat and sobbed, not knowing if I would ever see her again.

Two days later, she was back to report that all went beautifully; she was met right on time and driven to the suburbs to an immaculate doctor's office. The procedure was quick and painless, and she met another couple there who gave her a ride back to college.

I vowed to myself at that moment that I would do everything in my power to keep anyone else from enduring what Susan had, even though in her case things had a positive ending. I have been an avid supporter of Planned Parenthood for all of my adult life, and whenever anyone asks, I tell them adamantly, "It's not about the abortions — it's about preventing millions of them every year!!" Education is, of course, the key.

Michael Carrera

EdD

AASECT Certified Sex Educator

New York, NY

PROFESSIONAL LIFE

Current workplace: Vice President, Adolescence Division, Founder, Carrera Adolescent Pregnancy Prevention Program, The Children's Aid Society, New York, NY

First workplace: Junior High School Teacher, Bronx, NY

Favorite workplace: Teaching sexuality education at The Children's Aid Society, Milbank Center, Harlem, NY

EDUCATIONAL LIFE

Favorite course: Human Reproduction and Sexual Development, taught by Dr. James Malfetti, Columbia University, 1969. I never took a full course in our field that disappointed me. I have taken some conference workshops that did not meet expectations — mostly because presenters failed to take into account the multiple aspects of a young person's life when they discussed issues, such as helping young people reduce risk-taking behaviors.

TEACHING LIFE

Favorite topic to teach: Sexuality and Sexual Expression across the Life Span

INSPIRATIONS

Sex educator: Dr. Lester Kirkendall

Book: *The Spiritual Life of Children* by Robert Coles, 1990

NATIONAL SEX ED CONFERENCE

Title of presentation: *ABOVE THE WAIST: Family Life & Sexuality Education Beginning with the Brain*

Presentation description: My 45-minute presentation will be part of a 3-hour pre-conference workshop. I will provide reflections of the almost 50 years I've spent as a sexuality educator — my grievous errors, the exhilaration of observing people of all ages unfold when provided opportunities to learn about their sexuality and the sexuality of others, and other stuff.

How I Got Into Sex...Ed

In the 1959–1960 school year, I had my first teaching job at a New York City public school in the Bronx. It was a "special service" junior high school, meaning girls and boys who were doing poorly in their respective schools in the borough, and whose behavior was seen as disruptive by school officials, were placed in separate schools away from other students. I filled the position because the annual teacher turnover rate at this particular school was extraordinarily high, and "fresh" college graduates were desirable. While I was somewhat prepared to be a health educator, no such positions were available, so I was given a schedule filled with language arts and social studies classes. I was dazed and confused each day, emotionally exhausted, in bed immediately after school, and wondering if my career choice was a mistake. I had zero classroom management skills, and I had no idea of the economic and social suffering experienced by these young girls and boys; nor did I fully understand the extraordinary racism they experienced every day. Overall, I was lost, really lost, and secretly began contemplating a transition. But providence took over, and I was rescued. This is what happened. One day, in a language arts class, I made mention of dating. In those days, people dated — dating was big. At the mention of that word the class became still! I was thunderstruck! I regained my composure and said I would discuss dating and anything else they wanted to discuss if they would agree to give me half of each class to cover the material I was expected to teach. It worked. The seas parted, the classroom was suddenly orderly, and other young people wanted me to be their teacher. Teachers marveled at the classroom transformation. Now it was just simply a matter of trying to find things to discuss. Remember this was 1960; no sexuality field, no women's movement, no public reproductive health initiatives, zero public discussion of the subject. I read sociology, psychology, anthropology, psychiatry, and family therapy books, trying to mine them for material. I began taking courses in all those areas, trying to retrieve nuggets of information. I enrolled in a master's program, and followed that with nine years in the evening at Teachers College, Columbia University, working on my doctorate. From 1960 through 1970, the sexuality field was beginning to take root and blossom. SIECUS, AASEC (no therapists in title yet), and SSSS all began a more public discussion of sexuality.

I left that junior high school in 1964 and began teaching at Kingsborough Community College in Brooklyn, NY. Then in 1970, when I completed my doctorate, I began teaching at Hunter College in the undergraduate and graduate Community Health Education Program, which soon became an accredited MPH Program. From 1964, and through my almost 30 years at Hunter, I taught courses in Marriage and the Family, Human Sexuality 101 on the undergraduate and graduate level, and Clinical Aspects of Human Sexuality on the graduate level. During these exhilarating years as an educator in a public school, community college, and at a major college of the City University of New York, I was honored to serve as vice president, then president of AASECT, and chairperson of the SIECUS board of directors. But it all began because of one word — dating.

Jenny Caruso

MEd
Teaching Certification in Health Education

Bronx, NY

PROFESSIONAL LIFE

Current workplace: Sexuality Education Coordinator, Carrera Pregnancy Prevention Program: The Children's Aid Society, Bronx Preparatory Charter School, Bronx, NY

First workplace: Sexuality Educator at Binghamton University & Sex Advice Columnist for the Binghamton University Newspaper

Favorite workplace: Advance Africa Volunteer Program: International HIV Educator

EDUCATIONAL LIFE

Favorite course: Teaching Human Sexuality with Stanley Snegroff

Least favorite course: Um, every Math course

TEACHING LIFE

Favorite topic to teach: Gender Roles & Stereotypes

Most challenging topic to teach: I teach a parent class that focuses on talking with your kids about sex and sexuality. It can be challenging to open up this conversation with a room full of adults who have conflicting values and long-standing beliefs about these topics. (It is also extremely fun and exciting.)

INSPIRATIONS

Sex educator: Lindsay Fram. She basically taught me everything I know about being a sex educator, and continues to challenge my thinking and push me to grow and be better each day.

Book: Everything by Dan Savage

<u>**NATIONAL SEX ED CONFERENCE**</u>
Title of presentation: *Let's Get It Started: Starting a GSA*
Presentation description: Starting a Gay Straight Alliance (GSA) can be tricky. What are the first steps? Who should you talk to? What are the laws? Get ideas, tips, and suggestions for starting up a rockin' GSA at your school. Every student deserves to feel safe at school. LGBTQ youth often have a difficult time feeling supported within their school community. A GSA is a safe space that is welcoming to all students regardless of sexual orientation or gender identity. While one of the goals of a GSA is to help LGBTQ students find a safe space to be themselves, it also helps to build a school culture where students and teachers are accepting and respectful of one another.

How I Got Into Sex...Ed

Never in my wildest dreams did I think I would be doing what I am doing. As an awkward, shy girl growing up on Long Island, NY, I thought I would be married with children and a house in the suburbs by this point in my life (or I would at least be living out my secret fantasy life as a writer). Never, EVER, did I picture myself standing in front of a room full of teenagers talking about penises, vulvas, and all of the other wonderfully exciting things that we sex educators talk about every day (did I mention never, EVER?)!

So how did I wind up on this path? I wish I could say that I knew that I wanted to do this all along and that I worked really hard to reach my goals. In reality, it was a complete accident. In 2003, I began my college years at Binghamton University in New York. Unsure of my goals, and with limited motivation to commit to anything besides gaining twenty pounds at the dining hall "salad" bar, I considered my major to be "undeclared." What this actually meant was that I was randomly registering for whatever classes my friends were in that started after 1 P.M. I was passionless, without a path, and as a result, pretty darn unhappy.

My junior year I was forced to choose a major. Still lagging in adult-like decision making skills, I chose Human Development, by default. I had always enjoyed helping others and found people to be more interesting than, say, economics — so it seemed like a good idea at the time (it ended up being a great idea, phew!). Turns out that Human Development majors are required to complete a year-long internship in a community-based organization. Most students set up internships with nonprofit organizations where they wish to someday have a job. I had no idea what kind of job I wanted, so I waited for the right internship to come to me. (Evidently, life doesn't work this way.) The deadline to find an internship was fast approaching, and without an answer in sight, I desperately asked the girl who sat next to me in class for help. She had that put-together look about her that told me she had her life together. She handed me a flier for a program called REACH (Real Education About College Health), and told me that they were accepting last-minute internship requests for the upcoming semester. She told me that she, herself, had turned down the opportunity because she didn't feel comfortable talking about sexual health to college students, but "maybe that is something you would be comfortable with." I wasn't. But, did I mention that I was desperate?

I took the internship with REACH, and my life was never the same. Suddenly that passion that was missing in my educational path was shooting out of me like...[insert ejaculation metaphor here]. I never cared about anything as much as I cared about this internship. I quickly came to realize that I never wanted to work in a field where I did not feel this way.

The internship was challenging. Really challenging. I was talking about sex with my peers for the first time in my life in an open and honest way. I had to check my insecurities and inhibitions about sex at the door. Not comfortable saying the word "vagina"? Feel funny about handling condoms? Think you can only talk about sex and relationships with your own gender? Too bad. All of my sexuality hang-ups, and more, quickly became part of my daily conversation. I adopted the "fake it 'til you make it" philosophy about teaching sex ed. I thought, "If I pretend I'm OK talking about this stuff, eventually I will be." It actually worked!

A few months into the internship, I contacted the Binghamton University campus newspaper. I had admired the Columbia University "Go Ask Alice" Q & A model for sexual health advice-giving, and wanted to create a similar program at my college. My proposal was quickly approved, and before I knew it, I was writing weekly articles and answering the sexual health questions of my peers. Through this project, I learned a lot about the sex lives of the students around me, but the most important thing I discovered was how much of it they were getting wrong (half of my letters the first week were about being afraid of contracting STIs from the dorm toilets!). I have always been an autodidactic learner, so I knew a lot, even if I was afraid to talk about it. But these people had crazy misconceptions and shame attached to their understanding of sex. Many of them disclosed that they had no one else to talk to about these issues and felt completely alone. I quickly came to realize that sex ed was not just a hobby for me, but it was my responsibility to share what I knew about sex and sexuality with others.

Today, I work for the Carrera Adolescent Pregnancy Prevention Program at The Children's Aid Society where I am the Sexuality Education Coordinator at a charter school in the Bronx. This means that I get to train other sexuality educators while also providing sex ed classes and sexual health counseling to my own group of curious 8th-graders. This specific group of students has been taking my class since they were in the 5th grade. If I had any doubts about my career choice prior to taking this position, this group of kids has certainly reaffirmed my decision. I am excited to say that the students I work with are gaining the knowledge and the skills needed to learn and communicate about sex and sexuality in a healthy way. They are not only learning how to protect themselves from STIs and pregnancy, but also how to communicate about their bodies, about sexual orientation, gender identity, pleasure, and consent in a way that is not shaming or shameful. Teaching these students to have a holistic understanding of sexuality is the reason I wake up in the morning — it is my passion.

Rebecca Chalker

MA, PhD
Certified Sex Advisor

New York, NY

PROFESSIONAL LIFE

Current workplace: Women's Studies Department, Pace University, New York, NY

First workplace: Editor of *A New View of a Woman's Body,* for the Federation of Feminist Women's Health Centers (FFWHCs), Los Angeles, CA

Favorite workplace: Teaching a course that I developed: "A Cultural History of Sexualities from Prehistory to the Present" at Pace and at Florida State University

EDUCATIONAL LIFE

Favorite course: Numerous videotaped lectures from the Institute for the Advanced Study of Human Sexuality, including those by Erwin Haberle, Wardell Pomeroy, William Masters, Gayle Rubin, Alan Ginsberg, Karla Jay, and numerous others

Least favorite course: A required anti-communism course at Florida State University in 1966!

TEACHING LIFE

Favorite topic to teach: A Cultural History of Sexualities

Most challenging topic to teach: Job Opportunities in Sexuality Education and Reproductive Justice in the Nonprofit Sector

INSPIRATIONS

Sex educator: Betty Dodson

Book: What a hard question! Okay, for one: Eva Keuls's classic study of ancient Greek sexuality, *The Reign of the Phallus*

How I Got Into Sex...Ed

After I finished my Masters in English at Florida State University in 1975, I had no job and no prospects, so I volunteered at the Tallahassee Feminist Women's Health Center (FWHC), which was founded by my roommate and two other women. There I met Carol Downer, founder of the first FWHC in Los Angeles in 1971, who was visiting Tallahassee. This association of eight woman-owned clinics was staffed primarily by lay health workers and focused on abortion, contraception, well-woman healthcare, and self-help information. (Indeed, these clinics gave out personal plastic speculums like other businesses gave out ballpoint pens.) In 1978, Carol hired me to edit a book, *A New View of a Woman's Body,* that she and a group of the staff were writing, so I moved. "A Feminist Redefinition of the Clitoris" was one of the chapters, along with others on reproductive health. Using Dr. Mary Jane Sherfey's clarification of Masters and Johnson's detailed study of genital anatomy, along with several nineteenth-century anatomy texts, these women, who had no advanced degrees, no medical training, and no desire for profit, brought the definition of women's genitals up to modern anatomical standards for other organ systems! Suzann Gage, a clinic staff member who was a largely self-taught artist, did the illustrations. The idea that women's genitals (a dark subcontinent of neglect in that era) were a complex and powerful organ system was a revelation, and working on this chapter was precisely where I fell down the rabbit hole.

After I moved to New York City in 1982, I began doing what I now call "A Walking Tour Through the Clitoris," using Gage's exquisitely detailed drawings featured in *A New View of a Woman's Body.* As I continued lecturing and telling women why looking at the clitoris as a complex and powerful organ system like the penis, rather than as a pea-sized nubbin, is useful and empowering, a question kept lurking in the back of my mind: If the clitoris is equivalent to the penis in extent and power (and some have argued that it is even more powerful in certain respects), how *did* this information get lost? I began to think that besides my colleagues at the FWHCs, I was the only person on the planet who was curious about this, or cared about it. So I kept reading and noodling for clues. Then one day, as I was perusing the sexuality section in a bookstore, Thomas Laqueur's *Making Sex: The Body and Gender from the Greeks to Freud,* seemed to jump off the shelf into my hands. I had no idea who Laqueur was at the time, but after reading this erudite and extremely enlightening book, I knew that the FWHC's redefinition of the clitoris was spot on! I tell this story entitled "The Case of the Missing Clitoris: An Anatomical Detective Story" in my book, *The Clitoral Truth.*

The FWHCs and other feminist clinics participated in the revival of the cervical cap, a barrier method of birth control similar in effectiveness to the diaphragm, but smaller and more convenient and, hence, preferred by many women. I wrote a book on the cap for users and practitioners, *The Complete Cervical Cap Guide.* That same year, I was a featured speaker at a special symposium on the cervical cap at the World Congress of Sexology (now World Congress of Sexual Health), in Heidelberg, Germany. As "WomanCap," two other women and I provided the cap and trained practitioners in New York City for 10 years. Sadly, due to inept business decisions by the cap's British owners (they knew more about playing golf than they did about distributing latex products), the cap is now and, apparently forever, unavailable.

In 1991, I attended the first (and as it turned out, *last*) *International Conference on Orgasm,* in New Delhi, and continued going to World Congresses on Sexology and SSSS meetings, and wrote other books: *Overcoming Bladder Disorders; A Woman's Book of Choices: Abortion, Menstrual Extraction, RU-486;* and *Brachytherapy: The Best Kept Secret in Modern Medicine,* as well as articles on sexuality and women's health.

Over the years, I had also lectured on women's health topics at various universities around town (Barnard, Columbia, New York University, The New School), but I couldn't figure out how to put my knowledge into a coherent narrative, and I certainly had no idea, or even any ambition, to become a historian of sexuality. But looking at sexuality through a feminist lens, another question dogged me: *How did men get on top, economically, socially, and sexually?* Without a plan, I kept reading further and further back in time to prehistory, and I eventually found myself with enough material to put together a university-level course focused on how successive cultural constructions of sexuality have impacted women. Then I found Gerda Lerner's classic study, *The Creation of Patriarchy.* This book enables us to theorize how women's reproductive ability, which was likely a vital community resource in prehistory, became a family asset and, along with other cultural developments, became a key building block of patriarchy. Then one night I went to a reading on women's health, and afterward went to dinner with Karla Jay, an early lesbian activist and chair of the Women's Studies Program at Pace University, whom I greatly admire. Karla mentioned that she had two teaching slots to fill at Pace. I mentioned that I had a course proposal, faxed it to her later that night, and got the job! A few years later, I began teaching it at Florida State University in the summer. And the rest, as they say (whoever *they* are), is history!

So, like Alice, I fell down the rabbit hole, but instead of meeting outlandish animals and wacky people, I met many who think about sexuality in positive, constructive ways, study it and write thoughtfully about it, do ethical research, and are committed to teaching comprehensive, evidence-based sexuality education.

Karen B. K. Chan

MA

Toronto, Ontario

PROFESSIONAL LIFE

Current workplace: Sex Educator, Fluid Exchange Consultation (fluidexchange.org) and Health Promotion Consultant, Sexual Health, Toronto Public Health, Toronto, Ontario, Canada
First workplace: Education and Outreach at Asian Community AIDS Services, Toronto, Ontario, Canada
Favorite workplace: Puberty classes with 10- and 11-year-olds, as a Sexual Health Promoter with Toronto Public Health

EDUCATIONAL LIFE

Favorite course: Nonviolent Communication
Least favorite course: Nonvascular Plants

TEACHING LIFE

Favorite topic to teach: Puberty
Most challenging topic to teach: Pregnancy

INSPIRATIONS

Sex educator: Esther Perel
Book: *Action Theatre: The Improvisation of Presence* by Ruth Zaporah. (It's a book about dance, improv, and the body, and has everything to do with sexuality.)

NATIONAL SEX ED CONFERENCE

Title of presentation: *Sex as a Jam Session: How & Why*
Presentation description: This interactive workshop is based on my stop-motion animation *Jam,* a proposal for rethinking how we have sex. A common framework about sex renders bodies and pleasure into goods that are better when they're new, scarce, selfishly owned, and/or standardized. In this model, sexual consent is often a mere technicality, and partners are like traders with opposing interests. *Jam* is based on Thomas MacAulay Millar's essay, "Towards a Performance

Model of Sex," and proposes an alternate framework borrowed from musical improvisation. In this proposal, experience and pleasure are valued, partners are collaborators in unscripted journeys, and consent is ongoing and reciprocal, just like in any musical jam session. This workshop will screen the video, and invite participants to explore exactly how we can go about transposing theory into reality.

How I Got Into Sex...Ed

If I had set out to become a sex educator, I would never have taken the path I did. In retrospect, all of the smaller passages that make up my journey thus far feel like tangents, distractions, and miscalculations. But as it shapes up, I feel like saying, "Oh cool, yes, yes, I get it!"

For many years, I did what I thought I was supposed to do. Near the end of high school, my mother imprinted me with, "You can be a doctor who makes art as a hobby. You can't be an artist who doctors for a hobby." Full of the guilt of an only child from an immigrant family, I opted out of graphic arts and stayed the course of overachieving in the sciences.

I chose to move to Vancouver, 2000 miles away, to be close to my first girlfriend and far from Mom. And I chose to major in Cell and Molecular Biology for no better reason than that it sounded complicated, and none of the other options excited me. Excitement was not a determining factor in plotting my career path.

A year into studying biology full time, and deeply feeling the rift between myself and the other science types, I took up Women's Studies as a minor. Just to keep myself sane, that was how I had justified it. Feminism fueled the flames that science was dousing; it became my new "hobby." To pass the time, I lingered at the Women's Center on campus, and haunted awkward queer meet-ups. Eventually, I met a group of queer Asian folks who were organizing potlucks and conferences and softball teams. They were talking about sex and gender and liberation, and I was excited. More hobbies!

When I returned to Toronto I fell into a series of jobs in medical research and within the genetic engineering industry — jobs many of my fellow grads would have killed to score. But my soul suffered. I felt out of place and lonely, and I wasn't good at what I was doing. I wanted a different life but had neither the vision nor the courage to follow through.

Outside of work, I started to volunteer madly — for peer counseling phone lines, anti-violence initiatives, and on projects with queer Asian folks. My community felt like an extended family. I felt belonging and did good work. I also started to feel fulfillment for needs I didn't know I had: meaningful work, service, and healing. Wounds I had taken for granted — as a person of color, an immigrant, a queer, a gender weirdo — were all being touched. Sometimes it was painful; often it was fodder for hours of sharing and laughing and bonding. Always it was transformative.

I invested more and more energy into these "hobbies," all of which excited me. I fell in love with the idea of workshops — space crafted specifically for connection, experiment, critical exchange, and learning. Before this time I had only known teachers and coaches. The concept of a facilitator, as one who engages, challenges, inspires, questions, and animates, changed my worldview. I went to any workshop I could get into, to participate, yes, but also to observe the facilitator's craft. I felt enormously hungry, and I feasted.

In the meantime, in my other life, I was offered a research job in a cell regeneration study, to burn the hoof pads off live pigs. It was a sad, wincing moment, and a sobering message. I couldn't do it anymore. The hardest part was breaking the news to my family: I was going to quit a respectable, thriving industry to join the soft-skilled and under-waged. To soften the blow, I alluded to a possible return to science, knowing it was unlikely.

From that point on, I held job after job within the sector. And while every job was fulfilling in multiple ways, I continued to develop new "hobbies." They came into my life as ideas that excited me, practices that I wanted to learn, people I sought to emulate, and healing I needed to do. I pursued critical theories about gender and race, group work, assertive communication, empathy, principles of learning, embodiment and performance as resistance (I am a feminist taiko drumming collective), the production of culture, unlearning shame, creative problem-solving and play, redefining the erotic, redefining relationship structures, sexual diversities, sex positivity, and many more.

All in all, how I got into this work feels like a sprawling landscape and not a path at all. My current interests are in reimagining sex, widening what is permissibly erotic, being curious about the body, holding both the profane and the sacred together, and integrating play into all aspects of life. And I materialize these interests through workshopping, writing/blogging, making videos, conversation, and plain old living. I expect that all of these will change and shift over time, and I look forward to finding out how.

Julie Chaya
MA

Kent, OH

PROFESSIONAL LIFE
Current workplace: Kent State University, Kent, OH
First workplace: Kent State University, Kent, OH
Favorite workplace: Kent State University, Kent, OH

EDUCATIONAL LIFE
Favorite course: All of my Gerontology courses
Least favorite course: Sociology

TEACHING LIFE
Favorite topic to teach: Geriatric Sexuality
Most challenging topic to teach: Ethics

INSPIRATIONS
Sex educator: Peggy Brick
Book: *Older, Wiser, Sexually Smarter* and *Assisted Loving*

NATIONAL SEX ED CONFERENCE
Title of presentation: *Sex, Seniors, & Institutionalized Care: Healthcare Professional Training*
Presentation description: The purpose of this workshop is to educate healthcare providers about the importance of later life sexuality. Healthcare professionals who attend this session will learn how to be effective, knowledgeable, and sensitive practitioners to their sexually active geriatric patients.

How I Got Into Sex...Ed

My career goal has always been to work with older adults. Originally, I focused my education on the physical rehabilitation aspect of aging (i.e., kinesiology and physical therapy). On my significant other's mother's 50th birthday, she was told by her physician that she would need a hip replacement. Since my significant other and I were in the healthcare field at the time, she came to us very distraught, and asked us if she could still be sexually active with her husband after surgery. At that moment, the light bulb went on above my head. I needed to research this topic and find out if other people were having similar dilemmas. Currently, I am a PhD student at Kent State University in the Health Education & Promotion Department, and I am looking forward to the future, when I can provide older adults with the answers to their questions about geriatric sexual health.

Debra Christopher

MS

Boulder, CO

PROFESSIONAL LIFE
Current workplace: ETR, Corporate office: Scotts Valley, CA; Home office: Boulder, CO
First workplace: Teaching high school health education (including sexuality education) in Fort Morgan, CO (rural, conservative community in the eastern plains of Colorado)
Favorite workplace: I have truly enjoyed all of my workplace experiences and working with a variety of age groups.

EDUCATIONAL LIFE
Favorite course: Graduate course on Human Sexuality at the University of Northern Colorado, taught by Lloyd Kolbe
Least favorite course: WAIT training. Conducted by Friends First. Abstinence-Only.

TEACHING LIFE
Favorite topic to teach: Innovative, research-based instructional practices that lead to implementation and change. My passion is working with adult learners, in the field of sexual and reproductive health, who are motivated to strengthen their teaching and training skills.

Most challenging topic to teach: Understanding and supporting LGBTQ youth. I find it both challenging and rewarding.

INSPIRATIONS
Sex educator: Nora Gelperin, Answer, Rutgers University
Book: *A General Theory of Love* by Thomas Lewis, not specifically sex education, but focuses beautifully on the science of human emotions

NATIONAL SEX ED CONFERENCE
Title of presentation: *A Healthy Brain in a High-Tech World*
Presentation description: Each day, American children spend more time in front of electronic screens than any other activity, except sleeping. Facilitators will share key findings in the literature that help guide our understanding of the impact of technology and media on the developing brain, with special emphasis on personal health and sexuality. Strategies for maximizing brain health will be shared.

How I Got Into Sex...Ed

It started with my budding breasts. Anticipating the wonder of wearing a brassiere was the most exciting part of being an 11-year-old girl, when and where I grew up. It was 1965 in rural Colorado. My world revolved around wishing and wondering when my mom would give the green light for getting fitted for my first bra. My friends and I were giddy about the prospect of comparing our bosom-wear. So, when my elementary school sent out "the letter" to all parents of 5th-graders, stating that the school would be teaching a sex education unit and asking parents to please talk to their children and prepare them, my mom, though nervous and overwhelmed with the task, followed those instructions. One afternoon, she summoned me into her bedroom and asked me to sit down on the foot of the bed; I knew something strange was up. I sat; she was visibly nervous. She shared that she had received a letter from school and they were going to have a "special session" for us where they would separate the boys and girls and talk about changes in our bodies. Nervously, she asked me if I knew what it was about. I responded with an enthusiastic, "Yes!!" knowing for sure that they would be preparing us for wearing a bra. With a pronounced sigh she said, "Oh, good," and I could see that she felt a huge sense of relief and that her mission was accomplished. Her work was done, and she sent me on my way.

A few days later, as promised, the county health department health educator, Dorothy Strubel, showed up at our school and came to our classroom. We divided into a girl group and a boy group. The girls went first and were ushered to the "all-purpose" room. Dorothy introduced herself and shared that she was going to talk to us about changes in our bodies. She had set up a filmstrip projector (I wonder if anyone remembers what that is) and began showing us the filmstrip that led us through the changes in puberty, menstruation, and how babies are made. I am embarrassed to say that I spent at least the first half of that filmstrip thinking that the drawing of the fallopian tubes WERE breasts! I envisioned them to be inside my chest, just under my budding breasts. (Think of the two fallopian swirls; it makes sense, right?)

Finally, when I realized the teacher was talking about bleeding and sanitary pads, and penises, and vaginas, it suddenly struck me that I was off course and the fallopian tubes were really below the waist. I remember feeling embarrassed and ignorant, though no one else knew of my personal confusion, not to mention shock. I didn't blame my mom, but I was irritated with her for not sharing more and not preparing me for what felt like public embarrassment. I thought it was unfair to find out that way, in the midst of my friends, with a stranger in the room (the teacher). I wasn't sure how to approach my mom, so I remained silent. That left a mark. I needed information. I needed to talk, and I needed answers. I needed to find my comfort zone. After the boys received their session, Ms. Strubel left the building and the instruction and discussion ended. Silence. We now had to wait until 6th grade, when she returned.

Fast forward to gearing up for college. I knew from age 5 that I wanted to be a teacher. I was born to teach. Elementary? Not the best fit. Secondary? Probably, but what do I teach? Math? Too predictable. Science or language arts? Maybe, but I didn't feel the passion. I wanted to connect with youth at a "life-long learning" level and create a safe space where they could identify tough questions and find answers. The search for self-efficacy seemed to be key. I decided that to reach youth at this level, I would be a good candidate for becoming a school counselor. To accomplish that, it was a requirement that one had to teach a subject for two years. Between my freshman and sophomore year, I was a mess trying to figure out what to do. All summer I read, re-read, studied, and pondered the student handbook. In late summer, I was sitting on the floor in the large college ballroom not knowing what to do. In the days before computers, we had to appear at registration and stand in long lines to register for each class. Then a young man appeared and sat down beside me and asked if I was OK (I must have looked dreadful). I shared my dilemma, and he said, "Given what you want to do, have you ever considered the field of health education?" He calmly turned to those pages in the student handbook and shared the requirements with me. There wasn't anything on the list of required courses that didn't enthuse me (well, except maybe the chemistry requirements). Community health, nutrition, personal health, drug abuse prevention, tobacco prevention, and, there it was, "sexuality education." I wondered how I missed all of that but realized it was buried within the P.E. major and somewhat hidden as a legitimate degree. I signed up. I never saw this man again, and I don't know why he stopped and talked to me, but I will always consider him one of my angels. He opened a door to a career I have loved since day one. I graduated, proudly, with a BA in health education but was told by many I would not find a job. To the contrary, I was employed very soon after graduating by a rural school district where I taught (and LOVED teaching) sexuality education to high school students (and, as it turns out, to their parents, too). I knew I was making a difference. I still have the personal notes that my high school students sent to me saying "thank you!" I went on to teach middle school in an urban district before running sexuality education-related subjects — child sexual abuse prevention and HIV prevention education — at state departments of health and education. My greatest joy as a teacher has been teaching middle and high school students, not just sexuality education, but health education in general, all aspects of achieving healthy minds and bodies — it is ALL so interrelated.

Now, as a teacher of teachers (many of whom are sex educators) in the nonprofit realm, my professional purpose is to move educators and others who work with youth to embrace quality teaching and learning practices based on research, to impact change. My job entails sharing accurate information, embracing best practices, talking with other professionals, and collectively identifying solutions for positively impacting our youth.

Barbara Huscher Cohen

MA, MLA, MEd
Licensed Massachusetts Teacher

Boston, MA

PROFESSIONAL LIFE
Current workplace: SexEdConsultant, Boston, MA
First workplace: Independence House, Cape Cod, MA
Favorite workplace: Connect2Protect, Boston, MA

EDUCATIONAL LIFE
Favorite course: Creative & Critical Thinking Masters
Least favorite course: I honestly believe you can even learn from a horrible class, as you can learn what not to do when you teach. So, nothing has been the worst for me.

TEACHING LIFE
Favorite topic to teach: Puberty for 4th- and 5th-graders and sex after 60 to mature adults
Most challenging topic to teach: Abstinence-only

INSPIRATIONS
Sex educator: Peggy Brick
Book: *Our Bodies, Ourselves* by Boston Women's Health Book Collective and Judy Norsigian

NATIONAL SEX ED CONFERENCE
Title of presentation: *HIV-Prevention and Beyond: Transforming Sex Ed to Meet the Invisible Needs of Youth*
Presentation description: Youth in our classrooms suffer invisible struggles. In this workshop, participants will collaborate in adapting six basic sexuality education lessons to better acknowledge and support youth with a diversity of identities and histories. We will expand upon existing definitions of LGBTQ-inclusive and trauma-informed sexuality education as we articulate these transformative principles together. The facilitators are excited to share the work we've

been doing with colleagues in Boston and to learn from the perspectives of others.

How I Got Into Sex...Ed

Working on a suicide hotline, many of my calls were sex-related. While working at a domestic violence shelter, many of the clients had been sexually abused. Working in a large urban school district, students with behavioral issues often had backgrounds of sexual trauma or issues. Then I started teaching Health Education....

"When should I have sex?"
"My bottom is bleeding!"
"My boyfriend wants me to kiss his privates. Should I?"
"I think I am pregnant."
"Why do people do it?"
"Can I touch myself down there?"

I learned there were 1st-grade girls humping in the bathrooms, 5th-graders pregnant, blow-job clubs, sexual violence toward girls, bad touches, sexual harassment. Students needed sexual education classes instead of learning from porn.

I started as an elementary health teacher, under tobacco grant money, in kindergarten through 5th grade. No matter what lesson or what grade level I taught, it seemed like the students always wanted to talk about their bodies. They were hungry for the knowledge, and I was comfortable talking to them. I think some of my ease came from being a dancer and having my body as my instrument. Out of necessity, I started girls groups. I started boys groups. I began to train nurses, train teachers, hold workshops, work with principals, and have parent nights centered around sex ed. Many of the training sessions started with the students just simply learning to say the words "penis" and "vagina."

This grew into working under a CDC HIV grant as the sex ed teacher in our urban school district of 57,000 students. My work grew and grew as I developed more ways to reach more students and parents. This was difficult, as we then had no health education department, maybe six health teachers, and no designated learning time for health classes during the day. We got creative and kept pushing for Sex Ed as a formal discipline. We did parent, teacher, and student focus groups to find out what our community really wanted and how they really felt about sex education. It was very clear across the board that parents, teachers, and students all wanted sex education. They all knew pregnancy was the number one reason for dropping out of high school. We got parents to the schools by providing dinner — a healthy cooking experience along with sex education. The parents were taught about healthy eating, and received the recipe and its nutritional value. We ate together and then discussed sex. This proved to be very popular. Hyde Square Task Force got behind us, and they are a big force in our Latin community. The students were educated and then made a video. It was shown on CNC and got a lot of press in Boston and around the country. The students were asking for sex education. We reached out to city councilors and started having sex ed hearings. With the help of an outstanding city councilor, Ayanna Pressley, things began to change and the school committee began to listen.

A strong coalition and a very strategic plan were developed. Boston public schools eventually started a new Health and Wellness Department, after about 10 years of not having one, and I became the Health Education Program Director. I continued running the Youth Risk Behavior Survey for Boston Public Schools and the CDC, and by using those statistics, I emphasized the need for health ed and sex ed in the schools. I wrote new skills-based health education frameworks for kindergarten through 12th grade and encouraged the schools to start sexuality education in kindergarten and continue throughout high school graduation.

I felt like things were falling into place, all except for my desire — and the students' desire — to have access to condoms in the schools. I retired a year and a half ago, but I continued to pursue condom access with the help of community organizations and Councilor Pressley. Yes, we got there. Boston now has the beginnings of health education classes that include sex education and access to condoms, which started at the beginning of the present school year.

It was a long ride, but we did it. Presently, I am concentrating on making sure the schools follow through on their new policies in health education and condom access, and I insist on medically accurate and developmentally appropriate curriculum for ALL students as a private Sex Ed Consultant. I am focused on giving workshops, sharing my expertise as often as possible by volunteering for community health boards and education committees, guest lecturing in universities, helping other school districts reach sound sex ed requirements, and writing sex ed articles for the mature adult, as there are plenty of us sexuality active folks over 60!

Heather Corinna

Vashon Island, WA

PROFESSIONAL LIFE

Current workplace: Scarleteen, Seattle, WA

First workplace: See my essay, not sure how to answer this one! :)

Favorite workplace: It's a tie: love running Scarleteen, and love it as a workplace. However, I have equally loved the education work I have done at abortion clinics.

TEACHING LIFE

Favorite topic to teach: Consent, especially as a facilitator of/friend to pleasure

Most challenging topic to teach: Gender-related education, particularly in groups very socialized to think of gender as binary

INSPIRATIONS

Sex educator: Shere Hite

Book: *Our Bodies, Ourselves*, every edition, by Boston Women's Health Book Collective and Judy Norsigian

NATIONAL SEX ED CONFERENCE

Title of presentation: *Don't Fear the Router: How the Internet Can Save Sex Ed*

Presentation description: When it comes to sex ed, the Internet and other online tools aren't just second choices, or ways to supplement other, more traditional, kinds of sex education. They may actually be one of the best ways to provide sex and sexuality information and education, and to have one-on-one or group conversations about sexuality that can provide the safety and comfort that in-person avenues cannot. They also are far less regulated than other means of providing sex education, allowing a freedom in educational materials that can be difficult to find elsewhere.

How I Got Into Sex...Ed

Whenever I'm asked why I do this work, my simplest answer is because those who wanted my help asked me to do it, and I was able to help, so I did. The point at which doing sex education became my full-time job, and my life's work, started just that way. Someone asked me for information I was able to give, and so I gave it to them. The asks kept coming, and so I kept giving. But I'm never exactly sure when that all really started; rather, I can pinpoint a whole lot of times and places I could call the beginning.

It may have first started when, as a child, other children asked me questions about their bodies. I spent a lot of my time in the hospital where my mother worked as a nurse, and, surrounded by medical books I'd compulsively read; I knew the answers and was always delighted (probably a little too pleased, according to the comments on my report cards) to share them.

It may have started when, in high school, being not-at-all shy about my precociously busy sexual life, I was the go-to girl for sex questions from my peers.

It may have started when I was teaching general education in elementary and early childhood settings. Anytime sexual issues or body issues came up, and none of the other teachers wanted to deal with it (as often was the case), it got thrown to me, likely, in part, because I was the youngest teacher or assistant. So, I got the work others didn't want, but after a while, it became clear it wasn't work I minded doing in the least.

It may have begun during the times I found myself stepping up to be the counselor or educator to those who were asking for help while sitting in the waiting room at the sexual healthcare center, the abortion clinic, or heck, the bus stop. As I know some other sexuality educators have also experienced, there is clearly some kind of neon sign that glows over our heads. It blinks brightly at anyone who has questions or concerns, and it seems to indicate that this is the work we were born to do, whether we intended it or not.

And, of course, it may have started when I got the first email, and then the next one, and the next one, and the next (they have yet to stop), that facilitated the development of Scarleteen. That's certainly where, over the past 15 years, I have done the bulk of this work, and where I am asked for help, and give it, most often and most widely. I didn't see answering that one email as something that would result in this becoming such a tremendous part of my life, and all of my work; I didn't even see building one of the first sex education sites online as something that would lead to all this. Sometimes I say that Scarleteen, and providing sex education and support, ate my life, but when I do, I say it with love. It really did take up almost all of the real estate I had to offer, but I also love that it did.

I see so many reasons why I have been drawn, and am still drawn, to this work. As a survivor of sexual abuse before I was even 12 years old, sound sex education matters to me. As someone who knew they were queer before starting puberty, inclusive sex education matters to me. As someone who experienced parts of her life that were often a terrible struggle, my sexuality was a haven for me; alone or with partners, sex education that's about more than just sexual health and reducing health risks, but also about relationships, pleasure, and sexuality as part of who we are — that matters to me. As someone who came from politically radical roots, the activism involved in providing accurate, supportive sex information, especially for young people, matters to me. And as someone who craves a challenge, someone who loves to be creatively and intellectually stimulated, someone who wants to bring kindness and compassion into everything I do, and someone who wants work where I can use all my skills, heart, and talents, I couldn't ask for a better field to work in.

My very favorite thing about how I got started in this work is that no matter which door I'd pick as my entry, all the doors opened because someone asked me to help them, and told me what they wanted and needed. There's a freedom implicit in all of these entry points that remains core to the way I provide sex education and the way I always want to. It's a freedom I feel is essential. The world can push sex and sexuality unto young people, rather than allowing it to unfold naturally and providing support for that process. Instead, I find fulfillment in creating nurturing environments that are truly about learning and the free exchange of information and ideas.

Al Craven

MScEd

Michigan Teaching License: K–8 all subjects, K–5 self-contained, K–12 health & physical education

Adrian, MI

PROFESSIONAL LIFE

Current workplace: Adrian College, Adrian, MI

First workplace: Hamilton Board of Education, Hamilton, ON, Canada, Classroom Teacher of health, including sexuality education

Favorite workplace: TVOntario (educational television), Toronto, ON, Canada, Education Officer & Consultant in HIV/AIDS & Sexuality Education

EDUCATIONAL LIFE

Favorite course: TVOntario Train the Trainer Course on HIV/AIDS

Least favorite course: Principals Qualifications Courses Parts I & II, Ontario

TEACHING LIFE

Favorite topic to teach: Puberty Education

Most challenging topic to teach: LGBTQ Issues

INSPIRATIONS

Sex educator: Sol Gordon, Michael Carrera

Book: *The Joy of Sex* by Alex Comfort

NATIONAL SEX ED CONFERENCE

Title of presentation: Two workshops: *Move Your Feet 2, Lose Your Seat, Too!* and *The King & Queen of Puberty*

Presentation description: This is an interactive student-centered presentation based on the latest brain research and with an emphasis on movement in the classroom. It is a fun presentation to assist students in understanding basic physical, emotional, and social changes during puberty.

How I Got Into Sex...Ed

I began my career in Hamilton, Ontario, teaching a 5th/6th-grade class, but after one year was moved to the inner city to teach physical and health education at the middle-school level. During my five years in this position, I taught health education, which included sexuality education. Over the next few years, my various positions included elementary physical education specialist, teacher of grades 2, 3, and 4, plus a principal's assistant assignment.

A half-time health consultant's position was posted to which I applied and was successful. Over the next two years, I served as the district's health consultant for more than 100 schools. Although I was initially hired to focus on elementary education, I quickly assumed the responsibilities at middle and high school, all this while also teaching a 4th-grade class for half a day. My interest in the field of sexuality was continuing to grow. After two challenging years, they increased my health consultant position to a full-time job.

One fateful day in the fall of 1986, my life changed dramatically. I was sitting in my cubicle with my physical education consultant colleague who turned to me and asked what I knew about AIDS. I responded, "Not much," although I had just read a fascinating article in *Time* magazine about this emerging disease. He asked if I would be interested in attending an important meeting at the Ministry of Education to represent the Health and Physical Education consultants and supervisors in the province of Ontario. They were going to try to develop and implement a curriculum for all middle and high school students in the province, in record time.

Things really took off. I attended the meeting with representatives from numerous key agencies, departments, and unions. The development of the curriculum began immediately. TVOntario, an educational television network that had a history of working with the Ministry of Education, secured a grant of over $6 million to hire a team of educators to develop educational videos and provide workshops on HIV/AIDS for teachers and nurses throughout the province.

I was contacted by TVOntario and asked if we, the Hamilton Board of Education, would host a regional training on the AIDS issue. We were asked because we had a comprehensive sexuality program that had been in place for many years. At the regional training, I was asked to give an overview of what we had done and were doing regarding comprehensive sexuality education. After leaving the stage, I was approached about my interest in becoming a freelance trainer in AIDS for TVOntario. My district gave permission, and I was off to Toronto to participate in an intensive, dynamic one-week training. The course leader, Marion Bacon, was a fabulous, creative individual, who motivated and inspired me. She remains a good friend.

Over the next few months, I conducted a number of workshops around the province. I convinced our school district that we needed to do something to educate our current high school seniors about AIDS before they graduated. My superintendent agreed, and with the cooperation of the Public Health Department, we set up teams to present dozens of seminars for the students.

In August of 1988 TVOntario asked if I would like to take a leave of absence from my school district and be seconded[3] for one year to work on the AIDS Project. Initially, I said no. I felt that all the travel required would be too difficult on my family. About four weeks later I changed my mind, but I figured the position had been filled. I called and found out, to my surprise, they had been unable to fill the position. I immediately was given permission and traveled to TVOntario to assume my new role as an Education Officer on the AIDS Project.

Wow, what an experience awaited! Although the commute to work was a challenge, the next few years were the highlight of my career. To get to Toronto each day, I had to drive approximately 20 minutes to the train station where I boarded a GO Train for the one-hour ride to Toronto. Once there I still had a 15- to 20-minute ride on the subway to get to TVOntario. Thus, my commute time on a good day was three to four hours, round trip. When the weather turned bad, this travel time was dramatically increased. That first year, I presented numerous workshops around the province on AIDS and the effective use of TV in the classroom. I also consulted on video production and participated in radio and television panels. The organization was first-class all the way; our productions were top quality. Our team was passionately and seriously committed to the AIDS issue. We were on the cutting edge of a historic health issue, although at the time, we didn't realize quite how significant the matter was. It was very exciting work.

We attended and had a poster session at the World AIDS Conference in Montreal. I traveled to a one-week sexuality conference in Baltimore sponsored by ETR Associates. It was a fabulous week with Sol Gordon, Michael Carrera, Debra Haffner, and many more magnificent sexuality educators. Perhaps most importantly, I met my future wife, Su Nottingham.

During this year, my mother and I also continued to own and operate a costume store in Hamilton. One of the more creative things I developed was a "teaching condom" costume that I used in my presentations.

My secondment was extended for another year, and we continued to conduct HIV/AIDS and sexuality workshops all over Ontario. We experienced extensive professional development attending and presenting at provincial, state, and national conferences in the United States and Canada including AASECT and SAR programs.

The good fortune continued as I was again asked to stay for a third year. During that year, we developed a project to focus on drug education throughout the province. However, at the end of my third year, I had to return to my teaching position at the Hamilton Board of Education. Over the next four years, I continued to do freelance work for TVOntario in the area of sexuality and HIV/AIDS education, as well as spending two years in middle school and two years in high school teaching physical and health education including sexuality.

I married the woman I met at the ETR sexuality conference and moved to Michigan. I secured a position in Clarkston to develop and implement an elementary health program, which I taught over the next five years. The program included teaching puberty, reproduction, and personal safety lessons. During this time, I was awarded the Health Teacher of the Year by the Michigan Association for Health, Physical Education, Recreation, and Dance.

Then I moved back into a consulting role as a Health Consultant for an Intermediate School District, which consisted of three counties and more than 160 schools. I trained all the teachers in HIV/AIDS and sexuality plus provided support on key sexuality issues with advisory boards.

During this time, my wife and I traveled extensively conducting sexuality and HIV/AIDS workshops across Canada and the United States. We have presented at local, state, provincial, and national conferences, including the World Sexology Conference.

I often think back to what my life, personal and professional, would have been like had I not volunteered to attend that provincial AIDS meeting. Today, I am an Assistant Professor at Adrian College in Michigan where I teach Health Education as well as classes in the Teacher Education Department.

Melanie Davis

MEd, PhD

AASECT Certified Sexuality Educator

Somerville, NJ

PROFESSIONAL LIFE

Current workplace: Unitarian Universalist Association, Boston MA; Honest Exchange LLC, Somerville, NJ; and New Jersey Center for Sexual Wellness, Bedminster, NJ

First workplace: Patient educator and exam room assistant, Planned Parenthood: Flemington Health Center, Flemington, NJ

EDUCATIONAL LIFE

Favorite course: Two undergrad courses, Journalism 101 and Independent Study Creative Writing, both of which honed the writing skills I use today.

TEACHING LIFE

Most challenging topic to teach: Consent education, because we have so far to go as a culture to make the importance of consent universally understood and accepted.

INSPIRATIONS

Sex educator: Eli R. Green never ceases to impress me with his integrity, creativity, compassion, and generosity.

Book: *War Against the Weak: Eugenics and America's Campaign to Create a Master Race* by Edwin Black. But I also like my book, *Look Within: A Woman's Journal*!

How I Got Into Sex...Ed

When I was 7 years old, my two older sisters and I sat at the dinner table while our parents explained puberty and human reproduction. Reproductive organs were sketched on paper napkins, and when the conversation was done, Dad and Mom asked us not to share the information with our friends, whose parents might not be ready for similar conversations.

I was confused. Why would parents keep that from their kids? Wouldn't it confuse them to learn the truth later? Sure enough, a few friends told me later that when they started menstruating, they had been sure they were dying.

In my mid-20s, I volunteered as a patient educator for Planned Parenthood. I loved interacting with the staff and patients, even though I was often floored by most patients' complete lack of understanding of sexual anatomy, reproduction, and contraception. In time, I became an exam room assistant, prepping, cleaning, and remaining in the room during patient visits. Technically, I was there to assist the nurse practitioner or physician, but often patients asked me to hold their hand and ease their nervousness. A side benefit of that role was that it put an end to any embarrassment I may have had about getting pelvic exams.

I didn't realize it at the time, but my childhood at-home sexuality education and work at Planned Parenthood were an excellent foundation for the work that I do today. Much of my one-on-one time with students and clients is devoted to education on the fundamentals of sexual anatomy, function, and pleasure. I also do a lot of myth- and shame-busting.

I entered the field late in life at age 45, having spent 25 years as an independent marketing copywriter and journalist. When I entered Widener University's Graduate Program in Human Sexuality, my goal was to earn a master's degree to enhance my qualifications as a speaker on parent-child communication about sexuality. I considered my workshops for school and community groups as simply an avocation spurred by my facilitation of the *Our Whole Lives* sexuality education curriculum for my Unitarian Universalist congregation.

Early on in grad school, I found myself writing comments in the margins of my notes like "Great idea for patient education brochure...," "Idea for resource packet...," "Idea for a workshop," "Great research topic!" I also noticed that nearly all of my research papers involved some aspect of physician–patient communication about sexuality. I decided this might be a career path, so I switched into the doctoral program, figuring that physicians would be more receptive to a sexuality educator with a PhD.

One of my close friends at Widener was (and remains) Constance Bowes, a therapist with experience as an outplacement career counselor. As two of the oldest students in the program, we observed a need for emerging professionals to learn basics like resume writing, job interviewing, networking, and other aspects of career development. We pitched our idea for the Careers in Sexuality Education Professional Skills Conference to Betsy Crane, then director of the Graduate Program in Human Sexuality, who immediately approved it. I'm proud to say that the student-organized conference continues to grow, attracting students and professionals in and beyond the Widener community.

I founded Honest Exchange LLC in 2006 as a resource publishing company but then felt called to work with people face to face. The more I learned about how to teach and how people learn, and the more programs I presented, the more I realized that as a sexuality educator, I could touch people's lives in a significant way. I leapt at the chance to attend and speak at sexology programs and conferences. Every interaction with my fellow graduate students, faculty, and professionals increased my commitment to the field of sexuality education.

I landed my first academic position at Marymount Manhattan College in NYC, four days after earning my master's degree, thanks to a one-semester adjunct professor job opening that Don Dyson posted on the Widener student listserv. I thoroughly enjoyed teaching, but my interest in working in the healthcare environment continued, leading me to establish the New Jersey Center for Sexual Wellness with sex therapist Sandra Leiblum, PhD (creator of Sex Week at Robert Wood Johnson Medical School) and OB/GYN Judith Hersh, FACOG. Upon Sandra's unexpected death, sex therapist Melissa Donahue, LCSW, CST, joined our practice. My role in our venture is to provide clinical sexuality education to teens, individuals, and couples who usually are referred by gynecologists and family practitioners.

I promote my clinical practice using techniques honed during my marketing career as well as findings from my dissertation, *Sexuality Education as Perceived by Physicians and Therapists: An Assessment of Attitudes about and Interest in Referring Patients to Sexuality Educators.* My research showed me which types of physicians and therapists are most likely to refer patients for sexuality education as well as the types of patients they are likely to refer. Those findings have also come in handy as a basis for lectures to medical students and physicians in addition to workshops for sexuality educators and therapists.

I have taught two courses at Widener University and taught for 5 years at Moravian College before taking the 2013–2014 academic year off to focus on writing and speaking engagements. I recently developed a Human Sexuality course for a theological school as part of my growing interest in working with clergy.

I never imagined myself as a college professor, but I find the work tremendously rewarding (except for grading, which nearly every professor hates with equal passion). I've been privileged to support students who came out of the closet, who found the strength to leave unhealthy relationships, who struggled with chronic sexual health issues, and who disclosed their most private concerns, identities, and explorations.

Professional trainings and speaking engagements are challenging and fun, as this field offers an intriguing variety of clients and audiences. I also tremendously enjoy my part-time work for the Unitarian Universalist Association — in a weird twist of fate, I oversee and write resources for the *Our Whole Lives* sexuality education program that triggered my interest in becoming a sexuality educator many years ago.

My flexible work schedule enables me to serve as co-president of the Sexuality and Aging Consortium at Widener University. In this capacity, I am part of a growing, national organization devoted to enhancing and advancing the sexual health, rights, and education of older adults and the professionals who serve them. It is compelling work that engages me professionally and personally, as I am now part of the age demographic with which the consortium is concerned.

I have carved out time for creative projects, too. In 2013, I wrote *Look Within: A Woman's Journal,* which offers 60+ writing prompts that help women explore their sexuality, experiences, and expectations for the future. I have delivered workshops and a Unitarian Universalist Adult Faith Development course based on the book, which have inspired me to begin planning other writing and education projects.

Every day, I find joy and purpose in my work, and I know that I am not unique in this regard. It is an honor to be part of a profession populated by amazingly caring, creative, talented, and compassionate people. I was once concerned that I came too late to the party, but I couldn't have envisioned this career earlier in my life. It is never too late to become who you are really meant to be.

Kirsten deFur

MPH

Our Whole Lives Trainer,
Middle/High School and Young Adult/Adult

New York, NY

PROFESSIONAL LIFE

Current workplace: NYC Mayor's Office to Combat Domestic Violence, New York, NY

First workplace: Consultant for the Virginia Department of Education, Richmond, VA. I updated the sexuality education resource list for health educators in Virginia.

Favorite workplace: *Our Whole Lives* Facilitator, Arlington, VA and New York, NY (Manhattan, Brooklyn, and Staten Island)

EDUCATIONAL LIFE

Favorite course: Origins of Christianity, while I was an undergraduate student at the University of North Carolina at Greensboro. Since I did not grow up reading the bible, this was a fabulous opportunity to learn about Christianity in an academic context.

Least favorite course: Environmental Studies, while a graduate student at Columbia University. Vitally important topic, but poorly taught.

TEACHING LIFE

Favorite topic to teach: Sexual pleasure, because it piques most people's interest and many people have not had other opportunities to discuss the topic in an educational learning environment.

Most challenging topic to teach: Asexuality, because it's such a new and evolving concept that I'm still trying to wrap my head around it, both personally and professionally.

INSPIRATIONS

Sex educator: Debra Haffner. When I was still figuring out how to become a sexuality educator, I read an article in the *UU*

World (the weekly web magazine of the Unitarian Universalist Association of Congregations) that featured Debra Haffner. After reading the article, I sent her an email asking for advice about getting into the field, and she replied with some great insight. It has been amazing to witness her advocacy efforts in the field, and the resources she has crafted are essential.

Book: *But How'd I Get in There in The First Place?*, by Deborah Roffman. This book does such a good job of describing early childhood development and age-appropriate responses to some of the questions that adults really freak out about answering.

NATIONAL SEX ED CONFERENCE

Title of presentation: *YES! YES! YES! Teaching Enthusiastic Consent from a Pleasure Perspective*

Presentation description: No means no? How about yes means YES! Recent high profile cases such as the rape case in Steubenville, OH, highlight the need for sexual violence prevention initiatives. However, many approaches utilize fear-based messages and focus exclusively on sexual abstinence and refusal, omitting messages about giving and seeking consent. Alternatively, sexuality educators can teach participants how to actively articulate their desire to engage in sexual activities, and seek enthusiastic consent from their partner/s. During this interactive workshop, participants will define the term "enthusiastic consent," examine a teaching framework that acknowledges pleasure, and identify effective educational strategies.

How I Got Into Sex...Ed

"But Mom, I don't wanna go!" I said in response to my parents when they told me I would be taking a year-long SEX-ED class at CHURCH. I had just started 8th grade at Byrd Middle School in Richmond, VA. I was an angsty 13-year-old, dealing with feelings of being a social outcast, and I was not excited about spending my Sundays learning about sex. I refused to go, probably thinking I knew it all already. To that, my parents said that if I went to the first few classes and was really unhappy, that I didn't have to keep going. I figured that was a good compromise, so I agreed. (This was my first teenage lesson that my parents were not *always* wrong.) The class, and my classmates, turned out to be just what I needed — a social group that felt accepting and different from the "stuck-up" kids at school, led by two adults who were 100% comfortable talking about sex. The class made sexuality feel so normal and OK at a critical time in my personal development, both physically and emotionally. We talked about masturbation and condoms as if they were simply part of life, rather than something to be ignored, overlooked, or shunned.

That "About Your Sexuality" (AYS) class at the First Unitarian Universalist Church of Richmond, VA, was probably one of the best things that I did as I entered the tumultuous time of being a teenager. (Thanks, Mom & Dad!) Not only did I learn facts and information that the teachers didn't even begin to cover in the so-called "sex ed" classes in school, I also developed deep and lasting friendships. And many of those classmates are still my friends today, almost 20 years later (and not *just* as Facebook friends).

It wasn't until my senior year of college when I realized the impact that AYS class would have on my entire life. I was attending the University of North Carolina at Greensboro, pursuing a double major in flute performance and religious studies. I had spent the previous 11 years of my life focused on ear training, theory, crescendos, breath marks, and key changes. In college I regularly played my flute 3–5 hours a day, and served as principal flutist in the university orchestra. While I realized that I wouldn't become James Galway (not *my* favorite, anyway), I was considering a career in ethnomusicology as a way to combine my interests in music and religion. My studies had certainly leaned far toward the rigorous music program rather than the one class per semester I needed for my religious studies major.

In the beginning of my final semester, one of my religious studies professors suggested that I get a summer internship — I would be the first student to have an internship in the religious studies department. This was certainly appealing, since the six extra credits I would earn would give me a Bachelor of Arts in addition to my Bachelor of Music degree, and not just a double major. As I was searching for positions, I stumbled upon several intriguing opportunities at organizations such as the SIECUS and the National Campaign to Prevent Teen Pregnancy. In this search for an internship, I realized two things: First, there actually was a professional field of sexuality education, and second, I was really comfortable talking about sexuality with pretty much anyone. While my peers in North Carolina struggled to say words such as *orgasm* and *clitoris*, or ask questions about birth control options or sex before marriage, I talked with ease about sex with the saxophone players, the trumpet players, the vocalists, the cellists, the pianists, the kids in my dorm, friends from church, and so on. I realized that talking about sex is a skill not many people have. I recalled my own positive educational experience attending AYS and thought, I would love to provide the others with a similarly comfortable, safe environment to learn about and explore the complicated topic of sexuality. The realization felt so right that I didn't think twice about whether or not to pursue a career as a sexuality educator; it simply came down to *how* I could accomplish that goal.

That summer I did land an internship in the government relations department at the National Abortion and Reproductive Rights Action League (NARAL, now Pro-Choice America). I spent my time doing opposition research and attending hearings and press conferences, not really teaching sex ed, but it was a step in the right direction. And while I had always been vocal about sexual health issues such as abortion, I had perennially argued that we should be trying to reduce the need for abortion in the first place; an approach of prevention and education.

So, in the midst of preparing for my senior flute recital and wrapping up my degree in religious studies, I figured out that the career path of sexuality education fit me like a glove. While many of my peers were going on to teach high school band or get their masters at schools such as Julliard, I was on a very different path to sex ed stardom. My friends' reactions were affirmation enough; they all agreed that my "skill" of talking openly and honestly about sexuality would be put to good use.

After my big "aha" moment, I realized that I had spent a significant amount of time and energy honing my skills as a musician, and I would need to apply the same enthusiasm to building my knowledge base in sexuality — being a sexuality educator is much more than just being a sexual person. The next steps on this path included:

- Working as a consultant updating sex ed resources for the Virginia Department of Education (thanks to my aunt for the connection);

- Leading a workshop for my peers titled "Just Say Yes: Examining Ways to Say Yes to Sex" at the Southeast Unitarian Universalist Summer Institute (the room was bustin' at the seams with people wanting to participate);

- Volunteering as a sex educator for Richmond's Planned Parenthood (wow, kids really need this info);

- Teaching the 4th–6th grade *Our Whole Lives (OWL)* program at the Unitarian Universalist Congregation of Arlington, VA (omg, how did I manage without this class as a 10-year-old?); and

- Moving to New York City to get my Master of Public Health in Sexuality and Health at Columbia University (finally I could talk about sex in a thoughtful, academic environment).

Since finishing my masters in 2006, I have become a trainer for the adult/young adult and middle/high school age groups of the *OWL* program in addition to teaching almost all of the *OWL* levels. (Learn more about this comprehensive sexuality education program for humans of all ages at *www.uua.org/owl*. Fun fact: *AYS* was the predecessor to *OWL*.) My day job is directing the New York City Healthy Relationship Training Academy, a peer education initiative of the NYC Mayor's Office to Combat Domestic Violence. In doing this challenging and inspiring work in violence prevention on a daily basis, I have realized that in order to have positive, healthy, pleasure-filled sexual experiences, one must also have a healthy relationship, and that abuse and violence are often what get in the way. In recent years, the Center for Sex Education's National Sex Ed Conference has given me a chance to both explore some cutting-edge ideas in sexuality education and also meet some inspirational leaders in the field.

In January 2012, I started a blog about sexuality education, *www.fearlesssexualityeducator.com*, where I post about a variety of topics related to sexuality and how, as educators, we can take a positive, rather than fear-based, approach. Most frequently I post about sexuality in the media/news as part of my Friday FREAK OUT series. In addition, in the past year some fellow sexuality educators and I have been geeking out in a sexuality book club, reading those books that always sound so intriguing but can be hard to commit to. The book club makes me read the book, for better (*Mating in Captivity*) or for worse (*A Mind of its Own: A Cultural History of the Penis*).

Being a sexuality educator who is able to walk into any room and quickly engage a group in thought-provoking discussion is both a gift and a challenge. As a sexuality educator and trainer, my focus is on creating learning environments that encourage critical thinking and self-exploration about both the difficult and the everyday issues of sexuality. I hope that participants will be *comfortable* talking about sex, rather than *afraid* of it. Sexuality is an integral component of human existence, and our understanding of sex can enhance and/or inhibit our relationships. By offering educational opportunities that are open, honest, and affirming, individuals can really own and enjoy their sexual experiences.

And I'm having fun doing it all.

Melissa Keyes DiGioia

Graduate Certificate in Human Sexuality,
BA Psychology/Women's & Gender Studies,
AASECT Certified Sexuality Educator

Morristown, NJ

PROFESSIONAL LIFE
Current workplace: Planned Parenthood of Central and Greater Northern New Jersey (Morristown, NJ)
First workplace: Planned Parenthood of Central New Jersey (Shrewsbury, NJ)
Favorite workplace: Any alternative or specialized learning/life skills setting for people with disabilities

EDUCATIONAL LIFE
Favorite course: Politics of Sexuality

TEACHING LIFE
Favorite topic to teach: Pleasure! I try to infuse it in my sexual health and prevention topics.

INSPIRATIONS
Sex educator: Sue Montfort, CHES, MAT
Book: These are my two favorites. I cannot choose! *Because It Feels Good: A Woman's Guide to Sexual Pleasure* and *Satisfaction* and *I Heart Female Orgasm*

NATIONAL SEX ED CONFERENCE
Title of presentation: *Positive Images: Teaching about Contraception and Sexual Health*
Presentation description: My session will introduce attendees to the newest edition of *Positive Images: Teaching about Abstinence, Contraception and Sexual Health!* Attendees will experience strategies that focus on sexual health and a healthcare visit, factors that impact pregnancy prevention, and practicing interpersonal communication. As a result, they will be able to state common adolescent sexual health concerns,

identify factors that can impact contraceptive option selection, and describe two strategies to facilitate interpersonal communication about contraception and condoms.

How I Got Into Sex...Ed

I did not know as an undergraduate taking Women's and Gender Studies classes that it would lead me on my journey to the field of sexuality education. However, each class broadened my understanding of gender, sexual orientation, reproductive rights, oppression, and sexual violence. As a senior, my thesis allowed me to analyze representations of female sexuality in pop culture print media. I read research and theoretical constructs to better understand why media representations pigeon-holed women as "good girls" or "bad girls." As a result, I became passionate that women have access to positive, healthy constructs of female sexuality that facilitate autonomous, pleasurable, and safe sexual decisions.

After graduation I applied at a local Planned Parenthood, and my dream became a reality! Initially, I presented to adolescents and adults mainly about the topics of contraceptive choice and sexual health risk reduction. However, throughout the years, the populations I serve and the sexual health topics I deliver have grown exponentially. Training and collaboration with fellow sexuality educators have provided me with the knowledge and skills to create professional development workshops, develop multimodal education techniques, and co-author *Game On! The Ultimate Sexuality Education Gaming Guide* with my colleague and friend Jessica Shields.

Even after 10 years, I am still acutely aware that empowerment, information, and opportunities to practice skills are imperative for people to make autonomous, pleasurable, and safe sexual decisions. Of all the people I work with, people with intellectual and developmental disabilities often lack these criteria the most. Though I still continue to work with varying populations, I feel the most passionate about providing medically accurate, developmentally appropriate, and *positive* sexual health information to people with disabilities. In truth, I have learned how to be a better sexuality educator because of this work. Students with disabilities have taught me to be flexible in my approach and open-minded about topics in order to meet their needs and concerns. As I result, I think more critically about what I present, and I more carefully consider what types of materials and methodology I use.

Sometimes students will assume that I know everything about sex, and I chuckle, because sexuality information and the way we communicate information is constantly evolving. Applying new research, technology, and educational methodology in sexuality education is a daily and welcome challenge for me, one that I look forward to for years to come.

Shanna M. Dusablon Drone

MSW, MAEd

Apple Valley, CA

PROFESSIONAL LIFE

Current workplace: High Desert Juvenile Court School, Apple Valley, CA

First workplace: East Missouri Action Agency, Family Planning Intern, Cape Girardeau, CO

Favorite workplace: Human Sexuality Graduate Assistant, University of Illinois at Urbana-Champaign

EDUCATIONAL LIFE

Favorite course: Human Sexuality at the University of Denver for my Master of Social Work. The course stressed the importance of recognizing how sexuality is interwoven into all aspects of life, even when clients are not discussing sexuality. I also realized the importance of communicating about sexuality and how empowering it can be for couples and individuals to express their needs and desires.

Least favorite course: Anything with statistics! Only now at the PhD level am I beginning to understand this subject!

TEACHING LIFE

Favorite topic to teach: I enjoy speaking with adolescent males (adjudicated males, foster youth, and at-risk students) about their roles and responsibilities in their own sexuality.

Most challenging topic to teach: A challenging topic for me is aging and sexuality because I have zero experience with that population.

INSPIRATIONS

Sex educator: I am in absolute awe of Dr. Konnie McCaffree! I had the privilege and honor of being a student of hers at Widener University, and to me she is the epitome of a sexuality educator. She wants to empower all students to make the best decisions possible, based on accurate information. She teaches sex educators to be acutely aware of their methodologies and biases so that students can receive the best sexuality education possible. She creates a classroom of support, encouragement, and questions. She strives to engage all who want to learn about sexuality. She is my hero!

Book: *Guide to Getting It On* by Paul Joannides

NATIONAL SEX ED CONFERENCE

Title of presentation: *W.R.a.P. It Up: A Call to Action for Comprehensive Sexuality Education for Adolescent Males within Juvenile Detention Centers*

Presentation description: Incarcerated juvenile fathers are an at-risk group for poor sexual decision-making and responsibility. Let's start a conversation about the policies associated with juvenile delinquency and teenage fatherhood. "W.R.a.P. It Up — With Respect and Purpose" invites you to utilize your sexual education skills in assisting these youth with making responsible sexual decisions.

How I Got Into Sex...Ed

Becoming a sex educator was as simple as someone asking me to be a peer educator while I was an undergraduate student at Southeast Missouri State University in 1995. I had been involved with the Residence Hall Association and worked as a Community Advisor in the residence halls. Somehow word got out that I loved talking with students about sex, finding answers, and connecting the pieces of being involved in high-risk sexual activity (intoxication and sex, unprotected sex, date rape, etc.). I then did a 6-month internship as a family planning intern working with adolescents and parents about puberty, pregnancy, birth control, and STIs. Through these experiences as an undergraduate, I began to learn the importance of communicating about sexuality. I knew that I wanted to work in the field of sexuality; I just did not know how to break into the field.

So in 2000, during my first graduate school experience at the University of Denver for a Master of Social Work, I focused on the policy and politics of providing sexuality education as well as the financial aspects of prevention and welfare services for teenage pregnancies. It was an eye-opener to realize that sexuality education policy and funding are so closely related to "who" is running local, state, and national politics. I continued to realize that I wanted to work in this field, but I still could not find an in.

I worked at a couple of different universities as a health educator and residence director and continued to see a need for conversations about sexuality. At one Midwest university, I taught "Human Sexuality" in a discussion-based class as well as a lecture class. In those moments of speaking with college students, I again realized my strengths in teaching sexuality: I was comfortable with all topics. I realized that my ease helped students find their own comfort levels and that opened doors for questions and conversations that may not have occurred otherwise. When I was speaking with these students, it was as natural as breathing, and I loved it. I thought I had finally found my "in" for a sexuality educator position, but not quite yet.... Instead I found love, got married, and moved back to California from Illinois.

I then started working at a juvenile detention center and gave up my dream of working as a sexuality educator. I went back to school at Azusa Pacific University and earned two more Masters in Education in 2008 and 2011. I was happy and content in my classroom of incarcerated males. I enjoyed the everyday challenge of keeping these students interested and engaged in learning. I relished it. Funny thing though... questions about sexuality kept coming up in class. I began to realize how many of my students were dads before the age of 18. I kept noticing that this certain population of students were not receiving formal sexuality education and were continuously engaging in high-risk behaviors (sex while under the influence, intravenous drug use, unprotected sex, sexual assault, multiple partners, etc.). Who was looking out for this population? So what did I decide to do about it? Once again, I went back to school!

I enrolled at Widener University in Fall 2011 for the PhD program in Human Sexuality. I decided to merge my experience and training from having worked with incarcerated adolescent males with my passion for sexuality education. As I did more research on this population, I realized that there is very little attention paid to this particular group. Also, I learned that most pregnancy prevention is focused on females. I want to be a part of a revolution that calls for more focused sexuality education on adolescent males as well as engaging young men in the dialogue and action of being responsible fathers.

The journey of becoming a sexuality educator has been just that, a voyage. I would not trade the amount of time, education (including student loans), and experiences that have led me to where I am today. I am a sexuality educator who specializes in teaching at-risk adolescent males, training adults who work with these males in various systems, and promoting the importance of sexuality communication.

I know that my story is not titillating, sensational, or filled with lurid tales. I do not think that it needs to be; I think many sexuality educators came to the field because they saw a gap in education that needed to be filled. My story is one of knowing what has always been my passion, yet taking the road less traveled to find my way home.

Catherine Dukes
PhD

Newark, DE

PROFESSIONAL LIFE
Current workplace: Planned Parenthood of Delaware
First workplace: Internship at Division of Public Health as an HIV Educator
Favorite workplace: Planned Parenthood of Delaware

EDUCATIONAL LIFE
Favorite course: SAR at Institute for Advanced Study of Human Sexuality
Least favorite course: Statistics

TEACHING LIFE
Favorite topic to teach: Educating parents about talking to their kids about sex without dying from embarrassment
Most challenging topic to teach: Gender

INSPIRATIONS
Sex educator: My mom...she was my most powerful educator.
Book: *Promiscuities* by Naomi Wolf

NATIONAL SEX ED CONFERENCE
Title of presentation: *Slut Shaming & Stud-Baiting: Using the Courageous Bystander Model to Shift Attitudes in the Classroom*
Presentation description: An effective sex ed course depends heavily on the students' environment. Using the courageous bystander model, educators can empower their students to positively shift their classroom culture. In this workshop, participants will learn how to engage students as change-makers in confronting harmful stereotypes and creating a space of equality.

How I Got Into Sex...Ed

My mom always taught me the correct names of body parts. As I entered my teens, I thought that was weird. But looking back, I realize that her comfort with discussing anatomy and sex with me was my inspiration for becoming a sex educator and a sexologist. When I got older, I began to understand that much of what made my mom different was a cultural difference. Mom was born and raised in France — the country of love and lovers. So as a child, I would collect fake, cutesy names of body parts and bring them back to my mom asking, "Well is it a hoochie or a vagina?" and in her French accent, my mom would always clarify that it was actually called a vagina.

When I started college, I wandered between majors for a short time. I was in the Honors Program, and I took a class called International Women's Health with Dr. Kate Conway-Turner. During that class, a couple of graduate students made a presentation on their research on Asian-Americans and sexual behavior. I have no recollection what the results were but I was stunned. "You can study sex?" I practically ran up to my professor after the class asking, "How can I study THAT? How can I study sex?" And she smiled and led me to my major, Family and Community Services, with my area of specialization: Human Sexuality Issues. I was hooked. I took every sex class from every college and department in the University of Delaware — health sciences, anthropology, psychology, women's studies...everything! I also became interested in working as an advocate for those who experienced sexual assault as a Volunteer Rape Crisis Counselor.

In college, I tried to volunteer and then intern for Planned Parenthood of Delaware, but at first no one called me back, and then when they did, I was told no internships were available. But I was determined to become a sex educator. When I graduated from college, I accepted a job as a DUI Evaluator because I could also devote part of my time as an HIV Educator to those who were in drug and alcohol treatment. When I was 23, a job opened up for an Educator at Planned Parenthood of Delaware in the Education

Department. I was ecstatic, and I prepared diligently for the interview. Don Dyson, the Director of Education at the time, did NOT hire me. I was devastated. I learned that the candidate who had gotten the job had a master's degree. More education, I thought. I can do that. However, soon after that I landed a dream job as Director of Rape Crisis Services. I loved that job and led the rape crisis program for 4 years before finally following my dream to study...(more) sex.

I researched the programs: the Institute for Advanced Study of Human Sexuality in San Francisco or Widener University? I was torn as both offer diverse and wonderful programs. I decided to meet with Dr. Bill Stayton at Widener. He gave me a tour, and we talked for a long time. He asked me all about my interests and career aspirations. Afterward, "Oh, Honey," he said, "You NEED to be in San Francisco." And that was the final straw. I made my plans. I quit the job that I loved. I sold all my furniture. I left my hometown, my friends, and my family. I rented out my house. And then I drove what few possessions I had left across the country to San Francisco. It was a 3,000-mile-long, incredible leap of faith because I truly believed I was meant to be a sexologist and I was meant to be in San Francisco. What an amazing trip, and what a huge risk! I started at the Institute and fell in love with the program and everyone there. What an amazing education. The SAR, the classes, the professors, the students, and the experiences were unlike anything else I'd ever experienced. Amazing and life-changing. This is exactly where I needed to be. I made deep friendships quickly both in and outside of school, and everything fell into place (despite living in poverty).

As I was finishing my dissertation on "Women, BDSM & Body Image: A Comparative Analysis," I was aware I had to start preparing for life after grad school. I started a nationwide job search for program management jobs in sex ed. Impossibly, the first job that popped up on the first day of my national search was "VP of Education & Training" at Planned Parenthood of Delaware in my hometown...the same Planned Parenthood that had refused my offers of volunteering, then interning, and later my application to be an educator. Could this be it? I applied and received a call fairly quickly. I was interviewed over the phone and invited to come to Delaware for my second interview. I made flight plans and bought a suit and a new pair of glasses. I prepared endlessly for my interview. I cold-called other Planned Parenthood Education Directors across the country who were, like me, members of AASECT. I asked them for their insight on PP education work, funding, trends, target populations, and challenges. I even was able to speak with Don Dyson while in the airport on my way to the interview. I prepared for over 40 hours for that one 90-minute interview. I was back in San Francisco having just presented my dissertation when I got the call: I got the job! I accepted immediately. I loved San Francisco but was also so excited to be moving home to Delaware.

On July 31, 2006, I started my new job as VP of Education & Training at Planned Parenthood of Delaware. Nine years after I had first called PPDE trying to volunteer, trying to get my foot in the door, I had landed my dream job!

Over the past eight years I can truly say I've lived the dream. I've worked with and met some of the most extraordinary sexologists and sex educators in the nation. I've built my department from a department of one with no funding, to a team of six, and then finally a team of four with enough grant and contract money for our department to be essentially self-sufficient. Together we've successfully implemented a federal Personal Responsibility Education Program (PREP) grant statewide and formed positive collaborative relationships with our Department of Education, the Division of Public Health, and many local teacher and community service providers reaching more than 5,000 people per year.

What I love most about my job is the light-bulb moments from youth, from professionals, but mostly from parents. Parents are the most effective sex educators of their children, and it's rewarding to offer them the tools and teach them the skills to start a lifetime of sex ed conversations. Our programs allow parents to shed the fear that talking about sex will make their kids more sexually active, and they leave with the skills to start meaningful conversations about relationships, sex, decision-making, birth-control, and safer sex.

I've been teaching parents for eight years, but two years ago I became a parent for the first time...of twins. And I had to start taking my own advice. My kids knew the correct names of their genitals at 12 and 13 months old — awesome! Being the primary sex educator of my own children and seeing them learn about their bodies has been life-changing.

Then last year, I was asked to be the co-chair of the National Sex Ed Conference. It was an incredible experience to work with Bill Taverner and Jeffrey Anthony and to co-chair with the remarkable Dr. Karen Rayne. As VP of Education at a statewide affiliate, a mom of then one-year-old twins, and a co-chair of a national conference, my world last year was, to say the least, busy and exhausting, but inspiring and exhilarating as well! I still can't believe I was chosen to co-chair such a prestigious conference — the largest National Sex Ed Conference ever at that time. Also in 2013, my education department won a national Planned Parenthood APPLE Education Award for our work in bringing evidence-based programs into schools throughout Delaware by training teachers to implement with fidelity.

I'm so excited about being a VP of Education at a Planned Parenthood and being a mom to two amazing toddlers who are growing up in a sex-positive environment. I'm so proud to have been co-chair of the National Sex Ed Conference and to have led a national award-winning team. But most of all, I love to come to work every day with people I care about who are just as passionate about "the work" as I am. They inspire me with their creativity, their expertise, and their passion, and I can't wait to see what comes next.

Joycelyn Elders

MS, MD
American Board of Pediatrics,
American Board of Pediatric Endocrinology

Little Rock, AR

PROFESSIONAL LIFE
Current workplace: Professor Emeritus at Children's Hospital, Little Rock, AR
First workplace: University of Arkansas School of Medicine, Little Rock, AR
Favorite workplace: Arkansas Department of Health

EDUCATIONAL LIFE
Favorite course: Biochemistry
Least favorite course: Statistics

TEACHING LIFE
Favorite topic to teach: Human Sexuality and Pediatric Endocrinology
Most challenging topic to teach: Adolescent Sexuality

INSPIRATIONS
Sex educator: Eli Coleman, Pepper Schwartz
Book: *Solving America's Sexual Crisis* by Ira L. Reiss and Harriet M. Reiss

NATIONAL SEX ED CONFERENCE
Title of presentation: *Sex Ed and the Nation*
Presentation description: America is not a sexually healthy nation as manifested by intolerable statistics. The result of a lack of sexuality education, withheld information, and distribution of misinformation is America's sexual dysfunction; it can be measured by rates of unintended pregnancy and STIs that are higher than those of virtually every other developed country. Ignorance is not bliss.

On an individual level, preventable sexual health-risk behaviors among adolescents can expose them to lifelong consequences about which they are ill informed. This dysfunction threatens public health, disrupts family life, and generally imposes a high societal cost through poverty and misery. We can do better.

Preventing adverse consequences that occur with unprotected adolescent sex requires a broad-based approach that begins with the recognition that adolescents are both valued and vulnerable. Efforts in the United States that address adolescent sex have been directed toward preventing teenage sex as opposed to preventing its adverse consequences. Europe and other developed countries send the message to teens — safe sex or no sex.

Adolescents need education. To withhold basic facts of health, including sexual reproductive health, is child abuse. Sexually active adolescents need contraceptives, and the best contraceptive in the world is a good education. Strategies that we can employ to make America healthier and the creative role of health educators in accomplishing this change to improve sexual health and sexuality education will be discussed.

How I Got Into Sex...Ed

How I Learned to Swim in Jello

Looking back, I can see that life is about passages; development in one area evolves somehow into another area and into another. I began my profession as a medical doctor in pediatric endocrinology. Enlightening experiences and opportunities moved me into research and professorship at a medical school. More enlightening experiences led me into public health and to my position as the Director of Public Health in Arkansas, where I began to focus on the heart-wrenching problems at hand — teenage pregnancy and all the problems and suffering that go with it: poverty, lack of education, illegitimacy, low birth-weight babies, and high mortality.

My realization that the plight of youth in our society was vulnerable came gradually. Although I can look back and see the vulnerability of boys and girls throughout my younger life, it was in the years of my training in pediatrics that it became clear that we are not all the same at birth, neither in material things nor certainly in genetic makeup.

While many adults cringe at simply seeing the words, "adolescent" and "sexuality" paired together, the adolescent hormonal imperative continues its relentless takeover of youthful thinking and often, action. When children experience puberty, natural intensification of sexual feelings soon follows. Even worse for parents is when this normal process doesn't begin. I saw boys who should have gone through puberty but had not developed their sexual organs who were brought in by their concerned fathers. Children who were gender misidentified or had ambiguous sexual identification were all patients in my field of endocrinology. Humans are not always clearly male or female; we come in all manner of gradation. All of this helped me to understand that every one of us needs to be more informed — educated — in order to provide a healthy culture in which all people are valued and in which our vulnerable youth can develop to their full potential as human beings.

It became obvious to me that many young women were stuck in horrible predicaments that seemed to be inextricable. As a pediatric endocrinology resident, I saw young patients with endocrine problems, which included sex organs and sex hormones. But what struck me was a pretty 13-year-old girl from the Ozarks, who I will call Mary, who had a large goiter on her neck and bulging eyes — classic symptoms of hyperthyroidism. The doctor who referred her also wrote that she had severe nervousness, smothering spells, high blood pressure, bed-wetting, weight loss, and poor performance in school. After hospitalization, we were able to control her thyroid condition and were ready to release her to go home. When I told her, she began to cry and, after sitting with her for a while, said that she didn't want to go home. I thought, "Who doesn't want to go home from the hospital?" She finally explained that on Saturday nights at home her father and uncles got drunk and "used" her. When I tried to bring it up with the mother indirectly without making accusations, she denied knowledge of any problem. At that time, laws prevented us from interfering in a situation like this. In court or in a police station, it would just be the father and uncles' word against the young woman. So, I had no choice but to send her home. I saw her twice more in the clinic over the next two months. Her thyroid problem was doing fine, but the last time I saw her, she was pregnant. Her life seemed to be ruined; here she was at 13, pregnant by a close relative. Abortion was illegal even in a case like Mary's. How did she go on?

Stories like this continued throughout my residency and practice until the law changed. Thankfully, doctors and nurses went from not being able to do anything legally in these situations, to being mandated to report suspected abuse. I was a pediatric endocrinologist, not someone who would ordinarily run into the Marys in the world of medicine. If I was seeing this many patients who had been sexually abused, how many were there? What was education doing to address problems in sexuality?

When Governor Bill Clinton offered me the job as Director of Public Health in Arkansas, he said that he wanted me to improve the horrible teenage pregnancy statistics in Arkansas. Finally, in 1987, I agreed to take the job with him agreeing to back me up as I attempted to bring innovation to the Department of Health and "jump their engine," moving them into a new direction as he requested. This was an opportunity that ultimately evolved into a focus on sexuality education that would stay with me for the rest of my life.

Shortly after beginning the new job, Dr. Debbie Bryant, the maternal/child health chief, brought me up to date on the status of sexual health in Arkansas. We were the state with the second-highest percentage of teenage pregnancy, with the United States having the highest rates of all the developed countries in the world. Therefore, Arkansas had the second-highest teenage pregnancy rate for the developed world. Of course, we also had all the things that go with a high teenage pregnancy rate — high illegitimate birth rate, high infant mortality, low birth weights, poverty, and lack of education. Fifty percent of teenage mothers never finished high school, and only two percent went to college. This presented a picture of a culture that was clearly suffering and was keeping Arkansas from flourishing.

At a press conference with all the state department heads, Governor Clinton, whose heart was close to youth issues, asked each person to state briefly what they were going to do the next year with their agency in regards to the "Youth at Risk" conference in Washington, DC. When my turn came, many people looked as though they were about to dose off until I declared, "The health department is going to reduce teen pregnancy." In 1987, this was NEWS! Some reporters roused a little. One asked, "How are you going to do that?" I said, "We are going to have comprehensive health education and school-based clinics." Everyone was awake now. "Does that mean you are going to distribute condoms in schools?" I answered, "Yes, it does. We aren't going to put them on lunch trays, but yes, we intend to distribute condoms." That's how I became the Condom Queen. In that moment, I transitioned from pediatric endocrinologist, researcher, professor, Director of the State Health Department to Condom Queen. I still hold that title.

I began going out into the state to bring the message of sexuality education, healthcare, and hope for the future to young people. Also, I began the huge job of persuading Arkansas legislators that protection of our most vulnerable citizens — the youth — through education and access to healthcare was one of our most important tasks. Although resistant in public, behind the scenes most of the seemingly negative legislators were supportive of my ideas. All of this experience told me that we had to take education to the people — talk to them about subjects that were usually forbidden in public. We had to get people talking about sexuality using facts, not myth, or our people would be doomed to suffer in ignorance forever. I knew that we had to use multiple strategies, education of adolescents, schools, churches, communities, media — everybody. No one group could do it alone.

Each time I transitioned into another area, I felt as though I were swimming in Jello. Then, gradually, clarity came (after a lot of hard work). The nature of passages is not to make life easier. Rather, they are a way for life to present opportunities. It is always a good thing to remember that opportunities don't always come around again and again. So, it is best to grab the ones that matter most the first time around.

During the passages of my life, I learned seven things that were important for my successes.

1. *Be clear about your own goals; know what you want and what it takes to get there.*

2. *You must use common sense and realize that you never want to give anyone else your own personal power or the power of your office.*

3. *You must keep your eye on the prize; have stick-to-itiveness; be persistent. The prize for me was that all young people would have the opportunity to grow up healthy, educated, motivated, and have hope. Healthy sexuality is an essential part of that, and it is everybody's responsibility.*

4. *Never worry about who gets the credit; just get the job done.*

5. *You must have gumption. Ask for what you want; you might get it sometimes.*

6. *Look for the smartest people to help with your goals and collaborate with them to make a difference.*

7. *Remember all the shoulders you had to stand on to get there!*

Joanna Gattuso

Cambridge, MA

PROFESSIONAL LIFE

Current workplace: Cambridge Health Alliance (CHA), Cambridge, MA

First workplace: Spectrum Youth and Family Services, Peer Outreach Worker, Burlington, MA

Favorite workplace: My current position as a Community Health Educator and Family Planning Counselor at CHA

EDUCATIONAL LIFE

Favorite course: Culture, Health, and Healing

Least favorite course: Calculus

TEACHING LIFE

Favorite topic to teach: Gender and Sexuality

Most challenging topic to teach: Dating Violence and Consent

INSPIRATIONS

Sex educator: Al Vernacchio, of course!

Book: *Our Bodies, Ourselves* by Boston Women's Health Book Collective and Judy Norsigian

NATIONAL SEX ED CONFERENCE

Title of presentation: *Teaching Sexuality through Anti-Oppression Theory: Helping Students See Intersections*

Presentation description: In the classroom setting, opportunity is often missed for critical discussions about culture, gender, and power. If students are reminded consistently through the course of their sex education about the ways identity can intersect with sexuality, they will have a greater understanding of how to negotiate their needs, desires, and expectations in relationships. These complex and important topics won't seem so overwhelming if intentionally incorporated and mindfully discussed throughout the course.

How I Got Into Sex...Ed

I don't think any sex educator can discuss how they ended up in the field without drawing not only from professional experience and direction, but also from their own, deeply personal knowledge. I will, however, speak only for myself in saying that my drive for this work has been borne mostly of my own interaction with sexuality, gender, and health, with both my education and work experience informing and reinforcing that passion all the while.

As a young kid, I always felt different or abnormal. I was curious about my own body and the bodies of others. I felt unsure, unsafe, and unliked — and I thought I was alone. And, as a young woman, an abusive relationship caused me to question my worth. In becoming an educator, I see these struggles in my students every day. I notice their insecurities and their confusion, and I remind myself with every lesson that I had all these same questions. I still have questions every day.

Part of what drew me to this work was the notion that health, in general, is a complex equation that includes family, friends, identity, and politics. There is no piece of someone's health that is disengaged from larger social and cultural systems. I see this most saliently in reproductive and sexual health. As a student in Anthropology in my undergraduate studies, I learned that these systems mold and maneuver every fiber of our being. They inform our identity, our politics, our choices, and our beliefs. I knew that in my career, I wanted to focus on how reproductive health fits into that complex equation.

I started working at Spectrum Youth and Family Services in Burlington, Vermont, in 2009 as a Peer Outreach Worker. In this role, I acted as staff in a Drop-In Center for homeless and at-risk youth in the community. This is where I discovered how much sexuality meant to me and my career. In my time there, each young person I worked with struggled with questions about pregnancy, STIs, sexuality, and gender. Many, if not all, of the young women were either pregnant or parenting at least once during the time I knew them. Few had access to termination procedures, and many lost their children to state custody. It became increasingly clear to me how these young people were dealing with sharp intersections of oppressed identities (whether that be racial, sexual, socioeconomic, gender, or ability) that worked to disempower and disenfranchise them to the point of ill physical, emotional, and sexual health.

While I worked to excavate my interests and passions in this field, I also started to discover my own queer identity. This process of self-discovery showed me the ways in which I hold privilege and the ways in which I am oppressed — and how my sexuality is both a reaction to and a cause for those things. Recognizing these personal truths has allowed me to be a better and more understanding resource to my students. Sexual identity building is a lifelong process, one which I am actively working on and reevaluating all the time.

So, I've answered the question of how I got into sex ed. But I'd like to also answer the question of why I *stay* in sex ed, because it's so important for us to continuously reevaluate why we're in this field. I stay in sex ed because I believe that our young people have a right to health, and that includes a healthy sexuality. I stay in sex ed because it reminds me that I, too, have a right to health. I stay because the sex ed community is one that trusts, respects, and honors all people. The community allows me to keep learning and challenging what I know. I stay because I believe that sexuality education is going to contribute to the end of partner abuse, and I definitely want to end partner abuse. I believe that we can use sexuality as a platform to talk about race, gender, ability, orientation, and culture. And I stay because I feel that this field makes me whole, it is in my blood, and it keeps me happy.

Ashley Gaunt

Shrewsbury, NJ

PROFESSIONAL LIFE
Current workplace: Planned Parenthood of Central and Greater Northern New Jersey, Shrewsbury, NJ
First workplace: National Sex Education Conference 2010, Somerset, NJ
Favorite workplace: The Rainbow Room, Doylestown, PA

EDUCATIONAL LIFE
Favorite course: Human Sexuality with Professor Michael McGee
Least favorite course: Biology!

TEACHING LIFE
Favorite topic to teach: Sexual Orientation/Gender Identity
Most challenging topic to teach: How to Talk to Your Children about Sexuality. (There are no definitive answers!)

INSPIRATIONS
Sex educator: Rachelle Daniels of Rainbow Room!
Book: *A Kid's First Book about Sex* by Joani Blank

NATIONAL SEX ED CONFERENCE
Title of presentation: *Bringing Sexy Back to Education*
Presentation description: Often, educational strategies used to talk about safer sex and STI transmission inadvertently include scare tactics, thus making those who live with an STI feel alienated. It further perpetuates the myth that "this will never happen to me." Therefore, this session will explore common safer sex activities from the positive perspective.

How I Got Into Sex...Ed

I will never forget the day my mother came running down the stairs with a pile of papers in her hand waving them at me yelling, "Look! You can study gay people!" I think I froze dead in my tracks and thought to myself "Gee, she really IS crazy!" Who knew that what she was saying was actually *sort of* accurate? I had transferred from a community college to Montclair State University, trying to find my way in the world both personally and professionally. My mother had no idea at the time that I was in the process of coming out, but her statement really settled with me.

Of course, I wound up not majoring in "gay people," but in LGBT Studies. My eyes were opened wide to a field I never knew existed. I was beyond jazzed when I found out that I could potentially take this to the next level and become a real sexual health educator! I landed in classes with Michael McGee and Allyson Sandak who ever so gracefully opened more doors into the Planned Parenthood world. I took every single class I could sign up for on sexuality and sexual health. It was so interesting and so relevant to, well, everyone and everything! I became hooked instantly. I looked forward to writing papers and doing homework, and had finally found my niche! All of my college roommates became increasingly jealous of the fact that I could write papers on my feelings toward any chapter in the *Guide to Getting It On,* while they did research on economics and business. I became fascinated with people, and how no two people are exactly the same. I loved the inconsistency in people's attitudes and values. It was an uncertainty that I became very comfortable with. The more I learned, the more I wanted to learn.

Once at the end of my route, I picked up an internship with Planned Parenthood. I helped out on many different tasks around the agency, but of course, my favorite was anything that had to do with education. I loved sitting in on the other educators' classes. I used to fall asleep at night practicing how I would teach that concept if it were me. As the internship came to a close, my anxiety started to grow. Would I ever get to do this wonderful work? How would I ever settle for something else after I have already drunk the juice!? Luckily for me, they liked me, and they were in a bit of a pinch because a few things were changing, and they needed some administrative help. I stuck around and shimmied my way through patient services and did a full round back into education exactly a year and a day later. I have been part of the education department at Planned Parenthood of Central and Greater Northern New Jersey going on my third year this January. I am learning every single day. The education team I work with is so fabulous; I continue to learn more in so many different ways from every single one of them. I could not do my job without those fantastic people! One of the most valuable parts of teaching sex ed is all of the different ways participants value the information I give them. I start most of my sessions by explaining to people that I am not here to make their decisions for them, but to give them the tools they need in order to make the best decisions for themselves. They challenge me and open my eyes to new ideas nearly every time I step into a classroom (and by classroom I can mean anything from the basement of a senior citizen home to a college auditorium). My interests in the field are constantly changing as I become more interested in one particular topic for a particular reason. However, no matter where I find myself (and all of my friends and family can vouch for this), I'm always putting on my educator cap and going on about one subject or another. Being the resident "sexpert" goes over well at dinner parties and coffee dates. There is always an opportunity to educate! I was at a birthday party recently for a friend's 6-year-old daughter. One of the moms was telling a story about her child asking how to tell the difference between a boy and a girl. All of the sudden it was as if a red carpet was laid out for me, a perfect opportunity. On went my educator hat, in the middle of a princess birthday party! I am always looking for ways to show my pride in teaching sex ed. This is a field I never knew existed, but I am so happy to have found my home smack in the middle of it!

Charlie Glickman

PhD

AASECT Certified Sexuality Educator

Oakland, CA

PROFESSIONAL LIFE

Current workplace: Oakland, CA
First workplace: Providence, RI
Favorite workplace: Sex and relationship coach, Oakland, CA

TEACHING LIFE

Favorite topic to teach: It's hard to pick just one! It's one of these three: Sex-Positivity, Prostate Play, or Sex, Shame, & Love.

INSPIRATIONS

Sex educator: Megan Andelloux. She brings intelligence, humor, and wit together to create amazing sex ed.

Book: Another tough question! I'm a big fan of *Demystifying Love: Plain Talk for the Mental Health Professional* by Stephen Levine, *Speaking Sex to Power: The Politics of Queer Sex* by Patrick Califia, and *Arousal: The Secret Logic of Sexual Fantasies* by Michael Bader.

NATIONAL SEX ED CONFERENCE

Title of presentation: *Sex, Shame, & Love*
Presentation description: Shame influences and shapes sexuality for almost everyone, regardless of gender, sexual orientation, and individual desires. If we want to overcome and move past sexual shame, we need to understand how it works and how it affects us. To do that, we can unpack the mechanisms of shame, explore how it shapes sexuality, and look at what we can do to build shame resilience. When we have the tools to deal with this difficult but inevitable emotion, it becomes much easier to resolve jealousy, loss, and fear so we can create more space to give and receive love, explore our authentic selves, and build the relationships that suit us.

How I Got Into Sex...Ed

To be honest, I got into sex ed sort of by accident. When I was a sophomore at Brown University, I joined the campus queer student group, and started providing outreach to the dorms, fraternities, sororities, and other student groups.

While there is certainly plenty of anxiety and worry about sexually transmitted infections and HIV today, there was even more back then. In the early 1990s, the risks of HIV and AIDS were well-known, but there weren't yet any treatments. That meant that there were a lot of unknowns, and a lot of anxiety. As a bisexual man, people asked me all kinds of questions about safer sex, my personal decisions, and their worries about their own safety. Fortunately, one of the other students in our group had taken a year off from school to live in San Francisco and participate in AIDS activism, so she became our unofficial trainer in safer sex issues.

Of course, once I started learning about those topics, people started asking me about a lot of other things. They had questions about sexual identity, how to navigate relationships, how to negotiate sexual interactions, and what they could do to improve their sex lives. I quickly learned that if you're going to start talking about one sexuality topic, many other ones start showing up. It was the first time that I realized that sexuality really does touch on every aspect of our lives, and I started learning everything that I could about it.

After I graduated and moved out to Oakland, California, I became a volunteer at the Pacific Center in Berkeley, the nation's first LGBT hotline. I also volunteered at Bay Area Women Against Rape, the world's first sexual assault crisis intervention hotline, and I was trained as a Community Health Outreach Worker. I had already discovered that many sexuality educators aren't really well-versed in the experiences of sexual assault survivors, and I wanted to learn as much as possible because I knew how important it was. As part of that experience, I developed my first training on working with male survivors and significant others. I've continued to offer this training for nonprofit organizations and community groups for more than 20 years.

But I knew that I wanted more than that. I wanted to get back to working with people to help them improve their sex lives and relationships. So when I saw the job posting for a position at Good Vibrations, I jumped at the opportunity. My training in the store was the first time I'd received so much information on sexual pleasure and relationships. I knew that this was the course I wanted my career to take.

While I was working at Good Vibrations, I had the opportunity to learn about the many ways that people experience sexual pleasure, as well as the challenges they face. I got to learn about different communities of erotic affiliation, sexual and relationship practices, medical concerns that affect pleasure, and of course, all about sex toys. We needed to be prepared to talk to customers about whatever was happening for them. These days, a lot of this information is available in books, in trainings, and on the Internet, but at the time it was passed down from one educator to another.

A couple of years later, I started teaching workshops on topics such as polyamory, BDSM, and different sexual practices. I quickly discovered how much I enjoyed offering sex education in this format. Working with adults is very different from working with youth or even college students. The challenges people face and the goals they have change over the course of a lifetime, and I realized that helping them have the best sexual experiences and the happiest relationships possible was what I wanted to do with my career.

Eventually, I decided I wanted a more formal education. I

attended a few classes at the Institute for the Advanced Study of Sexuality in San Francisco, but it wasn't quite the direction I wanted to take. I eventually found the doctoral program in Interdisciplinary Studies at the Union Institute and University in Cincinnati. I was able to put together an independent study program in Adult Sexuality Education, which was a wonderful opportunity. Unfortunately, the program has since become much less flexible due to changes in the federal student loan requirements. So until somebody else develops a program in it, I have the world's only doctorate in Adult Sexuality Education.

For my doctoral research, I surveyed Unitarian-Universalist ministers about their training in sexuality topics, the preparation to work with these issues in our congregations, and their educational needs. I used that information to develop a semester-long class that I taught at Starr King School for the Ministry, which I evaluated using both qualitative and quantitative means. You can find my dissertation online at *www.bit.ly/GlickmanDiss*.

I originally thought that I wanted to go into academia. Unfortunately, teaching at the university level has become a difficult proposition for professors in any field, but especially in sexuality. With the shift toward adjunct teaching, I saw many of my colleagues scrambling to work at three or even four universities in order to have a full-time income. I was still teaching workshops, training medical and mental health professionals, and speaking at conferences and universities, mostly on an occasional basis. I hadn't yet figured out how to make it my primary work, especially since I had a full-time job.

That changed with the 2013 release of *The Ultimate Guide to Prostate Pleasure*, which I wrote with Aislinn Emirzian. I left Good Vibrations in order to go on tour and promote the book, and to launch my sex coaching business. As a sex coach, I work with individuals and couples over Skype to help them overcome their sexual challenges, enhance their relationships, and discover new pleasures. I love this one-on-one work because I can see the positive changes sex coaching brings to people's lives. It's a great complement to the seminars I offer and the workshops that I teach, and it brings me a unique sense of job satisfaction that nothing else does.

One of the things I've learned about being a sex educator is that there's no one structure that will work for everybody. Some people prefer individual work, some people enjoy workshops, some people like to read my blog or other articles that I post on social media. There's no one way to have sex, and there's no one way to be a sex educator. It does get a little bit tricky sometimes, juggling all of these different pieces of my life and career. But that's also what makes it exciting.

This is an interesting time for sex educators because there's so much information available on the Internet and in books. Rather than being the gatekeepers of sex education, we can take on a new role in which we help people figure out what questions they have in the first place, where the most useful information is, and how to decide what works for them. In essence, we help people learn how to learn about sex and to develop critical thinking skills for their relationships.

The field of sex education has changed a lot in the 20 years that I've been working in it. It can sometimes seem like there's no clear path to follow. But that also opens amazing opportunities. You can chart your own course, whether that's in academia, at a nonprofit organization, working one-on-one, coaching, or anything else. I'm looking forward to seeing how the field develops over the next couple of decades. We're only just beginning to discover how to integrate social media and new technologies in sex education, and who knows what new opportunities will develop?

Amy Jo Goddard

MA
Certified David Neagle Miracle of Money Mentor,
NYC HIV Pre/Post Counselor

Napa, CA
New York, NY

PROFESSIONAL LIFE
Current workplace: Napa, CA, and New York, NY
First workplace: City Kids Foundation, New York, NY
Favorite workplace: Assisting Betty Dodson—until I became CEO of my own business!

EDUCATIONAL LIFE
Favorite course: Sexuality & Human Rights with Carole Vance, Institute of Sexuality, Society and Culture, Amsterdam
Least favorite course: Research Methods (when the instructor really didn't teach—go on, retire!)

TEACHING LIFE
Favorite topic to teach: The Fine Art of Dirty Talk, How to Drive a Vulva
Most challenging topic to teach: Healing from Sexual Trauma

INSPIRATIONS
Sex educator: Betty Dodson, Carol Queen
Book: *Real Live Nude Girl: Chronicles of Sex-Positive Culture* by Carol Queen

NATIONAL SEX ED CONFERENCE
Title of presentation: *"I'm Sick of Being Broke When I'm Good at What I Do!" Why Sex Educator Poverty Exists and What We Need to Do About It*
Presentation description: Ever believed the myth that "sex educators can't make money?" There is a history to sex educator famine and struggle. I convened a Sex Summit in 2013 of veterans in the sexuality field to discuss the

experience of struggling to make ends meet and being able do sexuality work full time. From our activist roots in a world where no one was funding anything that had to do with sexuality, to a world that doesn't value sexuality in a serious way, and an increasingly expensive world to live in, it's time for sex educators to change the way we think and perform our work and how we get paid for and value what we do. I share my key findings from the Sex Summit.

How I Got Into Sex...Ed

Like many sexuality educators, the trajectory from disempowered girl to powerful educator was fraught with many of my own sexual challenges, as well as confusion and disappointments. My own personal path led me to wanting to help others.

I felt disempowered sexually when I was growing up — and totally in the dark. I had no information. No parent who talked to me about sex. No Internet. No books. I was completely isolated about sex.

I grew up with my Dad, and I have so much respect for my father, and all he gave my sisters and me as a single parent. He was in the military and was strict, and there was a lot of structure in our house. We saw our mother one weekend each month and on some holidays. She lived near us in southern California, until my dad got stationed in Maine — about as far away from our mother as we could possibly be. I lived there during a pretty critical time in my life. The day I started menstruating was in the middle of a blizzard. (Those are serious in Maine!) So my dad, dedicated father that he was, hopped on the snowmobile and went to the BX (the department store on an Air Force base) to get me some pads. He came home, handed me the bag, and didn't say a word.

I started having sex while we lived there, at age 13. My first sexual experience was not a choice I made. How could I have? I'd never had a conversation with myself about it, much less anybody else. It became a sexual relationship I was totally unprepared for — complete with pregnancy scares. It was one of those regrettable experiences that pained me for years. I couldn't even talk to my boyfriend about it and how scared I was. I couldn't utter a word about what we were actually doing. I'd had no training, no education, zero preparation for this. I remember not feeling like I could talk to anyone — not my girlfriends, certainly not my father or my mother, nor was there any other adult who could help me. It was not an easy place to be on an isolated air force base at the northern tip of Maine.

Later in my adolescence, we went back to California, and I had a pretty healthy relationship where love and communication were modeled for me, and that helped me break the shell around the topic of sex. However, I had two unwanted pregnancies and knew little to nothing about birth control. Luckily, my stepdad had opened the door to communication, and I was able to look to him for support when I was in these very tough and scary situations. My mother was a self-identified prude, and a "recovering Catholic," so she was pretty sex-negative overall. She had scared me away from masturbating or knowing my sexual body at all in a shaming experience when I was eight, when she said harshly one day at Rosicrucian Temple, "Stop touching yourself and smelling yourself!" I just thought my genitals smelled neat, and I would touch them through my clothes and take in the smell with curiosity. Apparently, that was not OK! That moment kept me from touching myself for another ten years.

I went to three high schools and somehow got out of taking health class, so I never even had two weeks of scare tactics in high school to get me on *some* road to sex education. Nada.

It wasn't until I got to college and took a human sexuality class that my world opened up. During the first quarter of the first year I took Sociology of Human Sexuality 152 with John and Janice Baldwin at the University of California, Santa Barbara. They were incredible! They taught with openness and ease about all of the things no one had ever taught me and which I'd never heard anyone even speak about before! I felt upset that I had to wait so long to get this very important information. Let me tell you, that Masters and Johnson text was the only textbook I ever read cover to cover!

I finally had permission to masturbate and explore my own sexuality; I was learning how to talk about it, and finally learned how to have an orgasm at long last after years of frustration that I couldn't, even with my loving, sweet, hard-working boyfriend who really had tried his best! But I didn't know how to do it, so how was he going to figure it out? It was sad and frustrating for both of us.

That class planted the seed for my becoming a sexuality educator. I became an activist while at college, and I was a part of an underground group called the Creative Underground Network of Truthful Sisters. We raised a lot of clandestine hell at our school over the high rates of rape and sexual assault that occurred on campus and in frat houses, about reproductive rights that were being heavily slammed by then president George Bush, Sr. and his Republican Congress. I got super activated about helping to empower women in their bodies, sexuality, and relationships.

When I left college, I felt strongly that I wanted to do work that would empower women and girls, but I wasn't sure exactly how to accomplish that. When I got rejected from women's studies programs (How could that be? I was such a good feminist!) I had to ask myself what it was that I really wanted to do. One day it hit me like a ton of bricks: I want to do what the Baldwins do! I want to help people with their sexuality!

Now I had to figure out where I could study sexuality in a graduate program. At the time, there was no Internet. I actually went to a library (remember those?) and found that there were three promising programs in the country. One was at NYU, and living in New York appealed to me. I was accepted, and I came to New York to study Human Sexuality. How perfect. I had amazing mentors and teachers who taught me academically, but also took the time to guide me on my personal journey of self-empowerment.

I was fortunate enough to meet Betty Dodson and count her among my close mentors. I worked with her on many projects and, via Betty, I was invited to join a professional women's sexuality group. I was beginning to be surrounded by some of the greatest minds and strongest feminists in the sexuality field. I felt so intimidated; what did I have to offer? But I knew that one day I wanted to offer something special to women, something that could help them have powerful experiences and knowledge about their sexuality. I had a mentor in Betty Dodson who had worked to change thousands of women's lives over the course of 35 years. I was a young, queer woman with a similar story. Carol Queen came into my life. I went to study in Amsterdam with Carole Vance. I made sure I got the best mentors available, and I created relationships with them that are still strong today. I feel really blessed for the many mentors I've had throughout my life who have helped shape me. And now, I am committed to being that mentor for others.

For me, it all started in the mid-1990s. In some ways, as a culture, we haven't come very far since then. We are still fighting many of the same fights. On a personal level, I know what it's like to be in a place of disempowerment—to the point where it hurt me. Many factors went into my becoming able to talk about sex, my ability to have fulfilling sexual relationships, my being able to more fully understand my sexual identity, to really carry my own sexual power, and so forth. Most people, including most good sexuality educators, have gone through their own experiences of feeling isolated, alone, uninformed, and scared about sexual situations, relationships, or their bodies. It has been a process to come into my own sexual power and feel like I can really hold it authentically in a place that is what I want and of my own making, rather than one that is prescribed socially or culturally in some way. And now I get to help other people along their journey. I absolutely love it.

I developed my Women's Sexuality Empowered Life Program out of this herstory — it's the program I wish I'd had all those years ago! I wanted other women to have a space to work on their sexuality in a deep and meaningful way. Now women travel from all over to work with me.

What I didn't know then was that my dream job didn't exist. I had to create it. I had to learn business skills and get comfortable charging for my worth, so I could actually bring my skills and gifts to the people who need them in the way I wanted to do it. I had to go through my own sexual challenges in order to authentically help others. I know the power of my work comes from the deep effort I have expended on my own sexual, emotional, and spiritual self, alongside my training, mentoring, education, and life experiences in the queer, women's, and spiritual communities I call home.

Eva S. Goldfarb

MA, LHD (Hon), PhD

Montclair, NJ

PROFESSIONAL LIFE
Current workplace: Montclair State University, Montclair, NJ
First workplace: Philadelphia College of Textiles and Science, Philadelphia, PA
Favorite workplace: My current job: Montclair State University, Montclair, NJ

EDUCATIONAL LIFE
Favorite course: Every Sex Education course I took at Penn
Least favorite course: Related to sex ed? None.

TEACHING LIFE
Favorite topic to teach: Pleasure, Sexual Response, Relationships
Most challenging topic to teach: Pornography

INSPIRATIONS
Sex educator: Konnie McCaffree
Book: *It's Perfectly Normal* by Robie Harris

How I Got Into Sex...Ed

A Love Story

My path into sexuality education is not typical, if there is such a thing. I am one of the rare people who never worked for Planned Parenthood and didn't even discover the field until well after college, and then pretty much through serendipity. I was always an excellent student and a very curious person. This meant I had many interests and followed several paths of inquiry in my life. Sexuality was always something that acutely piqued my interest but it never occurred to me that it held any possible career path. I also knew that I wanted to be in academia and pursue an advanced degree; I just didn't know in what field. There were many things that interested me on an intellectual level but nothing — other than musical theater and the dream of starring on Broadway — that I really felt committed to and passionate about. When I was getting ready to graduate from college, my mother urged me to continue in my studies and earn a PhD. "But Mom, I don't know what field to go into." "It doesn't matter what field," she told me, "just get a PhD." My mother was worried that if I took a break in my education I might never go back. After taking a year off after graduation and working at a computer software company, I went back to school at the University of Pennsylvania's Annenberg School for Communication. The Annenberg School is one of the top Communications schools in the country, and I was going on a full scholarship. Nonetheless, while I loved being in graduate school (yes, I am a nerd), I was not passionate about what I was studying.

At the same time, I had a boyfriend, but not just any boyfriend. This was a man I had been in love with since we were teenagers. Though we were friends in high school, he was two years older than me and about to go to college (where, presumably, there would be lots of women). He had no interest in a romantic relationship with a high school sophomore. Though we kept in touch following high school and through college, it took six more years for my persistent and unrelenting affections to be fully noticed and returned by him and for us to become a couple...just four months before I was to move to Philadelphia to pursue my graduate studies. So, when my faculty advisor informed me that I would need to take a summer course in order to graduate on time, I was devastated at the thought that I would be spending the summer away from my love, who was two and a half hours away in New Jersey. Who knew that love (or was it lust?) would ultimately propel me into a whole new future. Desperate to get back to New Jersey for the summer (it had to be lust), I discovered a graduate course, the entire duration of which was only one week, being offered during pre-session by Penn's Graduate School of Education. Taking this course meant I could be back home by the second week in May. As a bonus, the course was entitled "Human Sexuality." Perfect!! A class, completed in five days, fulfilling my course requirement, and about sex to boot. This was the basis upon which I decided to enroll. I could not possibly have known how profound an impact that decision would have on my life.

The course met eight hours a day for five days — an intensive format that had a Sexual Attitudes Reassessment (SAR)–like quality to it. On the very first day I felt like I was struck by lightning. Every part of my body from my brain to my toes was buzzing and alive. This was the eureka moment I had been waiting for but didn't expect to ever really experience. The class connected to every part of me: woman, daughter, sister, lover, feminist. It spoke to my sexual curiosity: my ignorance and my intuition, my naïveté and my wisdom. That very first night I called my mother and told her, "Mom, I'm getting my PhD, and I found my calling." "That's wonderful. What is the field?" she asked. "Human Sexuality Education." Silence. Then, "What kind of job can you get in Human Sexuality Education?" To which I responded with something like "I don't know exactly, but I suspect there will always be lots of important and amazing work." Although I'm sure she had no idea what this field entailed (after all, neither did I just 12 hours earlier), to her credit, she simply said, "I'm so happy for you." That course, taught by Dr. Ken George and Dr. Andy Behrendt, changed my life. As soon as the course was over, I was in Ken's office applying to the doctoral program, and I have never looked back.

As hard as it is to believe now, at that point I was still yet to meet and to learn from Dr. William Stayton, the first person I had ever met who truly embraced the concept that pleasure should always be in the forefront of our conversations about sexuality; Dr. Richard Friend, master of group process; and Dr. Ryda Rose, an intellectual's intellectual and the one who turned me on (yes, turned me on) to the intersections of philosophy and science that have informed my work throughout my career. Hardest of all to comprehend, however, is that I had not yet even met Dr. Konnie McCaffree. Konnie is the person who would become my lifelong mentor and who would have the greatest impact on me throughout my professional career, on how I think about, create, plan, prepare, teach, discuss, defend, and evaluate my work and how I see myself as a sexuality educator. Until that time, I could never fully appreciate just how profound an impact a true mentor can have. I am the luckiest person in the world to have studied my craft under Konnie.

And so, with my Master's degree in Communications in hand, the following September I started the PhD program in Human Sexuality Education at the University of Pennsylvania's Graduate School of Education. I graduated three years later, and have been happily and meaningfully employed ever since in a field where I know that I, along with all of my amazing colleagues doing this work, are having a profoundly positive impact on people's lives.

Oh, and P.S.: I married that boyfriend, and he has been my partner on this journey ever since.

The Rev. Debra W. Haffner

MDiv, MPH, DPS (hc)
AASECT Certified Sexuality Educator

Westport, CT

PROFESSIONAL LIFE
Current workplace: Religious Institute, Westport, CT
First workplace: Population Institute, Washington, DC
Favorite workplace: I've loved all of them.

EDUCATIONAL LIFE
Favorite course: 6th-grade social studies
Least favorite course: Anything to do with math

TEACHING LIFE
Favorite topic to teach: Adult sexual enrichment
Most challenging topic to teach: Sexuality issues with conservative clergy

INSPIRATIONS
Sex educator: Dr. Bob Selverstone
Book: I can't decide.

NATIONAL SEX ED CONFERENCE
Title of presentation: *Snapshots and Lessons from a Life in Sexuality Education*
Presentation description: For more than 35 years, the Reverend Debra W. Haffner, co-founder and president of the Religious Institute and former president of SIECUS, has been a leading force and influencer in shaping sexuality education. Come learn about how sexuality education has changed over three decades from her unique lens — from the depressing to the exciting; from the missed opportunities to the opportunities to come. Learn how we can integrate love, values, compassion, and, yes, faith, into a new generation of sexuality education. This keynote will summarize lessons learned from and for professional sexuality education over the years.

How I Got Into Sex...Ed

I had the good fortune to grow up in a home where sexuality was discussed openly and often. I knew a lot and was a "neighborhood sexuality educator" for my elementary school friends. I gave my first talk on the Women's Movement in a 10th-grade speech class. In college, I was trained to teach gynecological self help, and with my best friend, gave many talks at colleges on why women should learn to look at their cervix and take control back from gynecology. That led to my interest in taking a graduate-level, one-week course on sexuality education in the summer of 1975. The course was sponsored by AASECT at American University, and taught by Dr. James Maddock. I was so moved by that week that I decided to stop pursuing a job in Congress (where I was finishing an internship), postponed going to law school, and went searching for my first job in the field. The rest, as they say, is history.

Lynn Hammond

Columbia, SC

PROFESSIONAL LIFE
Current workplace: South Carolina Department of Health
First workplace: Buford Elementary School, Lancaster County School District, Lancaster, SC
Favorite workplace: South Carolina Department of Education, with the SC Healthy Schools Program

EDUCATIONAL LIFE
Favorite course: Curriculum Design
Least favorite course: Statistics

TEACHING LIFE
Favorite topic to teach: Coordinating School Health Programs
Most challenging topic to teach: LGBTQ

INSPIRATIONS
Sex educator: Dr. Shelley Hamill at Winthrop University and Dr. Darrel Lang
Book: *What Your Mother Never Told You About Sex* by Hilda Hutcherson, MD, and *Prime* by Dr. Pepper Schwartz

NATIONAL SEX ED CONFERENCE
Title of presentation: *Meeting the Needs of Special Education Students in Human Sexuality Education*
Presentation description: Through audience participation, individuals will be able to see or visualize how to teach human sexuality to students with various disabilities. Each teaching technique will be processed to show how one would teach a topic to the general population and then how to adapt and modify the teaching technique for students with various disabilities.

How I Got Into Sex...Ed

I started my teaching career as an elementary physical

education teacher with every intention of this being my career focus. After having two children, I decided to stay home with them for a few years until they were attending school. It was while I was expecting my third child that I started teaching pregnancy and postpartum exercise and care classes. While it wasn't sex education for school-age youth, it was certainly an education for many women about their bodies and how they function during and post pregnancy. I co-taught this class with a nurse instructor. Later, when I decided to reenter the field of teaching, I worked as a short-term and long-term substitute teacher while waiting on an opening for an elementary PE teacher. I would always get called to sub at a particular middle school, and it always happened to be when the sex education unit was being taught! I then took a position as a regional public health educator. While my primary responsibilities were related to promoting physical activity, I was called on to work with schools to look at their health education curriculum with a particular focus on sexuality education. During this time, the principal of a new high school called to ask if I would come and teach health and physical education at his new school. His wife had been one of the middle school teachers that I had substituted for (and taught sex education)! I took this position and was hurled into the world of teaching high school sex education within the health education course. My degree was in physical education, and my teacher certificate allowed me to teach health and PE kindergarten through grade 12 even though I had never had a content or methods course in teaching sex education. So I drew on my own good high school health education course and went about finding the best interactive skills based teaching methods I could find. It was during this time that I learned to work with secondary students and with special needs students to provide them with health and sex education.

Later I became the manager of the SC Department of Education's Centers for Disease Control — a cooperative for implementing a Coordinated School Health approach to improving nutrition and physical activity and preventing tobacco use and HIV/sexual risk among students. Our team was able to provide teacher training and resources to teachers who found themselves assigned to teach sex education and who felt they had not received adequate preparation to teach this important and sensitive subject.

Joyce Hunter

LCSW, DSW

New York, NY

PROFESSIONAL LIFE

Current workplace: HIV Center for Clinical and Behavioral Studies, at the Division of Gender, Sexuality, and Health, New York State Psychiatric Institute and Columbia University, New York, NY

First workplace: The Door, Center of Alternatives for Youth, New York. I had done my MSW internship there and was later hired as a full-time social worker. At the same time, in the early 1980s, I was working with Dr. Emery Hetrick and Damien Martin and others to do advocacy work for LGBT and homeless youth. We decided that these young people needed a safe space to be themselves, make friends, and to be able to explore their sexual orientation. Eventually, we founded the Institute for the Protection of Lesbian and Gay Youth, now The Hetrick-Martin Institute.

Favorite workplace: As one of the founders of the Institute, it was my favorite place. My position there was Director, Social Work Services, as well as Clinical Supervisor.

EDUCATIONAL LIFE

Favorite course: There were several courses on health and sexuality that were very important to me, as they coincided with my work.

Least favorite course: Swimming!!! I passed the course because I didn't drown.

TEACHING LIFE

Favorite topic to teach: Sexual orientation, sexuality, gender identity, stigma, and Human Rights

INSPIRATIONS

Sex educator: Mary Lefkarites, Peggy Brick

Book: *Our Bodies, Ourselves* (first edition) by Boston Women's Health Book Collective and Judy Norsigian

NATIONAL SEX ED CONFERENCE
Title of presentation: *Working with Transgender and Gender Non-Conforming Youth: Lessons Learned*
Presentation description: This poster supported participants' awareness of the issues for transgender youth and their ability to plan interventions to respond to the complex challenges that face this population.

How I Got Into Sex...Ed

To begin with, I majored in Health Services (BS), then Social Work (MSW), and Social Welfare (DSW). But before I even enrolled at Hunter College, I entered the field of sexuality education as a human rights activist, working with young people at Hunter College who were confronting their sexual orientation and were being stigmatized or were in need of resources for their sexual health. As a member of the Lesbians Rising Collective at Hunter College, I worked as a volunteer peer educator at their Student Health Society's Student Counseling Center. Students would even bring in high school students or homeless adolescents for counseling. In 1972, a Hunter College professor, Mary Lefkarites, asked me to speak in her human sexuality class, the beginning of many speaking engagements at colleges and high schools.

The Student Health Society was formed by students, as they felt they couldn't talk with their college counselor about their sexual health (i.e., birth control, abortion, sexual behaviors, sexual orientation, STIs), as the information would be recorded on their college records. I was then motivated to learn everything that I could about sexuality and sexuality education. When I finally enrolled as a student at Hunter, my volunteer work and activism became my career. I was able to incorporate my movement work into my school work, wrote papers on my experiences, and continued to learn. As a social work student, I became aware of calls requesting help for LGBT young people, some of whom were being mistreated elsewhere and many who were not getting help anywhere. At that point, the mission of the Institute for the Protection of Lesbian and Gay Youth (now the Hetrick-Martin Institute) changed its focus from advocacy to direct service delivery. Then, as the agency opened its doors in 1982, I worked there with young people who were at risk for STIs and HIV, and I needed to address their sexual behaviors and institute a risk-prevention curriculum.

One particular kid, a 14-year-old boy from the Bronx, inspired me to do more in the field. He would call once a week to talk and ask questions about being gay and about sexuality. He was not able to travel by subway until he was 15. I met him the following year, and he told me how important it was to talk to someone who could answer his questions. Sex education is very important to all youth.

Jacqueline Jaffe O'Duor
LCSW

Philadelphia, PA

PROFESSIONAL LIFE
Current workplace: Clinical Practice: Still Waters Holistic Health Therapies, Philadelphia, PA; Behavioral Research: Perelman School of Medicine at the University of Pennsylvania, Philadelphia, PA
First workplace: Refuge House, Inc., Tallahassee, FL
Favorite workplace: Dual roles: clinical practice at Still Waters Holistic Health Therapies and research at the University of Pennsylvania

EDUCATIONAL LIFE
Favorite course: Sexual Attitude Reassessment
Least favorite course: 10th-grade sex ed

TEACHING LIFE
Favorite topic to teach: Coping with chronic illness in intimate relationships
Most challenging topic to teach: Engaging in a healthy sex life after a sexually transmitted infection diagnosis

INSPIRATIONS
Sex educator: Nancy Gambescia, PhD
Book: *Rekindling Desire* by Barry and Emily McCarthy

NATIONAL SEX ED CONFERENCE
Title of presentation: *Sex Doesn't Stop after a Positive Diagnosis: Motivators to Negotiate Safer Sex*
Presentation description: It can be difficult to help individuals and couples find the drive to change their behavior to engage in safer sex after a sexually transmitted infection (STI) diagnosis. Often people either refrain from sex or use inconsistent methods of protection. The discussion will include an explanation of how stigma is internalized and the burden of

secrecy. Participants will learn about the concept of risk compensation and its impact on the prophylaxis use and safer sexual behavior. Moving a step beyond defining STIs and exploring sexual risk behavior charts, this workshop will delve into the process of making safer sex a comfortable conversation for the families, students, and patients we serve.

How I Got Into Sex...Ed

The transition into sexuality education sparked from a pursuit to enhance people's lives within their families and communities. I moved into the field after I took advantage of the opportunity to volunteer at Refuge House, Inc., a regional sexual and domestic violence agency. I learned about recovery from sexual trauma and the importance of strengthening relationships. We discussed topics not normally discussed in typical conversations, from the impact of sexual education on behavior to societal messages about gender. In a culture with conflicting sexual standards, I learned healthy, positive messages about sex and relationships that I could share with others.

The professional culture highlighted individual resilience and social change. At the time, I was studying architectural design and working for a community design firm. Though I enjoyed my work, I noticed my focus was shifting toward my efforts at Refuge House. I had always been a dedicated student, but I increasingly spent my time volunteering. I finally decided I needed to make a career shift when I accepted the fact that I was skipping class to work for free. Initially, I was hesitant to make the transition because it seemed to be a drastic change. I realized my interest in community design and development was fueled by the desire to create public spaces that would provide optimal individual functioning and social interaction. This paralleled my newfound desire to work directly with people to improve their personal growth and interpersonal relationships. Once I understood the common thread in my interest, I was able to navigate my transition to the field of human sexuality.

After assisting in crisis intervention, I was soon hired as a staff member. My responsibilities grew to include counseling, advocacy, and community education. The work reaffirmed the messages about healthy sexuality I had heard from my mother. It also confirmed what my father taught me. He told me to pursue a career I could be passionate about, explaining that anything I would spend over a third of my day and the majority of my life doing should be worthwhile. I bet they didn't think being a sex therapist would be how I interpreted their message!

I pursued graduate studies in clinical social work at the University of Pennsylvania School of Social Policy and Practice. I continued to delve into sexual trauma and recovery counseling at the Joseph J. Peters Institute. I began to see the discomfort, anxiety, and fear people have in discussing sexual functioning, sexual desires, and safer sex. I noticed how people benefit from discussing these topics with healthcare providers and sexual partners. This led to the decision to broaden my practice to include sexual health and functioning for individuals and couples.

Understanding how elements of the therapeutic process work became of great interest to me. This led me to join a research team for the Perelman School of Medicine at the University of Pennsylvania, developing and examining behavioral interventions to improve health. This has allowed me to work closely with physicians, nurses, pharmacists, and public health specialists to help people better manage their health and stay in care.

My clinical practice at Still Waters Holistic Health Therapies is focused on addressing sexual identity, sexual functioning, and the impact of past trauma and chronic illness on mental health and intimate relationships. Patients often report living in sex-negative and sexual-neutral environments in which asking questions or obtaining support is rarely encouraged, if at all. I observe clients' confusion about what is "normal." Many psychotherapy sessions include providing education to differentiate what is common or healthy or a natural part of development. My work has expanded to include sexual health education in addition to training and clinical supervision for healthcare practitioners working in various aspects of sexuality.

Sexual education makes up a significant part of my clinical practice. Sexuality is often compartmentalized, and it is thought to have an insignificant association with other areas of life. When people learn sexual functioning can be symptomatic of other physical and psychological issues, they can learn how to improve their overall health. Understanding the influence of interpersonal conflict and social mores on sexual desire and behaviors provides people with the incentive to improve communication in relationships. Giving parents, educators, and healthcare providers the tools they need to provide accurate sexual education only furthers the goal to enrich families', students', and patients' physical and emotional health.

My mission has been to help people experience sexual wellness in order to improve individual and relational functioning. Every component of my professional experience has been built upon efforts to address concerns I have observed working with patients and collaborating with healthcare providers. Sexual education has served as the link across each element of my career. This has allowed me to develop a deeper understanding of how sexuality influences various aspects of life, a lesson I apply to my work each day.

Paul Joannides

PsyD
Supervising Psychoanalyst

Waldport, OR

PROFESSIONAL LIFE
Current workplace: Waldport, OR
Favorite workplace: Speaking at colleges, so that can be in any state

EDUCATIONAL LIFE
Favorite course: A tie between a course in classical rhetoric and one in journalism
Least favorite course: Trigonometry

TEACHING LIFE
Favorite topic to teach: My new college talk on sex is what "I teach," and I have a lot of fun with it. I've put more than a thousand hours of work into creating my one-hour talk.
Most challenging topic to teach: Anything having to do with transgender

INSPIRATIONS
Sex educator: There are many who I find to be truly inspiring; I couldn't just say one.
Book: I've been lucky to have learned a great deal from a number of books.

NATIONAL SEX ED CONFERENCE
Title of presentation: *The Conversations We Are NOT Having with Our Teens and Pre-Teens*
Presentation description: Putting condoms on bananas doesn't cut it anymore for sex education when today's 11-year-olds are watching porn on the Internet. In this keynote, we look at the sexual world of today's teens and pre-teens, and the conversations they need to be having with their parents, teachers, counselors, and healthcare professionals.

How I Got Into Sex...Ed

I didn't take a single course on sexuality while I was in college. That's a sad thought, considering I was in college for 12 years! If you had told me then that I would someday be the author of an almost 1,200-page book on sex that's used in college and medical school courses, I would have asked what you'd been smoking. The idea of being in sex education was that far from my consciousness.

So how did I end up writing my book on sex — which was my entry into sex education? I usually tell people it was revenge for eight years in Catholic school. But if revenge for Catholic school had been the sole motivator, the first chapter alone would have been 1,200 pages.

I had actually planned to write a series of books on science for students who weren't doing well with the usual boring texts. The first in the series was titled "The Chemistry of Bikinis, Surfboards, and Skateboard Wheels." It introduced chemistry by showing the different forms that urethane could take if you just tweaked the molecule a little here and there. Unfortunately, the book had too much personality to ever be used in the school system. So there I was, pretty much broke and with a useless book in hand.

As part of the series, I had planned on eventually doing a book on sex for surfers. So I figured if I wrote that one next, it would provide the money to finance the others. (I was seeing a couple of teenage boys in therapy at the time who desperately needed a good book on sex, but there were none that even came close to engaging them. So I thought there would be a market for such a book.)

I assumed it would only take six months for me to write my book on sex for surfers. But then I discovered that with each new page, signs of the harsh, judgmental God from my youth would appear. This was shocking to me, because I honestly didn't think He was such a force in my life anymore. So I had more work to do than I'd anticipated!

After almost two years of researching, writing, and rewriting, I proudly presented my 200-page manuscript to a friend who was a playwright. She handed it back to me a few weeks later. There were maybe 10 lines in the entire 200 pages that were highlighted in yellow, and I thought "Wow, this is great! Only 10 lines to fix!" And then the hammer dropped. She said, "The lines I highlighted were the only lines in this entire dog that spoke to me. If you can write a book that captures the tone of these few lines, you'll have a winner on your hands." Interestingly, these were the few lines where I'd allowed my own voice and personality to come through, unhindered by my need to make the book sound upstanding and proper.

So I spent the next six years trying to take complex research and speak it with my own voice. (Tequila proved to be a helpful inspiration.) And then, when I finally finished my book on sex, no legitimate publisher in the country would publish it. They said a how-to book on sex that has a sense of humor would never sell. Dumb it down and make it a *Joy of Sex* clone, and they might reconsider.

Something didn't seem right about their estimation of the American people. So against the advice of many, I decided to start my own publishing company and to publish the book myself. Within the first year, the book had won its first award.

I can't say there's a single part of this journey that has been easy. And I'm almost certain I would not have gone down this road if I had known it would take ten times more work than I ever imagined. But it's a good thing I didn't know any of that, because if I had, I would never have gotten to meet the people in sex education who I have learned so much from and who I enjoy having as my friends. And I never would have ventured upon this amazing journey.

Amy Johnson
MSW
Certified Sexuality Educator, Planned Parenthood University;
Licensed Independent Clinical Social Worker, WA;
Certified School Social Worker, WA

Federal Way, WA

PROFESSIONAL LIFE
Current workplace: Diligent Joy Training, Education, Coaching in Federal Way, WA

First workplace: Teaching *Our Whole Lives* at Wayside United Church of Christ in Federal Way, WA

Favorite workplace: Teaching and Training Facilitators in *Our Whole Lives* regionally on the West Coast

EDUCATIONAL LIFE
Favorite course: *Our Whole Lives* Facilitator Training

Least favorite course: It wasn't exactly a course, but I saw Ed Ainsworth (a/k/a "Sex Ed") speak at an after-school assembly in my community, and I had to call a good friend and sexuality educator at Public Health to talk me down afterward. He was demeaning — spreading misinformation and incorrect facts — and charismatic at the same time.

TEACHING LIFE
Favorite topic to teach: I love teaching about how to incorporate faith into sexuality education in a comprehensive and inclusive way for all people.

Most challenging topic to teach: I sometimes find it challenging to teach about termination of pregnancy, because of misinformation coupled with strong values/opinions, often different and in the same room.

INSPIRATIONS
Sex educator: Ann Hanson

Book: I really love *The Parent Guide to Our Whole Lives K–1 and 4–6* by Pat Hoertdoerfer

NATIONAL SEX ED CONFERENCE
Title of presentation: *Five Engaging Ways to Connect Text, Values, and Scripture to Your Sexuality Education Presentation*
Presentation description: This poster presentation is designed to help people consider how to add text, values, and scripture to sexuality education presentations done in faith communities.

How I Got Into Sex...Ed

I have been a Social Worker for almost 30 years. Most of that time, I have worked with children, teens, and families in some capacity. As a school social worker, I was often working with teens that had little understanding of sexuality, boundaries, healthy relationships, and safety. Again and again, young people would be in my office due to sexual abuse, relationship strife, lack of clear communication skills, misunderstandings about consent, and more.

I remember thinking one day, "If I meet another 9th-grade girl from an abusive home who decides the best way out is to move in with her boyfriend, I think I'm going to scream." Over and over, this pattern would occur. The girl would then become at least emotionally dependent on her boyfriend. More than likely, she would also become financially dependent on him, and way too often, she would become pregnant. And the cycle would start again. At times, it seemed unbreakable.

I realized that a lack of education was a key component in this cycle. At the last school where I worked, there was an excellent teen parenting program, and even a great health class for teens that included some sexuality education—but, based on results, it was too little, too late.

Even though I had some opportunities to work on a short-term basis with youth who had been abused, and to try to help them do some healing, it wasn't enough.

I also had sporadic opportunities over the years to counsel youth about choices, provide resources for them for contraception, and talk to them individually and in couples and groups about healthy relationships. It still wasn't enough.

At the same time, I began as Youth Director at my place of worship, and I heard about *Our Whole Lives: Sexuality and Our Faith.* These lifespan curricula, co-written by the United Church of Christ and the Unitarian Universalist Association, teach comprehensive and inclusive sexuality education in faith communities. I took the training, began offering the classes at my church, and it changed my life.

The ministry was so relevant, so stunning, and so beautiful. The youth were grateful, engaged, and enthusiastic about coming to class and bringing friends. I was witnessing first-hand how I could fill in the holes made by lack of information for these youth—some of whom were from really great families who just didn't have a clue how to deal with talking about sexuality, even though they were smart and engaged parents.

I saw that by giving youth the opportunity to practice scenarios they might encounter someday, and to talk with each other in scripted ways about uncomfortable topics, we were giving them skills they didn't even know they were going to need. But we adults knew — and we all wished we'd had this type of education when we were younger.

Shortly after we began this ministry, we were contacted by National Public Radio (NPR). They were doing a story about churches taking on the task of sex education. They wanted to interview us. After checking with the youth, the parents, and the church council, everyone agreed it was a worthwhile endeavor. NPR did the story featuring the youth group in our small church, and it aired in March of 2007.

After taking some youth to the Sexuality Education Advocacy Training in Washington, DC, in 2010, we came back even more energized. We got a small grant from Spiritual Youth for Reproductive Freedom and held a "Faith and Sexuality Fair" at our church. We had tables with activities for each of the circles of sexuality (Dennis Daly's model). We had music — some of the participants played a song called "Physical Spiritual Sexual Bodies" and called themselves the "Safer Sex Pistols." I found the poster in my garage the other day, and it made me smile.

We watched "The Education of Shelby Knox" (which includes Ed Ainsworth and his "True Love Waits" program), and we discussed the ineffectiveness of abstinence-only education. We had a panel of folks from NARAL (formerly the National Abortion and Reproductive Rights Action League, now called Pro-Choice America), the Chaplain from Planned Parenthood, my friend from Public Health, and our pastor — all discussing the importance of sexuality education in faith communities.

I began to see how this work was changing our youth group, and how they were going out and correcting misinformation among their peers. Gray-haired congregants were praising the leaders for the work we were doing. People were asking for more information about more programs.

The damage that has been done, intentionally and unintentionally, to sexuality through faith communities in our country (and world) is enormous. I was watching people reconnect with the beauty, the holiness, the wonder of their sexuality. All ages were supporting the work we were doing. It wasn't only great for youth; it was healing for everyone in our church. The different facets of me that love working with youth, hunger for social justice, and want a spiritual connection were all coming together, in joyful, meaningful work.

Eventually, I became an *Our Whole Lives* trainer so that I

152

could help train others in faith communities to offer high-quality, relevant information in a safe format with trained adults to young people in their communities. I also went through the Planned Parenthood University to become a Certified Sexuality Educator, and I began offering workshops to parent groups and agencies on working with youth and sexuality issues.

Before I became involved with *Our Whole Lives* and doing sexuality education work, I had heard of people saying they knew they were "called" to do something. I had an intellectual understanding of that concept, but had never felt it. Now, I know. I truly feel called to do this work, and while I do it in secular environments, too, the joy I feel when I can help people of faith embrace a sexuality education ministry is the best. The healing ripples outward, and people blossom before my eyes. It is good.

Sam Killermann

BA, MA

Austin, TX

PROFESSIONAL LIFE
Current workplace: *It's Pronounced Metrosexual*, Austin, TX

EDUCATIONAL LIFE
Favorite course: Social Psychology of Marriage

TEACHING LIFE
Favorite topic to teach: Gender Identity
Most challenging topic to teach: Masculinity

INSPIRATIONS
Sex educator: Heather Corinna
Book: *S.E.X.* by Heather Corinna

NATIONAL SEX ED CONFERENCE
Title of presentation: *Breaking through the Binary*
Presentation description: What happens when you take an incredibly complex, borderline unsolvable, Rubik's Cube of a socio-psycho-biological puzzle, and present it as a cookie with four easily digestible labels? The same thing that happens when a subject that has traditionally been roped off from the general public by indecipherable "acadamese" is presented in layspeak: People freak out.

Gender is something that's always been on Sam's mind. After years of educating himself and exploring his own gender, he turned to educating the public. His mega-popular version of the Genderbread Person was one of the first tools he created, but he has been busy in the years since. In this talk, Sam will take you through his journey of understanding gender, discuss the tools and resources he's created to help others understand, and provide you with a few concrete takeaways to help you provide comprehensive, queer-positive sex education.

How I Got Into Sex…Ed

In improvisational comedy, we have a rule referred to as "Yes, and!" It's a pretty simple rule to follow, but it leads to what the audience perceives as a complex, intricate, improvised performance. Before I was a sexuality educator, I was a comedian. Looking back now, it's hard for me to separate the two. This sexuality stuff, for me, all started as one huge "Yes, and!"

As an undergrad student at Purdue, I was magnetically drawn to "diversity"-type activities and workshops. I likely would have been interested in such things before college, but they didn't exist in my high school. "Diversity" was a bad word, and "sex" was whispered. The lessons I took away from my health class can be summarized in two quotes that I can still recall in vivid detail: "Don't do drugs or you'll end up in a dumpster eating cabbage" and "I just don't think it's right for a 'grown-ass man'[4] to be talking about vaginas and uteruses to a bunch of kids."

When I got to college, it wasn't long before I found myself engaging in conversations about diversity and identity, then facilitating them in a variety of capacities. I was leading activities and discussions on class, disability, gender, race, religion, and sexuality. I liked it. No, I loved it. And I wanted more of it.

While at college, I also started doing comedy, or "comeding" as we might say (we don't). I was comeding any chance I could get. I did a lot of stand-up at different venues around town, and I also started dabbling in improv.[5] It was during my first improv workshop that I learned the "Yes, and!" rule. Simply put, the rule works like this: When someone presents a reality (e.g., "Yikes, this family reunion is stressful!"), you accept that reality ("It sure is."). Then you add something ("At least you don't have the pressure of someone trying to prevent you from discovering you were adopted."). I embraced this rule onstage, making for better and funnier improv, but also offstage, saying "Yes, and!" to different opportunities in life, making for more awkward and embarrassing stories (i.e., better stand-up).

Out of the blue, I got an email from an organization on campus. The president of the organization had been in one of the trainings I had facilitated focusing on issues of gender and sexuality, and he had a proposition for me. Their membership had gained a bad reputation on campus (I believe the president's phrasing was "our sexual exploits have been upsetting people"). They had tried bringing in a campus staff member to talk about sex, but the professional was unable to connect with their membership. "We meet on Tuesday nights. Can you come in and give a two-hour presentation about sex and healthy sexual relationships? Is this something you do?"

What I probably should have said was, "That's not something I *do,* or have ever done, though it does sound like something I would love to help with. But I'm going to have to decline. Sorry I couldn't be helpful."

What I did say was, "That's not something I *do,* or have ever done, though it does sound like something I would love to help with. Yes, let's do it! And does this Tuesday work?"

That Tuesday, which was then's tomorrow (or today's *super-duper* yesterday), came more quickly than I was ready for. I spent most of the time preparing, working on a little lesson plan, making a PowerPoint, and doing a lot of other things that I didn't realize at the time would have no role in the "training" that was to come. When I finally entered the room, excited to be a grown-ass man talking about vaginas and uteri, the whispers, awkward laughs, and intense avoidance of eye contact commenced immediately.

I started my presentation, realizing quickly that nobody was truly focused on me, but instead on the giant "sexual exploits" elephant[6] in the room. A few minutes in, I stopped mid-sentence. "You know what, let's talk about why I'm here. Tell me about these 'sexual exploits' of yours I was told about," I said, "and why you think they're earning you a bad reputation."

One hand went up, breaking the dam that would flood the next two hours of our time. They asked question after question after question, punctuated by confessions of frustration (some focused on a few other student orgs, some on our campus climate in general, and a few were of the "I blame society" variety). For many of the questions, I didn't have the answers. Somehow my PowerPoint presentation entitled "Sex and Healthy Sexual Relationships" didn't contain the answers to every question someone might ask about the very narrow, easy-to-summarize concepts of "Sex and Healthy Sexual Relationships."

"I don't know," I was saying a lot. "Does anyone know the answer? No?" Then I'd make a note. "I'll look into this and get back to you." Those notes started to add up. I was starting to realize how many questions I had about things that I previously had never wondered about. I quickly realized the inadequacy of my *Mean Girls*–esque, "Don't have sex, because you will get pregnant, and die" high-school sex education. Furthermore, I began to realize how intense my curiosity was for knowledge in these areas.

The presentation ended up being zero parts presentation, and 110 parts question-and-answer (it spilled over into time they were supposed to use on other organization endeavors). But we asked a lot of great questions, and answered a few of those great questions. So I'd be remiss to mark it as a total loss.

Little did I know that many years later, after earning a couple of degrees and embarking on a few unrelated professional endeavors, I would be dedicating my life to asking and answering those same questions. I couldn't have guessed I'd be referred to as "a gender and sexuality person"[7] in a professional capacity, or that I'd be viewed as an authority by anyone about anything — my only goal was to not end up in a dumpster eating cabbage.

So, it seems my entire career is the result of my following an improv comedy rule, perhaps a bit too fastidiously. Everything has been an elaborate and fully committed improvised scene that's been playing for many years now, and will hopefully carry on for many more. From the outside, it may seem complex and intricate, but from the inside, I know it boils down to two words: "Yes, and!"

After the presentation, I pulled the president of the organization aside. "Hey, do you think I could come back in a week or two with the answers to all these questions and do a supplemental presentation?" Without hesitation, he replied, "No. But they're never going to stop talking about this stuff, thanks to you. You did a great job; we just can't spend any more meetings on this."

Well. *Somebody* never learned the first rule of improv.

Darrel Lang
MS, EdD

Emporia, KS

PROFESSIONAL LIFE
Current workplace: President, Health Endeavors: Consulting and Training, LLC
First workplace: Teaching Health Education at Camden Central High School, Camden, NY
Favorite workplace: Professor of Health Education, Emporia State University, Emporia, KS

EDUCATIONAL LIFE
Favorite course: Current Issues in Health Education
Least favorite course: Philosophical Issues in Education

TEACHING LIFE
Favorite topic to teach: Human Sexuality Education
Most challenging topic to teach: LGBTQ

INSPIRATIONS
Sex educator: Dr. Sol Gordon (deceased)
Book: *Raising a Child Responsibly in a Sexually Permissive World* by Sol Gordon

NATIONAL SEX ED CONFERENCE
Title of presentation: *Meeting the Needs of Special Education Students in Human Sexuality Education*
Presentation description: Through audience participation, individuals will be able to see or visualize how to teach human sexuality to students with various disabilities. Each teaching technique will be processed to show how one would teach a topic to the general population and then how to adapt and modify the teaching technique for students with various disabilities.

How I Got Into Sex...Ed

My first introduction to teaching human sexuality education came with my first teaching position as a health education teacher in Camden, New York, in 1970. My undergraduate degree was in Physical Education, Hygiene, and Biology. I had an undergraduate course in human sexuality, but it was through the biology department and didn't prepare me for teaching human sexuality education, except for the "plumbing." One fortunate experience for me was that I started my graduate work for my master's degree right away and took a graduate class in the teaching of human sexuality. This course really assisted me in delivering various teaching techniques that could be utilized in human sexuality education. I also took a course in human sexuality education for special education students. The combination of these two courses benefitted me immensely. They helped me to understand how to reach the needs of all students in human sexuality education.

I was also professionally involved with various state health education associations and attended many of their conferences. I always attended the sessions on human sexuality education to expand my understanding and also my teaching techniques.

In my doctoral graduate work, I took more courses related to human sexuality education and also taught at the university level, specializing in human sexuality education. In 1987, I worked with the Kansas Department of Education in the development of the *K–12 Human Sexuality Education Curriculum Guide.* This guide was a scope/sequence for schools to utilize to assist them in developing their own scope/sequence for their particular school district.

I have also conducted many professional development workshops for school districts and state associations throughout the United States. In 1996, I became the HIV/AIDS and Human Sexuality Education Program Consultant for the Kansas State Department of Education. This position was funded through the Centers for Disease Control/Division of Adolescent and School Health (CDC/DASH) cooperative agreement, and it gave me an excellent opportunity to be trained on various "Programs that Work." With this training, I was also able to train many teachers and others who work with youth on these highly effective programs in human sexuality education. Five years ago, I was elected to the Board of Directors of SIECUS. In this position, I have been able to assist SIECUS in the promotion of comprehensive human sexuality education. This summarizes my 43+ years in human sexuality education.

Erin Livensparger
Certified HIV Counselor, Tester, and Educator

New Haven, CT

PROFESSIONAL LIFE
Current workplace: Planned Parenthood of Southern New England (New Haven, CT)
First workplace: Oberlin College (Oberlin, Ohio)
Favorite workplace: Work for the Health Quarters (formerly Healthcare of Southern New England). I worked with female inmates at the Barnstable County Corrections on relationships and family planning services (Barnstable, MA).

EDUCATIONAL LIFE
Favorite course: Anatomy and Physiology at Oberlin College
Least favorite course: N/A

TEACHING LIFE
Favorite topic to teach: Teaching parents how to talk to their children about sexuality in an age-appropriate way or teaching teens about safer sex
Most challenging topic to teach: Teaching foster parents how to talk to their foster children about sexuality in an age-appropriate way

INSPIRATIONS
Sex educator: Elizabeth Schroeder and Susan Hellen
Book: *Teaching about Sexuality and HIV: Principles and Methods for Effective Education* by Evonne Hedgepeth and Joan Helmich

NATIONAL SEX ED CONFERENCE
Title of presentation: *Sexuality Education and Developmental Disabilities: What Works, What Doesn't*
Presentation description: People with developmental disabilities are often excluded from sexuality education, almost as if they are incapable of having sexual thoughts, feelings,

and needs. In reality, they, too, need the information and skills for making healthy decisions. This workshop will explore effective ways for teaching people with developmental disabilities about sexuality.

How I Got Into Sex...Ed

There was a room in my house growing up that was my mom's office. Really it was a tiny side room piled high with art supplies, books, a sewing machine, VHS movies, and baby dolls. Yes, baby dolls that were life-sized, and when they were turned on, they would cry. When they were filled with water, they would pee. My mom taught home economics and teen-parent Lamaze classes. She helped teens who were pregnant be better moms. Of course, I watched kids' shows such as *Sesame Street* and *Mighty Mouse*, but I also watched cartoons about how sperm travels to the egg and what to do if a woman's water breaks. My mom was the mom that all my friends went to for information about their bodies, menstruation, and pregnancy.

You would think this upbringing is what motivated me to be a sexuality educator. Nope; it was not. First I had to explore creative writing, marine biology, neuroscience, midwifery, and ecology.

It didn't occur to me that people could be sexuality educators for a living while I was facilitating a women's health class for my fellow college students while studying biology at Oberlin College.

It didn't occur to me that people could be sexuality educators for a living while I was volunteering for NARAL Pro-Choice America while living in Woods Hole, MA, researching Atlantic Salmon life cycles for the National Marine Fisheries Service.

It occurred to me when I needed family planning healthcare

myself. I was an uninsured fisheries biologist, so I looked up family planning clinics in my area. I made the connection when I was sitting in the family planning clinic in Falmouth, MA, waiting for the reproductive health counselor to come back with contraceptive information. That was when I noticed a small certificate above her desk that read "Certified Reproductive Health Counselor." When she came back into the room I exclaimed, "Is that really a thing?" (How rudely that was phrased, now that I'm looking back on it!) It was in that moment that I knew I wanted to be a reproductive health counselor, too.

So while looking at salmon scales under the microscope to see how old they are (they are like trees; you have to count their rings), I would sometimes do Internet searches on reproductive organizations. Luckily, there was an opening at the Hyannis, MA, Family Planning Clinic so I applied. I got the job as Reproductive Health Counselor, and they had health insurance!

I quickly became a certified HIV counselor and tester and soon found myself at the Barnstable County Corrections facility providing reproductive healthcare to the female inmates. They became patients while incarcerated, and when they were released, they had an established place and relationship with us to continue their care and support.

I explored other areas of women's health as well. I became a doula and have supported women in labor and during their births. I have expanded what my own definitions of reproductive justice mean. I have new ideas of what human rights means. I want women to be able to make their own decisions about their bodies, their families, and their health. I want that for men and for transgender people as well. I have expanded my thinking about youth development and what it means to help young people have safer sex and make healthy decisions. I incorporate harm reduction in my daily life and try to remember that everyone has a noble intention behind everything they do. Everyone is as human as I am and deserves that grace.

My mom's work with pregnant and parenting teens shaped my ability to help and educate others. My Women's Health student-taught class at Oberlin also shaped my abilities. The older women who volunteered with me at NARAL taught me, too. They would lecture me that young women need to be more involved. I would look at them and say, "I am young, and I am here!" They would say, "Yes, but where are your friends?" I have taken their mini lectures to heart, and expanded upon them. It isn't just young women that are needed, it is everyone. So now I am an educator of parents, of teens, and of professionals. They can help me reach everyone. I can't do it alone. My mom couldn't and my Oberlin classmates couldn't, but we all can together.

Now I am living in Connecticut where I work as a trainer and educator for Planned Parenthood of Southern New England. We serve so many people and are able to talk openly with them about all manner of sex-related topics.

Luca Maurer

MS
AASECT Certified Sexuality Educator, Certified Sexuality
Counselor, NCFR Certified Family Life Educator,
National Wellness Institute Certified Wellness Practitioner,
AASECT Approved Provider of Continuing Education

Ithaca, NY

PROFESSIONAL LIFE

Current workplace: The Center for Lesbian, Gay, Bisexual, &
Transgender (LGBT) Education, Outreach & Services, Ithaca
College, Ithaca, NY

First workplace: First volunteer position in the field — Gay
Awareness Program panelist, University of Delaware, Newark
DE; first workplace in the field — educator, Planned
Parenthood of Delaware, Wilmington, DE

EDUCATIONAL LIFE

Favorite course: A humanities colloquium on Gandhi's
principles of nonviolence and social change, in which the
capstone project was each student putting into practice one of
Gandhi's principles toward effecting some sort of social
change in the world that was important to them

Least favorite course: I try to glean something useful out of
every learning opportunity; however, Intensive Elementary
German was not my favorite.

TEACHING LIFE

Favorite topic to teach: Intersectionalities

Most challenging topic to teach: Any topic where people have
complicated and conflicting feelings about the themes

INSPIRATIONS

Sex educator: My current and former students who serve as
LGBT Awareness Program panelists to educate their peers
and teachers, just as I did when I was a college student

Book: *Lessons for Lifeguards* by Dr. Michael Carrera

How I Got Into Sex...Ed

Two transformative experiences shaped how I got into sex...ed. Neither was a "conventional" career path, but both were instrumental in how I became the professional I am today. Both took place while I was a teenager and continue to fuel my passion and commitment to provide accurate sex education in ways that are useful to people.

Everyone in 11th grade was required to take one semester of health to last them throughout their high school career and adult lives. The course covered the respiratory, digestive, and circulatory systems, nutrition, exercise, and just saying no to drugs and alcohol. Sandwiched in there somewhere between renal functioning and "this is your brain on drugs," there was one class period devoted to reproductive systems, conception, and birth control. All semester I had looked forward to those 42 minutes to learn everything my parents had never told me about sex.

The night before the class, I was giddy. Not only would all my questions be answered, but an actual person from Planned Parenthood was coming to class as a guest speaker and bringing a kit full of birth control we could actually see and touch. Sure, I knew nothing would be said about people like me (people of different sexual orientations and gender identities). I was content to learn about the sexuality of heterosexual, conventionally gendered people; perhaps I could just extrapolate the rest. At the time, it had never even occurred to me to expect more — the possibility to be acknowledged, respected...named even.

It was a budding baby sex educator's dream...until I woke up that morning with the most virulent case of the flu I had ever had. Try as I might, I couldn't get myself upright or stop throwing up for more than a few minutes. I tried — I was determined not to miss that class! But in the end, I wound up staying home sick, on the couch all day watching *Match Game* and *$10,000 Pyramid*. I was devastated. And I was probably the only kid ever to be so upset about watching TV all day instead of going to school. My one chance to learn about sexuality was sabotaged by microbes and bad timing.

A lot of folks can remember messages they received from their family about sexuality. The overwhelming message I received from my parents — crickets. Complete silence. Nothing to see here, move along. No, nope, la la la la, we can't hear you! This absence of a message — even in response to my direct questions from the time I was small through my adolescence — encouraged, even compelled, my curiosity and my determination that no one else would experience this eerie void of information. So, to the parents out there: If you want to avoid raising a child with career aspirations of becoming a sex educator, make sure you talk early and often about sex!!

I made it all the way to college without any information whatsoever about sex. I threw myself into all the quadrants of college life — studying, friends, dating, drinking. Somehow, even without Internet or apps, we sexually and gender diverse folks managed to meet and form a community. Down the hall, a dormmate's uncle was one of the first people to be diagnosed with a terrifying new ailment, at that time called GRID or "Gay-Related Immune Deficiency." We stayed up all night playing Trivial Pursuit, sharing coming-out stories, occasionally visiting the gay bar in the Big City...and we often talked in hushed tones about this new "gay plague" and what it might mean for us. Our small circle of friends was our refuge within a campus and town that vacillated between being covertly and overtly hostile.

There was also a lesbian, gay, and bisexual–themed student group on campus, and we had all that was needed to reach out and support each other in the 20th century — an office in the Student Union, with a desk and telephone. Amazing resources at that time! We organized presentations for classes and dorms, fielding questions from peers and professors about our experiences. The most supportive of our peers said we were courageous and bold for fostering understanding; others heckled, or threatened us as we walked home, or worse. Bold was not the way I thought of our efforts. It was simply that I could not imagine living life without authenticity. People needed a chance to talk; if I could help, I was happy to try. As myths and fear grew about HIV/AIDS, it became clear that many people didn't even understand the human sexuality basics.

Things went well until we were thrown into the most dreaded of college rituals for LGBT students — landing room assignments for the next year, scrambling to secure living situations as safe as we could arrange, or the least dangerous. My brilliant plan was to live on the "Quiet Floor" that was conveniently near my girlfriend's dorm. Rather than be in the general pool of thousands of students who'd be randomly assigned housing, I'd know exactly where I was living.

The plan backfired. My roommate and many of my hallmates had been assigned, against their wishes, to the Quiet Floor because they were on judicial probation for violations of the conduct code. It was their last chance to avoid being expelled. Those of us who chose that floor found ourselves being verbally and physically bullied by them. Constant threats, intimidation, damage to our belongings, and physical violence made our living situation unbearable. Gay people, people with disabilities, people of color, anyone who was just perceived as "different"; even our RA, who was studying for the ministry — all were targets. No matter what we did, the bullying did not stop. Some friends and a professor encouraged me to go see a particular staffer on campus. I didn't understand why. We had appealed to our Residence Director, and to other people up the chain of command. No one did anything to intervene, and several "authorities" told us the situation was our fault. This particular woman had nothing to do with that system at all. But eventually, when all avenues were exhausted and I had nothing left to lose, I went to see her to vent before packing and leaving for good. I told her I was dropping out, that no one would notice if I left school, that it was ridiculous to think I could make something of myself in a world that wanted to erase me. It just wouldn't matter. She looked directly into my eyes, paused, and said words I will never forget: "It matters to me." Long story short, I decided to stay and to eventually graduate.

THIS is how I came to be a sex educator — to pay it forward. I want to leave students with those same words. You matter. You matter to me; you matter to each other; you matter to the world.

Later, my dream job as a sexuality educator did materialize. In my interview I talked about these two central experiences, and landed the position! Drive to learn everything possible despite all odds and fearlessness at tacking even the most taboo of subjects were just the qualities being sought. Through good fortune and timing, I learned at the feet of the masters in the field, Peggy Brick, Sol Gordon, and many others. My appreciation for having these opportunities has only grown over the years.

Since then, I've provided sex education in diverse settings for students and teachers in the United States, peer educators in Namibia, Girl Scout troops, religious education classes, correctional facilities, daycare providers, and communities of elders, among others. I've seen quite a bit of change centered around how the field grapples with the needs of folks on the margins, and those even more precariously on the margins of the margins. Class, race, ethnicity, age, ability, sexual orientation, and gender identity are all parts of the conversation now — they're still not fully included, and in fact are often overlooked, but certainly they've been expanded from the time I entered the field.

Now I have a job that did not exist when I was in college. My role is to foster the academic success and personal growth of LGBT college students, and to provide opportunities to enhance understanding and appreciation of LGBT people and themes. What does this mean? I provide class presentations; professional development sessions; consult with students, staff, and faculty; support syllabus development to infuse and integrate the experiences and needs of LGBT people into the curriculum; keep an ear out for promising practices; and occasionally even get to share some of my own.

What's the result? Students who are eager to major in Queer Studies, or work in LGBT-specific jobs? Sometimes. And that's great. But more often than not, it translates into something much more radical — students studying whatever they want. Students pursuing all career paths, not just those they think they can settle for and face the least amount of discrimination. Students aspiring untethered, rather than getting by on something less in the belief that inevitably they would amount to nothing or live sad, doomed lives. My hope is that through comprehensive sex education, increasing numbers of students will be able to better access their right to an education that is free from harassment and fear, so they can achieve and aspire to love who they love, be who they are, and do what they want.

And what incredible, talented, committed, driven students I've come to know. They pursue their interests, somewhat more free of worries about discrimination or harassment, with vigor and abandon. I am honored to know them, if only for just a little while. I encourage them to go out into the world and make it a better place, and take care of each other along the way. It's a big, wide world, and that world will be all the better because of them and the work we do together to build more spaces in which gentle and spirited inquiry, common humanity, dignity, and respect become the norm.

Konnie McCaffree

MS, PhD

AASECT Certified Sexuality Educator and NCFR Certified Family Life Educator

Doylestown, PA

PROFESSIONAL LIFE

Current workplace: I live in Doylestown, PA, and am retired from a workplace, but I do a lot of consulting, journal reviews, curriculum development, and sexuality educator training out of my home.

First workplace: My first position teaching sexuality education (of sorts) was at Council Rock High School in Newtown, PA, where I was hired to teach a Marriage and Family course (and almost didn't get hired because they wanted to know how I could teach this course and not want any children or a "family"). NOTE: It is illegal to ask that question in an interview today.

Favorite workplace: Council Rock High School is where I converted that Marriage and Family course into a series of Human Sexuality courses for different age groups, and loved teaching the many sections of seniors who took the elective in Human Sexuality, where we could discuss anything and everything, have guest speakers, and really explore the many different sexualities and relationships.

EDUCATIONAL LIFE

Favorite course: Study Abroad programs as part of my PhD studies at NYU. We spent the summers in places like Sweden, Denmark, Japan, Kenya, and Thailand studying sexuality that always challenged our U.S. perspective.

Least favorite course: High school and college social studies courses were so boring. They studied wars and the history of men, and I felt no connection to my world or life as a girl/woman.

<u>**TEACHING LIFE**</u>
Favorite topic to teach: Everything and anything related to pleasure
Most challenging topic to teach: Pleasure and STIs

<u>**INSPIRATIONS**</u>
Sex educator: All my students have been the best sex educators I have ever had. I have learned more from them than any one person or book I have ever read.
Book: *It's Perfectly Normal* by Robie Harris

How I Got Into Sex…Ed

I always wanted to be a teacher but I couldn't decide what I wanted to teach. I graduated from college with a dual major in Biology and Physical Education with the hope that I would find my niche somewhere. It became clear to me after a few months of teaching biology and coaching sports that the adolescents were more interested in their personal relationship issues than most of the subject matter of school. I then chose to get a master's degree in Adolescent Psychology, hoping it would help me learn more so that I could really be of some guidance to these blossoming young adults. Not one part of any course even broached a topic connected to sexuality!

I moved to Pennsylvania, and as I was looking for a job, the only openings I found were for health teachers. I had avoided taking many health courses in college because they were so boring! But I secured a job in a large suburban high school where they wanted someone to teach Marriage and Family because none of the other teachers (with more seniority than me) wanted to teach it. The course was part of the physical education department, and I would take most of the "health" sections. I really didn't know much about Marriage and Family so I took a course at a nearby college that was really a sexuality course. I loved it; I learned so much, and I could see just how I could frame the course I was supposed to teach using all of the topics from sexuality. The professor loved me, and kept encouraging me to go to the NYU PhD program in Health Education where they had developed this new specialty in Human Sexuality. I loved applying what I was learning to my classroom, and my students loved it, too. My technique was to find out what they wanted to learn. Every semester at the beginning of the course, I would ask my students to tell ME what they wanted to talk about. They submitted anonymous 3 x 5 index cards with questions and topics that interested them and affected their lives presently and the future. I kept those cards, thinking they may come in handy someday if I was ever questioned about what I was teaching. The questions came directly from the students, and I developed the curriculum around them. At the time, my school administration was really naïve about the issues that adolescents were dealing with and thinking about, so they couldn't even imagine what students wanted to talk about. They gave me no boundaries, and for the first time in years, they heard positive comments from the students about the course. So the administration was happy, and even let me expand the course into more advanced study by seniors who would be leaving home soon and would be experiencing many issues. They had to have parent permission, which the School Board granted (thinking that most parents wouldn't give permission so the class would not fill!), and the number of sections of the class grew and grew.

I also grew as a teacher because I was going to graduate school, taking all these wonderful sexuality courses, studying abroad in the summer, and learning how to effectively motivate students to learn. I utilized what I was learning during my graduate program, went to every conference that was offered in sex education, and began to develop skills to utilize interactive learning, which had always worked well as my own personal learning style as well. There were books written on "values clarification," which were the basis for many of these learning activities. I also wanted to know more about what was going on in the heads of my students, and used journals to help them articulate their own thoughts, examining their activities and values. I read journals almost every night for over 30 years. I commented in a guiding way, asking thoughtful questions and, to this day, many of my students tell me they have kept their journals well into their adult lives, reading them many years later. I LOVE teaching sexuality education!

Connie Newman

MD

Warren, NJ

PROFESSIONAL LIFE
Current workplace: New York University Medical Center, New York, NY

EDUCATIONAL LIFE
Favorite course: Victorian Passion
Least favorite course: Physics 101

TEACHING LIFE
Favorite topic to teach: Familial Disorders of Lipid Metabolism
Most challenging topic to teach: Taking Sides: Should Sexual Problems Be Treated Pharmaceutically?

INSPIRATIONS
Sex educator: Dr. Ruth
Book: *Tess of the D'Urbervilles* by Thomas Hardy

How I Got Into Sex...Ed

I am not a sex educator, but a medical doctor and an endocrinologist, committed to ensuring access to reproductive healthcare and sexuality education. My interest in this topic began in June 1963 when I was 10 years old and preparing to leave my home in New Jersey to spend the summer in a camp in Reading, Pennsylvania. The camp had separate recreational and sleeping facilities for girls and boys, but there were some activities in which the girls and boys got together. My brother, one year older than myself, was attending the boys' camp.

My father, a pediatrician, supported my decision to go away for the summer, but decided that I could not leave home without being educated about sex. Thus, he met with me in the dining room, and began a "lecture" about sexual reproduction. He did not talk to me about boys and girls, or about kissing, touching, or the act of sexual intercourse. Rather, he explained to me the menstrual cycle, and how babies come from oocytes and spermatozoa. He described in some detail the processes of ovulation, fertilization, and the formation of an embryo, and if I recall correctly, the zygote and blastocyst. At the end of this fascinating story, he cautioned me to be careful of spending any time alone with boys.

Now, to be fair, I was not completely naïve at the time. I grew up with one older and two younger brothers, knew about the differences in anatomy between girls and boys, and even had heard that babies were created after a man put his penis into a woman's vagina. But I had never heard those words before — menses, ovulation, oocyte, ova, spermatozoa, fertilization, etc. — and I was intrigued by their foreignness, their length, and their sound. I felt that my father had told me secrets that no one else of my age knew. And, it occurred to me that if I were to become a doctor, I could learn more about these words and other secrets of the human body. But that was 1963, and there were very few women doctors then.

I went to camp that summer, but don't recall spending time with any boys other than my brother, who would faithfully visit me every Sunday and bring me a bag of popcorn. More recently, I asked my brother whether Dad had given him a sex ed lesson. Apparently he had not. Neither did the school that we attended. Sex ed in high school consisted of one movie that showed a teenage couple kissing in a car. In the very next scene, the young man was in a doctor's office asking about a lesion on his penis.

A few years later, when I was a teenager, my father introduced the topics of teenage pregnancy and abortion — this was before *Roe vs. Wade*. He told me that he had one or two teenage patients who were mothers, but that they, being children themselves, did not actually care for their babies. Care was provided by the grandmother. He also told me sad stories about back alley abortions with crude instruments in unsterile conditions, and about the devastating consequences that sometimes resulted.

In 1970 I entered college. It was a women's college, and during the first year, we had to be in the dormitory by 11 pm every night. That hardly mattered for me because I spent most of my time studying and did not have even one date during my freshman year. I was taking the birth control pill, at my father's suggestion, not because I was sexually active, but as a treatment for my severe facial acne. During one father-daughter weekend, my Dad brought up the topic of STIs — specifically syphilis, gonorrhea, and herpes. He also talked about love and marriage. My Dad was always trying to protect me.

My father died a few years ago at the age of 87, revered by his patients and loved by his family. Of the many memories that I have of him, one that stands out is that first sex ed lesson. He certainly was not trained in sex education, but he took his responsibilities as a parent and a doctor seriously. He sparked my imagination with those long scientific words, and although I did not realize it at the time, my interest in family planning, sexuality education, and reproductive endocrinology started long ago, during my childhood in Passaic, New Jersey.

Brandye Nobiling

PhD, CHES

Salisbury, MD

PROFESSIONAL LIFE

Current workplace: Salisbury University, Salisbury, MD

First workplace: Western Illinois University, Macomb, IL

Favorite workplace: Difficult to answer. I suppose it would be Southern Illinois University, Carbondale, as it was my "coming of age" era of learning how to be a sexuality educator.

EDUCATIONAL LIFE

Favorite course: My first Human Sexuality course as a doctoral student with Dr. Judy Drolet at Southern Illinois University, Carbondale

Least favorite course: My cervical adjustment course at Palmer College of Chiropractic. It was then I realized I was spending more time evaluating HOW I was being taught than WHAT I was being taught. This was pivotal in my deciding to go into education.

TEACHING LIFE

Favorite topic to teach: Contraception, because it marries my teaching and research passions

Most challenging topic to teach: Interpersonal communication, because it is difficult to get students to demonstrate those skills effectively in the classroom

INSPIRATIONS

Sex educator: Dr. Judy Drolet, FASHA, FAAHE, Professor Emeritus of Health Education, Southern Illinois University, Carbondale

Book: I have always been more of a read-to-reference person, so I would have to say *Contraceptive Technology* by Robert A. Hatcher et al., as it helped me get through my dissertation.

NATIONAL SEX ED CONFERENCE
Title of presentation: *Foundations of Sexuality Education: A Brief Look through History*
Presentation description: A glimpse into the past gives us an understanding of the present and future. The purpose of this lesson is to allow participants to reflect on perceived revolutionary events that have shaped our sexual culture in the United States. Participants brainstorm events they perceive as influential, share them on the board, and discuss the impacts of these events in our society. By the end of the lesson, participants can synthesize their perceptions with course content, giving them better comprehension of key events/people and their impact on us as a sexual society.

How I Got Into Sex...Ed

Growing up, I always knew I wanted to be part of a profession that helped people achieve a healthier quality of life. That passion stems from a long and often winding professional preparation. It was a "treasure hunt" that guided me to the "pot of gold" of being a sexuality educator. But I want to preface this metaphor by saying that I did not discover the "pot" all at once. Instead, there were many stops along the path that led me to this profession. I left some places empty-handed. I left other destinations with a small piece of gold that served as a sign that I was on the right track.

The journey began in my hometown of Jacksonville, IL, after I earned my undergraduate degree in biology. I pursued this degree because it seemed like the best fit for someone interested in health, but who attended a very small liberal arts college that did not have a health-specific major.

After graduation, the compass pointed due north to Davenport, IA, to the "fountainhead of chiropractic" in pursuit of a Doctor of Chiropractic degree. Much to my surprise, however, this point on the map was not as it appeared to be when I first arrived. Over my two-year stay there, it became evident that the curriculum lacked a holistic approach to health, and was not inclusive of integrative healthcare. Since the philosophy we were being taught greatly contrasted with my personal philosophy of health, I began searching for disciplines that were more aligned with my fundamental beliefs. At that point I searched the Internet for a different trail to travel. Through a search for advanced degrees in health-related disciplines, I discovered the field of Health Education, and found a nearby university with a strong graduate program.

The next "X" on the treasure map became Western Illinois University to pursue a Master of Science degree in Health Education. During this leg of the trip, I was given my first-ever teaching opportunity. It was to cover a topic of my choosing in a Human Sexuality course. Given my background in the natural sciences, I felt most comfortable with the biological dimension of sexuality, and was intimidated by the psychological and sociocultural dimensions of the subject. With my preparation at that time, I felt ill-equipped to teach topics such as relationships, communication, and gender roles. Therefore, I chose the more objective topic of Sexually Transmitted Diseases (the go-to term about 10 years ago).

After prepping my first sexuality education lesson, there I stood, a 24-year-old graduate assistant, in a lecture hall full of students not much younger than me, with large images of STDs projected on the screen behind me. The interesting thing was that I felt very comfortable teaching the subject to that target group. I figured if I could get through that experience successfully, I could teach just about anything to anyone...I just needed a bit more training. I collected a piece of gold for getting through that presentation effectively, and I moved forward.

After completing my MS degree in eight short months, I stayed put for two years and worked as an adjunct instructor at local community colleges. Those years solidified my passion for teaching at the postsecondary level. I realized that if I wanted to continue on this path, I would need a terminal degree.

I pulled out my compass once again, and it pointed due south this time — Carbondale, IL, to be exact. I was accepted into the PhD program in Health Education at Southern Illinois University, Carbondale. My interest in human sexuality continued into my doctoral program. There, I discovered I had a passion not only for teaching sexuality education, but also for researching the topic. In addition, I had the opportunity to co-teach a Human Sexuality course for two years with a couple of scholars in the discipline who became my mentors. This experience helped me gain knowledge and confidence to successfully teach the psychological and sociocultural dimensions of sexuality — topics I had shied away from a few years prior. I collected another piece of gold when I realized I was competent to teach all subject areas in human sexuality.

I also realized that not every health educator is interested in being a sexuality educator. Therefore, I saw a need to fill that void (and collected another piece of gold). I find it interesting that even though most of us are on this earth because two people had sex, we are so quick to brush the subject under the rug. And the United States has almost a passive-aggressive approach to sexuality. We use sex to sell products and get media attention, yet we don't want to discuss it in the context of healthy sexuality. I feel that as a sexuality educator, I am helping to address this double standard.

I finished my PhD in three years. Prior to graduation, I began searching for assistant professor jobs in health education. The compass pointed in a new direction for my first tenure-track job (and my first "real" job as a sexuality educator). I was headed due east to Maryland, a state I had never visited, let alone lived and worked. At this point, I collected a few pieces of gold for completing my PhD and moving forward on a new adventure.

Currently in my fifth year of teaching Human Sexuality Education at the collegiate level, I have found that students of all ages, races, ethnicities, orientations, and identities are thirsty for knowledge about the topic. I feel blessed that I get to teach at the level where restrictions are few, given that my target audience is composed of adults. At the same time, however, I realize that being the sole sexuality educator on campus means the magnifying lens is often on my curriculum and me. For example, it can take longer to approve a curriculum change for my sexuality course than a proposal for a "less controversial" subject. Nevertheless, I feel it is my goal to advocate for sexuality education, and to increase awareness that it is as necessary a course on college campuses as any other.

In the future, I hope to collect more gold as I continue to feel justified in what I am doing as a professional and representative of our field. I look forward to more adventures ahead of me on the treasure hunt. And someday, the compass even may direct me to "head west"!

Su Nottingham

MA

Mt. Pleasant, MI

PROFESSIONAL LIFE

Current workplace: Central Michigan University, Mt. Pleasant, Michigan

First workplace: My first job in education was at Crary Junior High School, Waterford, Michigan. I taught my first sexuality class at Waterford Mott High School, Waterford, Michigan.

Favorite workplace: Working with teachers who are looking for innovative teaching strategies to use with their students

EDUCATIONAL LIFE

Favorite course: Price and Price: Elementary Education and Learning Centers

Least favorite course: Nutrition...the instructor was a dietitian, a first-time teacher, and read to us from the textbook. Then there was the lab, which was really cooking, and I was a 36-year-old graduate student, returning to get a major in Family and Consumer Science (FCS). I eventually stopped going to the lecture, and only went to the lab. I hope the instructor got better with practice.

TEACHING LIFE

Favorite topic to teach: Relationships

Most challenging topic to teach: Abstinence

INSPIRATIONS

Sex educator: Carol Cassell, Peggy Brick, ETR Associates

Book: *The Dynamics of Relations* by Patricia Kramer and *But I Love Him* by Dr. Jill Murray

NATIONAL SEX ED CONFERENCE

Title of presentation: *Move Your Feet 2, Lose Your Seat, Too!* and *The King & Queen of Puberty*

Presentation description: The first seminar is an interactive, student-centered presentation on a variety of sexuality topics with an emphasis on movement in the classroom and based on the latest brain research. The second talk is an interactive fun presentation to assist students in understanding basic physical, emotional, and social changes during puberty.

How I Got Into Sex...Ed

I started my teaching career in a gymnasium as a physical education teacher for 7th- through 9th-graders in Waterford, MI, in 1974. Waterford was a white-flight community that was gaining in numbers as a reaction to bussing protests, urban fear, and proximity to Pontiac, the third-largest city in Michigan. I was totally unaware of this volatile situation, and simply happy to find my first teaching job. There was no sexuality education, in fact in the late 1960s, there were community protests *against* sex education in this district's schools. Again...totally unaware...just happy to get a job!

I became aware of the need for sex education as a relative innocent, in my second year of teaching. Walking to the teacher's lounge for lunch, I overhead an 8th-grade cheerleader (I still remember her name, but I will leave that out of this story) say: "The worst part is that the cum tastes so bad." This young person was rumored to be servicing several young boys outside the local roller-rink. (I remember the name of the rink, too!) I began having discussions regarding the need for comprehensive sex education with colleagues and the administration almost immediately, although I never told the story of what I overhead until many years later.

Waterford did have a teen mother program where about 25 high school girls each year would attend school at a site away from the three high schools. They were provided classes that counted toward graduation, and there was free daycare for their infants and children. There was no sex education as part of that program. (No shock there, eh?)

During my sixth year (1980) as a PE teacher, something happened that propelled our district into a renewed discussion about sex education. Pontiac, MI, was reported as having the highest abortion rate in the nation. We knew that our students were accessing services in our neighboring city, as we had no clinics in Waterford. Even the administration could see that the climate was different than it had been 10 years earlier, and it established a committee to write comprehensive sexuality programming for the secondary schools. Being a vocal supporter of sexuality education, I was on that committee. We were very successful in launching two semester-long course electives for both 8th grade and high school. We didn't quite get sexuality education as a required subject for all students — it was much too conservative a community for that — but a semester-long elective course in three middle schools and three high schools was a great start.

Personally, something happened to me just before I served on this committee. I was laid off due to declining enrollment. So, I was planning for a program that I would not be able to teach. Still, the program was launched, listed, and became available for students to take. The courses were listed as electives but too few students signed up for them, so they were "combined" with an FCS course called Human Relations. Meanwhile, I remained laid off for four years.

In 1984 I returned to Waterford School District, but this time I taught classes in my minor, Family Life Education. I took the place of a teacher on leave at the high school level. Six weeks became a semester, then a full-time position when the teacher returned from leave and took an administrative position with the district. I began canvasing the students to garner enough interest to get one full sex ed class. In 1985, 16 students elected to take Reproductive Health. Within the next few years, there were between five and seven semester-long classes in my teaching load, which were filled out with Human Relations (think sex education without the sex). This created the need to hire another full-time teacher to teach courses such as Parenting, Consumer Education, Foods and Nutrition, and Single Survival — all the courses I "could" teach, but never wanted to. I had a 20-year run of teaching sex education, semester-long classes to high school students. Eventually, our district separated the classes into 9th-10th–grade Reproductive Health and 11th-12th–grade Sexuality Education...yes, the word "SEX" finally appeared in our course description booklet! Eventually, our district was able to drop the Teen Parent Program due to lack of need. I wish I'd collected the data, done the research, and illustrated the correlation...I might have a PhD!

How I taught sex education evolved quickly. In the beginning, there was soooo much knowledge to impart, it was nearly all teacher talk and discussion. Honestly, if sex had not been the topic, and had there not been such great need and interest, it might not have gone so well.

While working on my master's degree in Curriculum and Teaching, I needed a three-credit elective course to fill out my program. In the summer of the mid-1980s, I took a two-week course with the Price sisters, two 2nd-grade teachers from Lansing, MI. This course was aimed at elementary educators, but it was right for me at the time! The Price sisters taught us interactive learning strategies every other day, with the days in between used to create teaching strategies to implement with our students. I was the only secondary educator there, and certainly the only sexuality educator there! Everyone else was working with letters, numbers, and all things K–5. I was working with STDs, pregnancy prevention, recognizing healthy relationships and all things sexual. It was fabulous! It was the beginning of a dramatic change in my teaching style, which continued for 25 years.

At the secondary and college level, we talk too much. Those two elementary teachers taught science, language, math, reading, social studies — all with the student as the focal point. Putting the student in the middle of the learning is a key component for all learning to take place. I learned this during that two-week course, and carried the flag to colleagues and eventually other teachers through workshops, conferences, and presentations throughout the United States and Canada. I also gained a huge amount of respect for the elementary classroom teacher!

I now teach pre-service teachers who are school health majors/minors at Central Michigan University to utilize student-centered learning in their future classrooms. I also get to teach a methods course in sexuality education at CMU and at Wayne State University. What fun! And I get to see these future teachers begin their journeys in the field of education.

This is how I began, and how I arrived where I am today. Throughout my almost 30 years in sexuality education, I have been honored to attend workshops with Carol Cassall, Peggy Brick, Sol Gordon, Michael Carrera, Deb Hafner, Nancy Abby, Mary Lee Tatum, and Linda Shortt and Randy Rattan. I have attended ETR Conferences; The Guelph Sexuality Conference; The World Sexuality Conference; American School Health Association; American Alliance for Health, PE, Recreation & Dance; AASECT Regional HIV/AIDS and Sexuality Conference with Darrel Lang; and now the National Sex Ed Conference through The Center for Sex Education. I've been invited to speak at each of these conferences. Who would have guessed that a PE teacher who one day overheard a girl's comment in the hallway would use that as the impetus for commitment to a life's work?

Joan O'Leary

Phillipsburg, NJ

PROFESSIONAL LIFE
Current workplace: Retired
First workplace: Northwest New Jersey Community Action Partnership (NORWESCAP), Phillipsburg, N J
Favorite workplace: Any Department of Corrections Juvenile Facility

EDUCATIONAL LIFE
Favorite course: New Jersey Department of Health AIDS/HIV "Train the Trainers" program
Least favorite course: None; I always learned something.

TEACHING LIFE
Favorite topic to teach: Anything and everything having to do with relationships
Most challenging topic to teach: All, depending on audience

INSPIRATIONS
Sex educator: Too many to mention
Book: Again, too many to mention, but two I really enjoyed were *As Nature Made Him: The Boy Who Was Raised as a Girl* by John Colaprinto and *And the Band Played On* by Randy Shilts

How I Got Into Sex...Ed

The road I traveled on the way to becoming a sexuality educator was not one I had any intention of taking. My mother, brother, two uncles, and several cousins were all teachers, and as much as I respected the profession, I knew that particular career was not for me. So, following high school, I attended a small business college, and my very first job was working in the advertising department of a large local industry. I enjoyed that job because there was a lot of creativity involved.

However, I met a man, fell in love, and got married. This was the 1960s, and that is what a lot of women did. In four years I managed to give birth to three children. Reality was a hard "row to hoe." I guess the first step on my road happened when I had my check-up following the delivery of my third child, and I asked my OB-GYN to put me on the pill. He refused, stating that it was very new and not fully tested. I should stick with my diaphragm.

Like that was working for me! He did tell me, however, that if I insisted on the pill, there was a Planned Parenthood clinic across the river in the neighboring state. A few days later, I became a patient there and started on "the pill." I no longer had to worry about becoming pregnant, but it was already too late for my marriage. I joined the ranks of "single parents," which did not sit well with my parents and other family members. Did I mention my Catholic upbringing? Divorce was not in their vocabulary. I also realized that I would have to go back to work to supplement my child support.

The next step in my journey happened when I went to work for an organization called NORWESCAP, an anti-poverty agency funded by the federal government. The program headquarters was located in my town, and the flexible hours helped me care for my kids after school. My first assignment was to recruit and work with low-income teens who were reported by their schools to be at risk of dropping out. A variety of programs were available to them to help with everything from after-school jobs, assistance with school work, health-related problems, and anything else to help them stay in school. I loved that job. Those kids taught me as much as I taught them. Many of them were from single-parent homes growing up in low-income housing, having little if any contact with their fathers, and dealing with involvement with drugs and alcohol. They helped me appreciate the relationship I still had with my former husband and his family, and how important it was for my own kids to have supportive family in their lives.

Then another twist of fate changed my direction. NORWESCAP received a grant from the NJ State Department of Maternal and Child Health to establish a Family Planning Center in my county. Remembering what Planned Parenthood did for me, I asked (begged) to be part of that program. It was to be a cooperative effort between NORWESCAP, the County Public Health Nursing Agency, and the state health department. My job was to coordinate the program among these three agencies. The state provided months of training in all aspects of the program. Now I was definitely headed in a different direction — one I never dreamed of. As part of my responsibilities, I would work at some of the clinic sessions providing patients with family planning education to help them make informed decisions about their choice of contraception, their reproductive healthcare, and related information about sexually transmitted infections, if necessary.

After several years, there was another change of direction for me. A federal grant involving supplemental Title X money became available to establish additional family planning centers in the county. Unfortunately, since NORWESCAP was only receiving state money, they were not eligible to receive the supplemental funds. The only other program in the county was a small one run by Planned Parenthood/Morris Area (PP/MA) in the eastern part of the county. They were already being funded by federal money and were therefore able to secure the grant. I knew that NORWESCAP's program could not compete should PP expand. At a meeting with federal, state, PP/MA, and NORWESCAP, the executive director of Planned Parenthood offered me the opportunity to come to work with them in a similar coordinator position.

I had recently remarried, and my husband would have been supportive of any decision I made. I became a Planned

Parenthood employee, and their presence in the county grew significantly.

One day a teacher from a local high school asked to meet with the clinic educator. I guess that was me, since I was the only one doing any kind of education at the center. The teacher's school administration was concerned over the number of female students leaving school because of pregnancy. She wondered if I would be willing to talk to her health classes about birth control methods. That was the first of many schools that I became involved with throughout my years with Planned Parenthood. Working with the administration, faculty, and parents, I established a Peer Education Program that received private funding from a Morris County–based foundation. It was the first program of its kind in any school in the county and lasted for many years. I still hear from several members of that first group of students, who I trained and who now have high-school or college-aged children of their own.

There were many benefits of working for Planned Parenthood. I received many opportunities for training in many areas of sexuality education, and I took advantage of as many as I could. This was also the early years of the HIV/AIDS epidemic. The state health department instituted a "Train the Trainers" program, and I was part of the first group trained in my county to provide training to other educators. The schools and other agencies were also requesting educational programs on HIV/AIDS. Filling all the requests was a full-time job in and of itself.

Just when I thought my plate was full, requests for educational programs came from an unexpected source. The Juvenile Justice Department had several residential detention programs for adjudicated juveniles in my area, and they were looking for someone to provide sexual education programs for those youth. And thus came another slight curve in my road, and I spent years providing educational programs at those facilities. And, not to be left out, the two adult correctional facilities in my area requested, and agreed to pay for, a variety of programs in both the male and female facilities. I spent a lot of time in prison. So much time, in fact, that my husband, a police officer, gave me a small gold police badge charm to wear. In working with the juveniles, it seemed that my road had come full circle, back to my roots, working with teens.

While I was busy doing programs, Planned Parenthood was also busy growing. When they merged with CFLE (since renamed The Center for Sex Education) I was honored to work for a new Education Director, Peggy Brick, for several years before her retirement and then with Bill Taverner. And I had worked almost from the beginning with Sue Montfort, all of them outstanding sexuality educators. I'll never forget the help and support they gave me along the way.

I retired after 29 years of doing what I thought I never wanted to do. But, do we ever completely retire? I have two wonderful grandchildren. My grandson lives fairly close to me, so I have been fortunate to watch him grow up. He has always gone to Catholic Schools and is now a junior at a Catholic high school. Can you imagine the conversations we have????!

Wayne V. Pawlowski

MSW, LICSW
AASECT Certified Sexuality Educator, ACSW

Wilton Manors, FL

PROFESSIONAL LIFE

Current workplace: Independent Consultant and Trainer primarily based out of Wilton Manors, FL (and sometimes out of Arlington, VA). At the moment, my only formal connection with a workplace is with Planned Parenthood of South Florida, where I have an ongoing contract for about one week each month.

First workplace: This is almost impossible to identify, as I slid into sexuality education, I did not land in it. If I had to pick one job/one place, it would be Director of Counseling for Preterm in Washington, DC, (an abortion-providing health center) in 1983.

Favorite workplace: NICHE (North West Institute for Community Health Educators) in North Bend, WA, sponsored by what was then the Region X Family Planning Training Center. Second favorite was working for the PPFA Education Department based in Washington, DC, (served as Director of Training). My favorite volunteer position ("favorite" is not the right word; "most meaningful" would be more appropriate): HIV/AIDS Support Group Leader for Whitman Walker Clinic in Washington, DC.

EDUCATIONAL LIFE

Favorite course: Believe it or not, English 201 at the University of Maryland. For the first time I had an instructor who really made me think about and analyze what I was reading. My favorite workshop/sexuality course was Human Sexuality at a Social Work conference in NYC taught by Harvey Gochros, a Social Work Professor from the University of Hawaii.

Least favorite course: Health at the University of Maryland (a course required of all freshmen). The course was supposed to have covered sexuality, but it never mentioned the word the entire semester.

TEACHING LIFE

Favorite topic to teach: First, Ethical Issues When Dealing with Client Sexual Issues (for adult professionals); Second, Experiential Group Process; Third, anything addressing working with boys/men

Most challenging topic to teach: Experiential Group Process, which is also one of my favorite topics to teach. Sexuality related: Talking with Your Kids about Sex (for parents)

INSPIRATIONS

Sex educator: Terry Beresford, hands down!!!! She is my role model and mentor from whom I have learned more than I could ever summarize.

Book: *Gay, Straight, and In-Between* by John Money. While an impossibly difficult book to read (Money apparently did not understand the use of periods), it is a fascinating and comprehensive review of an enormous amount of sexuality information.

NATIONAL SEX ED CONFERENCE

Title of presentation: *Understanding the American "Culture of Maleness": Working More Effectively with Boys and Young Men*

Presentation description: Understanding the "culture of maleness" is critical to establishing a meaningful relationship with male clients/students/participants. This workshop will explore messages American boys receive about how to "be a man" and how these messages impact communication and relationships. Strategies for more effective communication with males will be presented and discussed.

How I Got Into Sex...Ed

I became a sexuality educator through a combination of self-interest, being in the right place at the right time, and the AIDS epidemic. I didn't grow up wanting to be a sex educator. That "job" didn't exist when I was a kid.

No one provided sex education in the late 1950s and early 1960s. There were books available that parents could get from the "restricted" section of the library. One of those appeared on my dresser when I was in 5th grade. That book talked exclusively and clinically about heterosexuality. And that was the extent of my sex education!

When puberty hit, it became clear to me that the subtle disconnects I had been experiencing with my peers were actually significant. But, in the absence of any information or even a word for what I was feeling, my only option was to avoid sexual feelings as much as possible.

During my freshman year at the University of Maryland in 1964, I saw a book called *The Homosexual Revolution.* I instantly knew the word "homosexual" described me and my feelings. I have no idea how I "knew" that, but I finally had a word that told me who I was. At Maryland, I had a swimming scholarship, which meant I was surrounded by handsome and muscular young men in bathing suits nearly every day for four years. That was both exciting and stressful to me, and it precipitated more than one suicidal thought.

In the early 1970s, I spent two years in the Peace Corps in India. In 1973, I returned to the United States. My BA in secondary education landed me a job as a live-in counselor with a residential, therapeutic-camping program for "emotionally disturbed" boys in the wilderness of central Virginia. Not surprisingly, in a live-in setting for 12- to 14-year-old boys, there was some "homosexual acting out." Also not surprisingly, the program essentially ignored it or talked around it. I was too deeply closeted and fearful to say anything about it on my own.

I went from the "Wilderness School" to a job in Alexandria, Virginia, as a counselor in a co-ed halfway house for adolescents in the child welfare system. (Get the theme here? Another job "helping kids in need.") Now that I was living in the city instead of in the woods, I decided it was time to explore my sexuality...to start coming out as a gay man.

My first night "out," I met Don (not his real name) who immediately became NOT my sex partner but my gay mentor. He recognized a confused, young gay man who needed a friend and guide. He selflessly coached me through my coming out. I have always felt grateful that I had someone who eased my coming out of the closet and into the gay world of Washington, DC, in the mid-1970s.

But, as I went through that process, I found myself asking, "Where are the Dons (and Donnas) for isolated gay and lesbian youth? Why did I have to wait until I was in my late 20s to find someone who could help me understand myself and the subculture of which I am a part?" I made a decision that year to get an MSW so that I could continue to work with teens and be a "Don" for the next generation of gay/lesbian youth.

Fast forward another four years. I had earned that MSW and found work in child welfare. I learned in graduate school (Catholic University, 1975–1977) that social workers got NO education or training in human sexuality, other than in psychopathology (which is where information about homosexuality was still covered). None of the social workers I encountered had any idea what to do about "homosexual acting out," other than to refer "those" kids to a psychiatrist. As time went by, it became increasingly clear to me that child welfare was not the vehicle by which I would be able to help gay/lesbian youth.

In 1981 I got a job in Washington, DC, with a consulting firm that had a federal contract to write a comprehensive training curriculum for social workers involved in child welfare. I was hired to write the module, "Working with Adolescents in Need of Special Services." Drawing on my experience and the current research, I wrote about working with adolescents, including "Pregnancy and Parenthood," "Sexual Acting Out," and "Gay Youth."

Through our curriculum review process, I was regularly challenged about including information on gay youth. My reply was always: "This is a module on 'working with adolescents in need of special services' and gay/lesbian youth are in need of special services."

That reply worked until President Jimmy Carter left office and President Ronald Regan took over. During our first curriculum review by the new Republican administration, the pregnancy, parenthood, sexual acting out, and gay youth materials were all removed. So there we were, with a curriculum called "Working with Adolescents in Need of Special Services" that did not include one word about sex or sexuality.

The consulting firm let me "package" those deleted materials into separate modules, which we marketed at social work conferences and at the annual Media Fair of the DC-based, Sex Education Coalition.

Everything came together in 1983 when I left the consulting firm and became the Director of Counseling for Preterm (Washington's oldest abortion clinic). As dumb luck would have it, on my very first day at Preterm, a woman named Terry Beresford was doing an in-service for Preterm staff. Terry was a gifted trainer and educator, who had been with Planned Parenthood of Maryland and Preterm for many years. She was well known in the fields of abortion and sexuality. I knew immediately that I adored her and that I wanted to be like her. I have been working on that goal ever since.

As part of my job at Preterm, I did community education about abortion and sexuality, which allowed me to network with DC-based organizations that were working with adolescents and adolescent sexuality issues. That work also got me more involved with the all-volunteer Sex Education Coalition, through which I wrote an article about growing up gay and developed and presented a daylong workshop called "Homosexuality: Youth and Families." I was also able to serve on the Coalition Board for several years.

At this time, the Gay Rights Movement was taking hold in Washington and a strong gay community was growing. Through my work at Preterm and the Sex Ed Coalition, I met others who were committed to supporting gay youth. In 1985–1986, a small group of us founded SMYAL (then called the Sexual Minority Youth Assistance League, now called Supporting and Mentoring Youth Advocates and Leaders).

After three years at Preterm, Planned Parenthood of Metro Washington took over Preterm's abortion services and I became Director of Education and Training for PP Metro DC. As part of my new job, I provided sexuality education and training throughout the DC area and made contacts with many other sexuality educators.

In the mid-1980s one of those contacts asked me to do a session on "male involvement" for a National Family Planning Administrators' Conference in DC. Little did I know at the time that that session would launch me into doing some version of "male involvement" training for the next 30 years!

Enter the HIV/AIDS epidemic into DC. Suddenly, everyone needed training about sexuality, homosexuality, and safer sex. Due to my work with the coalition and Planned Parenthood, I had the credibility to position Planned Parenthood as DC's "Sexuality Expert." As a result, any HIV/AIDS training in DC, Maryland, and/or Virginia had Planned Parenthood (usually me) teaching the sexuality components.

In the early 1990s, I left PP Metro DC to become the Director of Training for Planned Parenthood Federation of America. That position enabled me to continue doing sexuality training and to work with sexuality educators all over the country.

Fast forward one last time to 2001. That year I was laid off from PPFA and launched out on my own as an independent consultant and trainer. Since then I've become an AASECT Certified Sexuality Educator, and served terms on the Boards of SIECUS and AASECT. And, as befitting my increasing age, I became a member of the Consortium on Sexuality and Aging at Widener University and have started doing training on sexuality and aging, including LGBT aging.

Several years ago my husband of 30 years (well, "officially" only of 5 years) and I moved to Wilton Manors in South Florida. From "down here" I continue to work as an independent consultant and do contract work for Planned Parenthood of South Florida — once a Planned Parenthood person, always a Planned Parenthood person.

Up until her recent passing, I still would pick Terry Beresford's brain from time to time. I learned so much about teaching sexuality from Terry, and she will be missed by me and by the entire community of sexuality educators. [8] Meanwhile, I continue to work here in Florida; my goal is to keep making the world a better place for all people, but for LGBT youth in particular.

Mary Jo Podgurski

RN, MA, EdD

AASECT Certified Sexuality Educator, AASECT Certified
Sexuality Counselor, Lamaze Certified Childbirth Educator,
Olweus Bullying Prevention Program Trainer

Washington, PA

PROFESSIONAL LIFE

Current workplace: Academy for Adolescent Health Teen
Outreach, Washington, PA

First workplace: Volunteered with pregnant and parenting
teens, 1975; Taught What's Up as You Grow Up? early
sexuality/puberty education at the Washington Hospital in
1984; founded Teen Outreach in 1988

Favorite workplace: Teaching sexuality education in our school
districts

EDUCATIONAL LIFE

Favorite course: Honestly? Children/Adolescent Literature,
undergrad in Education at the University of Pittsburgh, 1971. It
opened my eyes to youth culture.

Least favorite course: Statistics — grad and doctoral level. I
don't enjoy data, although I do enjoy research. Go figure.

TEACHING LIFE

Favorite topic to teach: 6th-grade sexuality education. I love
their hungry minds.

Most challenging topic to teach: I teach aspiring teachers at
Washington and Jefferson College. My Educational
Psychology course there challenges me to become more
creative and make the content relevant.

INSPIRATIONS

Sex educator: There are so many...really...but if I must name
one, it would be Peggy Brick.

Book: *Guide to Getting It On* by Paul Joannides

NATIONAL SEX ED CONFERENCE
Title of presentation: *Me Too: Sexuality Education for People of ALL Abilities*
Presentation description: Learn to really provide inclusive sexuality education! This workshop will explore incorporating interactive activities for people of all abilities. Techniques focus on providing comprehensive sexuality education for individuals living with cognitive, social, or physical disabilities. The presentation will include games, exercises, role-plays, and original techniques utilized in a partnership with The Arc of Western PA.

How I Got Into Sex...Ed

I didn't plan to be "the sex lady," but that's how I'm known in my small community. Recently the county commissioners honored the outreach program I founded for 25 years of service; during the formal photograph with my staff and our peer educators a commissioner quipped: "If I'd known you weren't going to mention being the sex lady in your remarks, that's how I would have introduced you." Being the sex lady is one of my greatest honors. I have no doubt I'll be referred to as the sex lady in my obituary.

There are other sex ladies; I've actually trained many myself, including a few sex men. But in my small community, I'm the original. How did I become the first person to introduce comprehensive sexuality education to schools in our county, the co-founder of the first-ever county GSA (gay–straight alliance), and the catalyst for seven youth development programs? The answer is easy. Life brought me here, led by a powerful young woman and her courage. What an amazing journey it's been!

As a 24-year-old nurse at Memorial Sloan Kettering Cancer Hospital in New York City, I encountered my own mortality through the deaths of my young patients on the pediatric/adolescent unit. When we moved to PA, I sought out birth and became a Lamaze certified childbirth educator. I thought I was finished with death, but I was wrong (ultimately, I returned to end-of-life care as a hospice nurse). However, my role as a childbirth educator brought me to sexuality education.

Early on I realized that teen parents didn't always fit into a traditional childbirth class. Even unhappy couples typically act supportive during a six-week class about birth. I decided to teach a special class for adolescents. It was the 1970s. I made myself available 24/7, and I didn't charge for the classes. I always fed them. Teens responded enthusiastically. They said I was "free, funny" and I gave them "food" — the "3Fs". The classes became very popular.

One evening during the last trimester of my own pregnancy, I received a call from the parent whose daughter was pregnant. Would I teach her? "Of course" I said. Class was on Tuesdays at 6 P.M. at my home. I started giving directions when she stopped me. Her daughter was in foster care. Could I do a home visit? I had no experience with home visiting except through hospice, but I reasoned that it was possible. After all, I had a portable uterus!

When I entered the foster home, I was directed to the young mother-to-be's bedroom. I hadn't yet completed my master's work in counseling but I didn't need a degree to know this child was depressed. All the blinds were drawn; she sat in the dark. I took a breath and said: "Hi. I'm Mary Jo, and I'm going to help you have your baby in the best way possible." She didn't turn around. Her "Who the fuck do you think you are?" didn't shock me. I simply responded: "I think I'm Mary Jo, and I'm going to help you have your baby in the best way possible." She almost smiled. During our first meeting she didn't speak. She was 12. Pregnant at 11, she was a hold-over 5th-grader. She was the most streetwise young person I've ever met.

I already knew not to assume, but my adult thinking reasoned that the conception was not consensual. I was incorrect. She wasn't "in love" with the 16-year-old father but, in time, she shared that she had initiated the sex. I knew little about female adolescent sexuality. I knew little about long-term reactions to child sexual abuse. It took her two years to disclose her childhood abuse to me but when she did, I affirmed her worth. She was my best teacher.

I'd only met with her twice when she called to say she was in labor. My home phone rang at 10:30 P.M., and she opened with: "Ain't nobody going with me." I ascertained she was in labor. I asked if she wanted me to meet her at the hospital. She said: "Who gives a fuck?"

My partner and husband Rich is my rock. He's supported me for 40 years. That night I told him I was going to the hospital and would return by midnight. Nineteen hours later, her baby was born.

During those long hours, I learned life-changing lessons. I developed a passion for doula work — serving a woman during labor and birth. I learned how protected I'd been in my own life. I began to grasp the concept of socioeconomic privilege. I learned a new respect for extreme depths of strength and resiliency. I learned how much courage a 12-year-old could have. I also decided I didn't want to give birth myself, although at 32 weeks, I was at a point of no return.

The young mom had chosen adoption. "I need my kid to find a better life than mine." She decided she couldn't go through "giving up my baby" if she saw the baby, or even knew the child's gender. Before ultrasounds were common, the first shout in a delivery room was "It's a boy" or "It's a girl." I alerted the DR staff to be silent and respect this brave teen mom's wishes. Ultimately, the only sounds were the mom's sobs and her newborn's cries; the baby was swiftly whisked away. She asked me for a soda; after making sure she was comfortable, I gladly left the room.

The nursery was between the soda machine and the labor suite. I entered and stared in awe at this beautiful, healthy, 9 lb., 6 oz. baby. Then it hit me — no one had yet welcomed this new little one to life. I scooped the newborn up in my arms, sunk into a rocking chair, and began to hum. My own baby kicked in utero. And I began to cry. I don't cry easily. Kodak commercials don't make me tear up. The other nurses asked if I was OK. I said no.

Like many women in the 1970s, I had huge plans for our baby's birth. I hoped to welcome our newborn gently with a LaBoyer birth. I planned to put the baby to breast immediately. I knew I'd sing one of the Italian lullabies my mama sang to me. I thought I'd baptize the baby right away, since, as my papa often said, you never know when there could be a nuclear attack. I actually made these plans a reality. What about this amazing 12-year-old? What about her baby?

The contrast between my life and the life of that young mother nearly overwhelmed me that day. I was on a pedestal in my Italian family. My papa called me three times a day to see if I wanted bing cherries or juicy oranges or fat peaches. I was treasured and honored and loved because I was giving life. Yet this young woman, whose courage and sense of purpose was infinitely higher than mine, this child who gave life no differently than I would, was treated like dirt under society's feet.

When I returned home, I told Rich I was going to talk with teens about sex. I began as a volunteer with pregnant and parenting teens in five local school districts, only receiving funding for that aspect of our outreach program in 1996. I'd

---

meet with young parents — both mothers and fathers — during their study halls or lunch. In 1987, a wonderful guidance counselor asked me: "Why don't you teach the rest of the kids not to have babies?" I said I would. I had no idea where I was going; I just knew I had to try. My local hospital, The Washington Hospital, partnered with me to form a school-business partnership, and I began in one school in October 1988. Since then, my staff and I have taught comprehensive sexuality education to more than 230,000 young people.

Initially, I simply wanted to change teen pregnancy rates; in time I learned from young people and realized I wanted so much more. I wanted to teach sexual health, not just the avoidance of pregnancy or STIs. I wanted to inspire healthy relationships. I wanted to "be there" for all kids.

I learned to involve parents and community. I learned to really listen to teens. I learned to be inclusive, avoiding heteronormative language and creating a safe place for all youth. I learned that peer educators' messages are heard as shouts, compared to the whisper from an adult. I learned to teach body-positive, affirming, interactive, teen-driven lessons. I learned that every person is a person of worth.

I made a promise in 1988, and I've never broken it. The day I don't look forward to teaching young people with joy is the day I'll stop. I don't expect that day to ever come.

Karen Rayne

MA, PhD

Austin, TX

PROFESSIONAL LIFE
Current workplace: Unhushed, Austin, TX
First workplace: Trinity United Methodist Church, Austin, TX
Favorite workplace: Unhushed, Austin, TX

EDUCATIONAL LIFE
Favorite course: AP American History in high school. For our summer project, we were asked to design and create a school — everything from the building to the pedagogical approach. That was the summer I fell in love with education.
Least favorite course: Algebra II, also in high school. My teacher told me to stop asking questions because they were stupid. It took me years to overcome my dread of math and remember that I am really quite mathematical.

TEACHING LIFE
Favorite topic to teach: Comprehensive sexuality — pulling everything together over many meetings is such a powerful thing. Within that spectrum, sexual orientation and technology are probably my favorites. I love to work with youth, parents, and teachers, in all of these contexts.
Most challenging topic to teach: Sexuality and religion

INSPIRATIONS
Sex educator: There are so many beautiful people in this field. I am honored to be among them, professionally and within this book. Learning so many of my colleagues' stories has been such an inspiration! Among so many stars, Pam Wilson, Bill Taverner, and Mary Jo Podgurski stand out as mentors.
Book: I am currently reading Danah Boyd's new book, *It's Complicated: The Social Lives of Networked Teens*. It's rare that I want to start buying extra copies of a book to put into people's hands before I even finish the Introduction — but Boyd's book is one of them. For anyone working with

adolescents or young adults, understanding how social media intersects with their lives and sexuality is imperative, and this book does that with such beauty, insight, and firmly grounded research that I would literally stand up and applaud it. It is even written in a way to withstand the fast pace of technological evolution!

NATIONAL SEX ED CONFERENCE

Title of presentation: *Learning a Lot about LARCs: How to Incorporate Long-Acting Reversible Contraception into Your Lessons*

Presentation description: Should we consider Depo-Provera a LARC? How do LARCs fit in with lessons on other contraception? How do we get teenagers to consider the implications of LARCs in their decision-making processes? In this workshop, we will discuss these questions and more, as well as introduce three LARC-specific curricula from the new 4th edition of *Positive Images: Teaching about Contraception and Sexual Health*.

How I Got Into Sex...Ed

I got into sex education by a trick of fate, by grace, by luck. My story is not, in its contours, very different from many the other ones that fill this volume. There was one short moment when this professional path opened to me. Through the door, I saw a pot of gold at the end of a rainbow, far in the distance, and it winked. I slipped through, even though the door was only open for a second and everything looked just the same on the other side. In the miles since, I've learned how very lucky I was to have jumped through.

My professional and academic calling has always been about teenagers. What I wanted, as a still optimistic and doe-eyed young graduate student, was to research how teenagers were integrated (or not integrated) into intergenerational communities. My goal was nothing short of a Bowlby-esque shift in how our culture perceived adolescents.

When the mists of optimism cleared and I saw what a life in academia would actually mean, it clearly wasn't the path for me. I had a toddler and was pregnant with my second daughter — there was no way I would enter the tenure process in the next two decades. But graduate school was fun, and I had a decent research position that was flexible and paid enough, so I stayed in. I assumed that a PhD couldn't do me any harm.

When my research position was canceled and I was given a year to finish (and also start) my dissertation, everything jumped into warp speed. I had two very young children, a dog, and a house to care for, nine course hours to complete, and a dissertation to propose, write, and defend in nine months. My partner, ever supportive and caring, was amazing, and I got it all done.

But I still didn't have a career path. I could (God forbid!) write and analyze SAT and other standardized test questions; I could do educational research for various programs; I could teach; I could write curriculum. But none of this really thrilled me. I imagined the opening line of my resume: "PhD in Educational Psychology for hire...in anything."

And then the door opened.

A friend's 14-year-old daughter had a pregnancy scare. There was no logical reason why she was scared — it was highly unlikely that she'd gotten pregnant the one time she'd had sex because she'd used a condom. She was still two weeks away from her next period, but she was worrying herself sick and ended up telling her mother what was wrong. My friend mentioned this to me, in passing, asking if I knew of a comprehensive sexuality education program in Austin. She wanted something more in-depth than what the high school and the local Planned Parenthood offered (which was nothing and contraception only). There wasn't a Unitarian Universalist Church offering age-appropriate *Our Whole Lives* sessions nearby, so I offered to talk with her daughter. We met for maybe seven hours over the next few months. I loved our time together. I met with my friend and her husband to talk about how to talk about sexuality at home. The family relationship grew in leaps and bounds. And, I suppose you could say, a sex educator was born.

The pot of gold at the end of the rainbow that I saw must have been a mirage, because there is no gold anywhere to be found. But the rainbow is real, and I dance in its dust every day. Writing this story at midnight on a Saturday, I can't imagine a better way to spend my time, better colleagues with which to surround myself, or a more meaningful professional compass by which to guide my life.

Rebecca Roberts

MEd, CSE, CHES

Newark, DE

PROFESSIONAL LIFE

Current workplace: Planned Parenthood of Delaware, Newark, DE

First workplace: Sheridan Japanese School, Sheridan, OR

Favorite workplace: Planned Parenthood of Delaware, Newark, DE

EDUCATIONAL LIFE

Favorite course: Human Sexuality at Linfield College. In graduate school at Widener University, it's a toss-up between Sexual Minorities and Sensitive Issues in Human Sexuality. Most of my sex classes were pretty great!

Least favorite course: Statistics in the behavioral sciences

TEACHING LIFE

Favorite topic to teach: Effective teaching strategies for human sexuality

Most challenging topic to teach: Cultural competency

INSPIRATIONS

Sex educator: Peggy Brick

Book: *Guide to Getting It On* by Paul Joannides

NATIONAL SEX ED CONFERENCE

Title of presentation: *SeXXX Ed: Teaching youth about porn from a media literacy perspective*

Presentation description: Sexually explicit material (SEM) is prevalent in our media and often accessed by youth. But what messages are youth receiving from this content? Sexuality educators have a unique opportunity to discuss SEM, especially pornography, with young people but may have reservations about how to approach this often controversial topic. As with any other media, students need to be able to deconstruct messages about SEM and analyze reality versus fantasy in order to better understand and appreciate the diversity of sexuality. Using a media literacy approach that won't get you kicked out of the classroom, this workshop will present specific strategies for incorporating the discussion of SEM with other media examples.

How I Got Into Sex...Ed

I wish I could say that I had a profound experience that solidified my intention to pursue a career in the field of sexuality, but that wasn't really the case. I guess my entry into sex education wasn't all that sexy, but rather, a practical decision that came about over a few years and some small movements in a general direction. In looking back, I now wonder how I could have ever thought about doing anything else.

In my youth, I certainly never had the intention to be a sex educator. Because I had such random and seemingly unrelated interests and no particular career path, my parents breathed a huge sigh of relief when I seemed to have settled on being a teacher (until they figured out what kind of teacher). When I decided on a general direction, the toss-up then became whether I was going to be a teacher of history or health — two largely unrelated topics, but certainly influenced by my high school teachers at the time. In college, I decided on health education because I felt that it was so relevant to everyone. As the saying goes, *if you don't have your health, what do you have?* I guess I took this to heart because anything health related interested me in some way (even the dissection of cadavers in anatomy lab...very cool!) and I felt it was all so applicable to people of any age (which subsequently turned into my same viewpoint about sexuality).

It really wasn't until my first human sexuality course as an undergrad that I realized how intriguing the topic of sexuality could be. It was my first time experiencing extra credit in the form of visiting sex shops and discussing sexual behaviors over coffee like it was the most natural thing in the world. I have my human sexuality professor to thank for my eventual move into the field. She taught me not only that sex was perhaps the most interesting topic to study, but also that it was possible to make a career out of it. She also gave me my first experience with sex ed as a teacher's assistant at a nearby Japanese school. I didn't actually make the transition into full-time sexuality education, however, until a few years later. In the interim, I taught health education to middle- and high-school students which, although I didn't fully appreciate it at the time, also gently pushed me in the general direction of sexuality. My students taught me that sex was probably the most intriguing topic to talk about, which was evident in how they came alive during class discussions. I realized in teaching the sexuality unit that it was by far the most fun topic I taught throughout the entire health curriculum. But I still wasn't quite ready to make the transition from health education to sexuality education, although the two are inextricably linked. I had my own process that led me into sex ed. I was 20-something, and I had a what-am-I-doing-with-my-life crisis in which I had the unique opportunity to drop everything I was doing, pack up my life in Oregon (where I was born and raised), say goodbye to friends I'd had since elementary school, and make a cross-country move to Delaware to see what the East Coast had to offer. Although this period was filled with turmoil and transition, I emerged with a concrete goal for my career — teaching about sexuality. So where did I go from here? To Planned Parenthood of course. I had known about Planned Parenthood for years and had even invited Planned Parenthood educators into some of my classes to speak to my students. I was fully aware of the high-quality sex education that this organization provided, and I loved the idea of being a part of it. So I began my search for Planned Parenthood job opportunities in Delaware.

This is where I'm sure a little luck (or perhaps the universe pushing me in the right direction) came into play, because educator positions with Planned Parenthood are somewhat difficult to come by. I had a unique experience in that while I was job searching, there were three availabilities in the education department within a few months of each other at the only Planned Parenthood in Delaware. I applied for the first position and was quickly told it had already been filled. I then applied for another position and after waiting some time, was again told it was filled. If at this point in the story you are unsure about my persistence and determination, let me be clear: I hate giving up. When I have finally made a decision about where I want to be and what I want to be doing, I go to great lengths to make it happen. So I applied again, for a third position, not knowing if there would be any other job availabilities anytime soon. And just for good measure, I also applied to work in the medical center as well as the volunteer program. I was going to get into the organization one way or another! And it was in the medical center, not the education department, that I finally got an interview. Although I didn't have as many qualifications to work in healthcare, I was more hoping this position would lead me to the education department at some point. And it did — actually much more quickly than I had anticipated. Immediately after my interview, the interviewer called up Catherine Dukes, the VP of Education and Training, to suggest she take another look at my resume. Two more interviews and one presentation later, I finally had the position for which I had been applying for months. This became my first full-time position as a sexuality educator and one I will never forget.

Working in a Planned Parenthood education department felt like coming home. It became evident quite quickly that teaching about sexuality was what I was meant to do. With that realization, I began to investigate graduate schools in the area, which led me to Widener University's Human Sexuality program. Who knew I could work in sex education and study sex education all at the same time? Brilliant! I applied and was accepted into the doctoral program, which served to further my knowledge and skill set. It was really the perfect program for me because I could directly apply my coursework to the work I was doing in the field. As I now write this story of my entry into the field of sexuality, I am nearing the end of the doctoral coursework (dissertation, here I come!), and I can honestly say that my colleagues at Widener are a huge asset to this field. I am excited to see all of the great work they will continue to do throughout their careers, and I've been blessed to have walked with them for a while on this journey.

I've also been with Planned Parenthood now for more than five years and I've had the most wonderful, memorable adventures in sex ed. I've been able to work with such a diverse group of people — students of all ages, adults, professionals, parents, grandparents, young men in prison, adolescents in juvenile detention, pregnant and parenting teens, kids in urban and rural areas, and I have learned more from them than I ever could have imagined. I don't know how many people can honestly say they enjoy coming to work every day. The amazing people I work with, colleagues and students alike, are such an inspiration. At some point I know I'll move on, perhaps to a college or university as a long-term goal, but when that day comes, I will never forget my experiences here. Sexuality education is, hands down, the most interesting subject to teach and learn about. It relates to everyone, is controversial at times, and is so uniquely diverse and complex...and Planned Parenthood does it fabulously!

Laurencia Hutton Rogers

DrPH, CHES

Towson, MD

PROFESSIONAL LIFE
Current workplace: Department of Health Science, Towson University, Towson, MD
First workplace: YWCA of Tampa Bay; Healthy Start Work and Gain Economic Self-Sufficiency Home Visiting Program, Clearwater, FL
Favorite workplace: Department of Health Science, Towson University, Towson, MD

EDUCATIONAL LIFE
Favorite course: Human Relationships
Least favorite course: General Chemistry

TEACHING LIFE
Favorite topic to teach: Pregnancy & Childbirth
Most challenging topic to teach: Sexual Orientation

INSPIRATIONS
Sex educator: Dr. Hilda Hutcherson
Book: *For Women Only* by Shaunti Feldhahn

NATIONAL SEX ED CONFERENCE
Title of presentation: *Spiritual Selves vs. Sexual Selves: Opportunities for Sexuality Education*
Presentation description: This is a poster presentation of the findings from a qualitative study that examined the religious/spiritual experiences and needs of LGBTQ college students.

How I Got Into Sex…Ed

How I got into sexuality education…wow, I don't think I've ever given this much thought. Probably because it has always been a part of me, even when I didn't know what it was called. I spent my early years in the Caribbean, and even though sexuality-related messages were all around me in the music, the dances, and even the children's games, I was raised in a very conservative household. My mother consistently told me to "study your lessons and leave the boys alone." She gave me a book on puberty and told me that I could ask her anything I wanted to, but of course, I never did! That was the extent of "the talk." However, that book was a great reference for just about everything — or so I thought.

At some point in high school I became an "expert" on everything. I took an elective parenting class and loved it. Hmm...maybe that was the beginning of this journey. This information would certainly come in handy, since at the time, I wanted to become a pediatrician. My boyfriend and I broke up every few months, but that didn't matter because "we were in love." Besides that, we went to the same church and saw each other every day, so we were destined to be married. Wrong!! Heartbreak came with the admission that he had cheated on me. That flipped a switch in me, and changed my approach to relationships. I majored in health education in college and was required to take a class on teaching sexuality. My group partner and I decided to do an afterschool workshop with 7th-graders. All I can say is, "What an experience!" I had the opportunity to volunteer, and I chose Planned Parenthood, but I really can't remember why.

After college, I did an afternoon program at my church that included domestic violence, and I was dumbfounded that there were male leaders who joked and suggested that the violence was the woman's fault. While pursuing my masters in public health with a concentration in maternal and child health, I worked on a study about infant mortality among African American women, and the church became a crucial component. While working on my doctorate, I attended a youth convocation, and the leaders started talking to the youth about their irreverent sexual behaviors. I couldn't sit still — I stood up, Bible in hand, and made my point in defense of the youth. To my surprise, it was followed by applause. Up until then, I didn't have a dissertation topic, but it was becoming clear: the intersection of sexuality and religion. A few years later, "The Relationship between Religiosity and Responsible Sexual Behavior among Adolescents and Young Adults" was completed.

In 2009, I was a stay-at-home mother looking for an adjunct teaching position. I interviewed and was offered a full-time position, and one of my classes was human sexuality. To be honest, sexual orientation was a difficult chapter for me to teach because I only had a heterosexual perspective, so I invited a panel of LGBT students to speak to my class. Their stories of rejection by their family and their faith nearly broke my heart. That was the impetus for our study, "Spiritual Selves versus Sexual Selves: An Exploratory Study of the Spiritual/Religious Needs of LGBTQ Youth." No matter how much I try to pursue a different path, I keep coming back to this place — that intersection where faith and sexuality meet. I am a Christian, so perhaps "the church" is my target audience.

So as you can see, I didn't set out to become a sexuality educator, but I'm confident that I am where I am supposed to be right now. Education alone won't solve all of the many issues, but it's a huge step toward creating a more healthy society in which we value and respect each other and are equipped to make informed decisions. What a responsibility, but one that I'm happy to assume!

Timaree Schmit

MEd, PhD
AFAA

Philadelphia, PA

PROFESSIONAL LIFE
Current workplace: Widener University, Sex with Timaree; Philadelphia area, PA.
First workplace: PersUNL, University of Nebraska-Lincoln
Favorite workplace: Impossible to choose, but training future sex educators now at Widener is amazing.

EDUCATIONAL LIFE
Favorite course: Another impossible question, but an elective on Black Sexuality pops into my brain more often than most.
Least favorite course: I took a History and Ethics course that was largely phoned in. It was bad simply because it had so much potential and was squandered on watching videos intended for the general public.

TEACHING LIFE
Favorite topic to teach: Media and sexuality
Most challenging topic to teach: Talking about sexual assault is always a challenge because you never know who is in the room and what they've experienced, or what the discussion might trigger.

INSPIRATIONS
Sex educator: William Stayton is and always will be a personal hero. Pat Tetrault (University of Nebraska) put me on the right path as a young person. Melanie Davis and David Hall always make me feel like anything is possible.
Book: *Not In Front of the Children* by Marjorie Heins is such an enormously important book because it demolishes the framework of childhood sexlessness that underlies all controversies around sex education, censorship, and talking about sex around young people.

NATIONAL SEX ED CONFERENCE

Title of presentation: *Your Org Needs a Twitter Handle*

Presentation description: Melissa Fabello and I are presenting on the need for sexuality educators to effectively use social media. Whether you're working for a nimble sex education group or a massive institution, there's a need for a significant, responsive, and professional-looking online presence. We're talking about how to make the best use of social media platforms and also how to build and maintain interfaces that are effective for educational interventions and can actually reach your intended audience.

How I Got Into Sex...Ed

I was going to be a cinematographer. There are surprisingly few women who do that, but it had been my plan, as I was starting to apply for colleges. I had a small group of friends with whom I regularly made films and music videos. A few of us planned to do it for real; some of them actually did go on to work in Hollywood. But one night, in the course of conversation, I heard about someone who had a job as a sex therapist. And that was it. It was over. I didn't even know that was a profession until that moment, but once it was an option, it was the only option. Why didn't EVERYONE want to talk about sex for a living?

It seems like sexuality education and counseling are callings in the way that clergy or doctors might feel compelled to devote their life's work to one subject. It made sense for me, as I was one of those kids who read all about sex as soon as I was literate. It ranged from art history books full of naked people to anthropological studies of sexual mores across cultures and, naturally, every single book about puberty that the library had. I had always felt comfortable talking about this stuff and gave off some kind of vibe that led to people I barely knew to ask me their extremely private questions (everything from questions about lube and contraception to wondering about sexual orientation). It was important, from the beginning, to honor confidentiality, to express no judgment, and to use what I had learned to facilitate mutually pleasurable and safe sexual experiences for my peers that aligned with their ideals, not mine. And from the sound of it, there weren't a lot of places they could go to get that kind of conversation, where facts would be relayed without critique.

Fortuitously, I have parents who are far better educated than most, especially considering where I grew up, and they provided all the resources anyone could ever want. My house was filled to the brim with books. There were works of hard science, feminist anthologies, mythologies from around the world, and more than a few comic books intended for adults. If I wanted to read about it, it was available. And if I didn't know what a word meant, I was directed to the dictionary. There was no clutching of the pearls about whether content was appropriate for my age. It was all about cultivating autodidactic skills and being given *carte blanche* to become the person I wanted to be, as long as that person was fulfilled. We had a computer the moment they became available to the general public, and we got the Internet as early as possible. So when people ask how my parents reacted to my becoming a sexuality educator, I'm lucky to say it was pure pride.

It would be easy to tell stories of heartbreak or tales about peers who inspired me: kids who were sexually abused, girls who got pregnant very young, the slut-shaming and harassment that was common. But to be honest, it was the positive stuff that really drew me in: pleasure, fantasy, awesome relationships. I love the weirdness that is human anatomy and physiology, I revel in finding out about new fetishes and uncommon practices. It's intoxicating to delve into the psychological processes behind different desires, habits, and behavioral patterns. So I got a psychology degree from one of the best programs in the nation (University of Nebraska) and then went to the only place in the United States where I could be challenged academically and study sex at the same time, Widener.

My areas of interest have shifted over the years since I started as an HIV prevention counselor, running HIV testing drives and doing peer education for college groups. But one common thread courses through from my early writing as a sex advice columnist for the *Daily Nebraskan* all the way through to my current podcast, workshops, and classroom lectures. It's all about expanding options, exploding restrictive boxes, and getting people to think about sex as fun, collaborative, exploratory, and fundamentally healthy. I admonish those who use sexuality as a weapon; those who judge, demean, or choose selfishness over cooperation. It's important to me to bring in as many vantages as possible, focus on inclusion, and ultimately let individuals decide what is right for their lives. Just as my parents granted me free rein to find out my truth, and gave me the resources that I needed to discover what that was, I hope to do the same for others.

Mark Schoen

BS, PhD
AASECT Certified Sexuality Educator

New Hope, PA

PROFESSIONAL LIFE
Current workplace: SexSmartFilms.com, New Hope, PA
First workplace: Health Educator, Burr's Lane Junior High School, Dix Hills, New York
Favorite workplace: SexSmartFilms.com, New Hope, PA

EDUCATIONAL LIFE
Favorite course: Human Sexuality at New York University Summer Abroad Program, Uppsala, Sweden, taught by Deryck Calderwood, PhD, 1974

TEACHING LIFE
Favorite topic to teach: Gender Identity
Most challenging topic to teach: Sexual Orientation and Gender Identity

INSPIRATIONS
Sex educator: Deryck Calderwood, PhD
Book: *Love and Sex in Plain Language* by Eric W. Johnson

How I Got Into Sex...Ed

This past year has been a journey of discovery for me. In 2012 my production company released the feature length documentary *TRANS,*[9] a human rights story about gender variance. In addition to the many DVDs sold, I have attended more than 30 college campus showings, and the film has been to more than 55 film festivals. *TRANS* received nine awards including Best Documentary and Audio Visual of the Year Award.[10] The screenings are emotional. This film touches lives and makes a difference.

Had I been told as an undergraduate student 40 years ago that my career would be in producing films related to sexuality education, research, and therapy, I would have thought the prognosticator out of his or her mind. I wanted to be a professional hockey player! Maybe a high school coach if that didn't pan out. Well, I have no regrets. I went from teaching health education to producing more than 50 films related to sexual health and gender identity. I have a very satisfying career. My work touches many more lives than I could have if I had followed my sports passion.

How did I get into sexuality education? In 1971 I started teaching a state mandated course in health at Burr's Lane Junior High School in New York. New York State mandated that a unit on "Sexually Transmitted Diseases" be introduced into the curriculum at that time. Each school district had the option of including sexuality education. Being a young, enthusiastic health educator, I jumped right into this new topic.

My first day teaching this unit is forever etched into my brain. I began by identifying the diseases we would be covering and then said they are spread by "sexual contact." Hands shot up. These 12-year-old 7th-graders wanted to know what I meant by sexual contact. I unflinchingly said "either sexual intercourse or oral–genital contact." Many more hands went up. What did those terms mean? The rest of the class was spent explaining what sexual intercourse and oral–genital contact was. As you might imagine, after a few oohs and ahs, the class was riveted to my every word!

I remember walking out of the classroom and meeting the school principal, Rod Penny, in the hall. Rod asked how this new class went. I told him what happened and said, "What a negative way to introduce young people to sexuality — via disease!" After a lengthy discussion he asked what I thought we should do. My response was to create another unit devoted to sexuality education and include the STI in the unit on communicable diseases. Without hesitation, Rod said, "Go for it." That moment changed the course of my professional life.

I prepared a letter/consent form and sent it to the parents of my 150 students, informing them how I wanted to teach sexuality to their children. They were invited to attend an evening meeting at which I would explain more about this new, optional unit. My plan was to use the book *Love and Sex in Plain Language* by Eric W. Johnson as my text. I encouraged parents to get a copy before our meeting. I further requested that if they decided their child was to take the course, they should give the book to their child and let their child know that they were completely supportive of this class.

Once the letter was sent out, the community was buzzing; 7th-grade students were chatting it up, and the 8th- and 9th-grade students wanted to know "Why aren't we getting sex education?" By the time the parent meeting came two weeks later, we had kids walking around school showing off their copies of *Love and Sex in Plain Language.*

The meeting was fantastic. There was a large turnout with much dialogue. Only four of the 150 students opted out and would take the optional First-Aid class. Finding there weren't many appropriate sexual health resources, I utilized my photographic skills to create slide programs to use in my classroom.

In 1972, I enrolled in the Intensive Teacher Training Program in Health Education at State University of New York, Stony Brook. There I took my first human sexuality course. I saw firsthand the impact of film. The instructor, Howard Lempert, used sexually explicit films. The process of introducing, screening, and processing these films was a valuable part of my education. I noted how powerful the experience of viewing Sexually Explicit Media (SEM)[11] in an academic setting was.

It didn't take very long to realize how important this class was to the students at Burr's Lane Junior High School. All were seated and ready to start as soon as the bell rang. Believe me, that didn't happen when I was teaching nutrition! I chuckle when I recall the time I was in the hallway after the bell had rung, talking to a fellow faculty member, when I was reprimanded by one of the students to start the class!

That next summer (1974) I enrolled in New York University's study abroad program in Human Sexuality in Uppsala, Sweden. We had two professors, Deryck Calderwood from NYU and Maj-Briht Bergström-Walan, the first authorized sexologist in Sweden. Early in the program, Maj-Briht spoke about a film she had been a part of called *The Language of Love*. [12] She showed us two short segments, "Sexual Intercourse" and "Sex and the Handicapped."[13]

I observed the impact these films had on a group of graduate students studying human sexuality. And to think this film had a theatrical release in Sweden, yet it was controversial to show films with nudity and depictions of sexual behavior in academic settings in the United States. Imagine studying human sexuality and actually wanting to observe the behavior! It really shouldn't be so shocking, considering both Alfred Kinsey and William Masters had to deal with public vilification when producing films depicting sexual behavior and using them in research. I remember writing a chapter for a book about using sexually explicit media to educate. The chapter was heavily edited to include numerous warnings about children seeing these images. I objected, considering the average American sees pornography on the Internet by the time they are 14 years old.

I continued my graduate education at NYU. Deryck Calderwood encouraged me to produce films. Soon he and I began a collaboration that would produce seven films from 1974 through 1980. Deryck was my mentor and the best human sexuality educator I have encountered. His creativity inspired our projects, which are still used in teaching human sexuality today. In 1980 I finished my degree and left my teaching position to focus on film production and distribution.

My experience of starting a sex education program and producing films with Deryck Calderwood helped me to see the importance of sexual health and how wide a field it was. It is composed of educators, researchers, and therapists. Production wheels began turning in my head.

In 1980 I wrote a children's book about body parts, including genitals, called *Bellybuttons Are Navels.*[14] This book was the focus of a film with the same title, depicting a grandmother reading the story to two 4-year-old children. Talk about controversy! I couldn't believe how much discussion the word clitoris created. The most common question was, "What is the appropriate age to teach the word clitoris?" My response? "What is an appropriate age to teach the word nostril?"

That same year, I received a call from a researcher named Beverly Whipple. She wanted to know if I would be interested in making a film about some recent research she was doing on the anatomical area in the vagina she called the G spot. Well, to be quite candid, I did not know much about the G spot, and I was a little skeptical about the project. But after a little investigation, I agreed to take this on. This nine-minute film, *Orgasmic Expulsions of Fluid in the Sexually Stimulated Female,* is one of the most viewed films I ever produced and is still relevant today.

In addition to my educational and research films, the 1980s saw my entree into sex therapy films. I am most proud of *The Couples Guide to Sexual Pleasure,* which is three of the exact same film, each depicting couples, one gay, one straight, and the third lesbian.

For eight years I produced sexually explicit educational home videos for the Sinclair Institute. The most well known was *The Better Sex Video Series.* These films were used in homes and academic settings. They covered everything a course for heterosexual couples could possibly want.

After leaving Sinclair, I went into the documentary world, producing among others, *Betty Dodson: Her Life of Sex and Art, Harry Benjamin, MD,* and most recently, *TRANS.*

Today I produce and acquire films for my streaming website, *SexSmartFilms.com.* We now have more than 400 films that are being utilized by viewers in more than 50 countries. We have been called "The Netflix of sex education."

Elizabeth Schroeder

MSW, EdD

Montclair, NJ

PROFESSIONAL LIFE
Current workplace: Sexuality Education Consultant, Montclair, NJ

First workplace: First volunteer-ship in the field at the Gay Men's Health Crisis, New York, NY, 1988–1991; First workplace in the field at Planned Parenthood Federation of America, New York, NY, 1993–1998

Favorite workplace: I don't know that I have one favorite. Each one has been amazing in its own way, and I have learned a great deal. I would say, however, that my work as a consultant was perhaps the most significant for me in terms of my own learning.

EDUCATIONAL LIFE
Favorite course: Human Sexuality for the Education Professional, two-part course taught at Widener by Dr. Konnie McCaffree

Least favorite course: What I remember of my own high-school sex ed, which encompassed one class period in a health class in which the teacher threw a tennis ball at students and, when a student caught it, the student had to repeat a sexual term the teacher said. After three terms, we rebelled and stopped catching the ball. He was so flustered and had no backup activities, so the rest of the class was a study hall.

TEACHING LIFE
Favorite topic to teach: Sexual orientation and gender identity
Most challenging topic to teach: STDs

INSPIRATIONS
Sex educator: Konnie McCaffree
Book: *The History of Sex* by Reay Tannahill

How I Got Into Sex...Ed

As an undergraduate French major whose first job out of college was working in fundraising for the New York City Ballet, it's easy to see how I ended up in the sexuality education field.

Wait, what?

Exactly. I'd love to say that my start in sexuality education was a natural job progression, or something I'd wanted to do since high school, but the desire to do this work actually hit me out of the blue, like a thunderbolt.

I loved working in the arts, but had a strong desire to work in social services in some way. After interviewing at Planned Parenthood of New York City (PPNYC) twice for fundraising jobs — and being turned down twice — I was lucky enough to be hired by Planned Parenthood Federation of America (PPFA), again in fundraising. One day, I was asked to attend a meeting with the education department so that I could write a proposal for their work. I walked into a meeting with the head of the department, Trish Moylan Torruella, and her two staff members, Michael McGee and a woman named Donna Alleyne. As someone who grew up in an Italian Catholic family, it was a big enough deal for me to be working at Planned Parenthood. But when I found myself ensconced in a discussion about sexuality, sexual development, how best to teach sex ed to youth, etc., I was blown out of the water by the ease with which they discussed the topic and verbalized the rationales for why sexuality education was so important.

In a word, I was hooked.

I saw in the education department's budget that they had a line for a new position — an administrative support position, starting at the lowest level on the administrative food chain, at a lower pay scale than the job I had at the time. I went to Trish the next day and told her that if she'd hire me for the position, I'd give notice that day. She laughed, but in a matter of weeks, I'd transitioned from development into education. And I've never looked back.

Michael eventually became the VP of the department, and I got to meet and watch Wayne Pawlowski in action. He was someone who knew more about effective facilitation skills than anyone I'd ever met. I attended the North Atlantic Training Institute in Sexual Health Education (NATISHE), which was sponsored by Cicatelli Associates. There I met this quiet, unassuming guy who was nice enough to offer me a ride home — Bill Taverner. That meeting resulted in years of collaboration and partnership, including the creation of the *American Journal of Sexuality Education*, which Bill graciously invited me to co-edit with him.

After a few years, I moved to Planned Parenthood of New York City, where I worked with Leslie Kantor, then the VP of Education, to create the agency's first training institute for youth-serving professionals, honing in on schoolteachers throughout New York's five boroughs. The curriculum we used was *Our Whole Lives,* Grades 7–9, which had been written for the Unitarian Universalist Association by Pamela Wilson. It was the best thing I'd seen produced for comprehensive sexuality education, and both youth and educators loved it. All these years later, Pam's wisdom, both from OWL and her other books, comes out of my own mouth easily when I'm working with colleagues, youth, and parents.

I don't think I'd been at PPNYC a full year when I had the amazing opportunity to attend Advocates for Youth's European Study Tour in 1999. We went to France, Germany, and the Netherlands — the countries with the lowest rates of STDs and teen pregnancy at the time — to learn how they provided sexuality education and sexual health services. This trip introduced me to colleagues who became close friends, some of whom have made some of the greatest contributions in sexuality education: Barbara Huberman, who passed away in the spring of 2014 and who coordinated the trip; Eva Goldfarb, who is as hysterical as she is a talented educator; Debra Hauser, the current president of Advocates for Youth, who may have the most brilliant mind in our field; Nora Gelperin, with whom I had the privilege of working every day as the director of training for Answer (then called the Network for Family Life Education), and too many others to name here.

In 2000, I embarked on the most exciting, yet terrifying, adventure of my professional career — the launching of my consulting business. This brought me into the arena of university teaching as an adjunct professor and marked the beginning of my international work with a project in Kathmandu, Nepal, followed by conferences in Austria, France, and Germany and consulting to schools in The Netherlands, Italy, Norway, and Russia. In every country, I learned lessons, the most salient of which is that no matter the culture, when it comes to curiosity and the need for information about sexuality, young people are young people. I could use what I learned in other countries in my work in the United States, and vice versa.

That same year, I began my EdD program at Widener University in the human sexuality program. How lucky I am to have studied with Bill Stayton, Pat Koch, and the person who changed my view of and improved my skills as an educator more than anyone I've ever met, Konnie McCaffree. I wrote my dissertation on how high school teachers in New Jersey, which has a strong sexuality education mandate on paper, addressed the topic of sexual orientation. I learned a lesson that is still true today: Even the most inclusive, comprehensive sexuality education mandate amounts to nothing if there aren't any accountability measures in place. Countless high schools did not teach sexuality education at all, and of those, even fewer addressed sexual orientation — even though doing so was required within the core curriculum content standards.

Consulting afforded me the time and opportunity to write more, which I enjoy immensely. Thanks to Bill Taverner, I ended up editing several editions of *Taking Sides, Family and Personal Issues* and worked with Dr. Judy Kuriansky to co-edit the four-part book series, *Sexuality Education: Past, Present, and Future.* I started consulting with the Network for Family Life Education both as a sexuality expert responding to questions from teens on their web site, *Sex, Etc.*, and as a trainer and general program consultant, getting to know this amazing woman named Susie Wilson. I could never have hoped or imagined that one day I'd get to join that amazing organization as its executive director but in 2008, that's exactly what happened.

Answer has a great leadership team and staff, and its mission "to provide and promote unfettered access to comprehensive sexuality education for young people and the adults who teach them" could not be more aligned with my own professional mission. I have met and continue to work with incredibly committed, talented colleagues and organizations around the United States, and still continue to occasionally consult with an international school or two on the side. But the thing I will always be most proud of during my tenure at Answer has been the organization's work with the Future of Sex Education (FoSE) initiative. FoSE was started just before I joined Answer as a collaboration between Answer, Advocates for Youth, and SIECUS. I have never before been part of such an open, honest, hard-working partnership, and the depth of the relationships between these organizations serves the field as much as it does the organizations. In the future, when I look back on my career, I will always be most proud to say that I was a part of the process that created the *National Sexuality Education Standards* in 2012 and the *National Teacher*

Preparation Standards for Sexuality Education, which will be released in 2014.

Like pretty much everyone, I imagine, I frequently wonder what's next — for me, for the field, for whoever our service populations might be — and the word that keeps coming to me is "more." This work that we do — the truly holistic definition of human sexuality as offered by Dr. Dennis Dailey — is so, so important. And it is about so much more than teaching facts and skills. It is a thread that runs through all aspects of human interactions, not just the ones that involve sexual and romantic relationships.

I'm not alone in joking that folks in our field will always have jobs because the general public will always be messed up about sexuality. I'm also not alone in saying that if one day the world weren't so messed up and we were all out of work, I'd be absolutely delighted. In the meantime, however, there is much left to do.

Robert Selverstone

MS, PhD
Licensed Psychologist

Westport, CT

PROFESSIONAL LIFE

Current workplace: Private Practice, Westport, CT
First workplace: Human Relations Director, Westport (CT) Board of Education
Favorite workplace: Human Relations Director, Westport (CT) Board of Education

EDUCATIONAL LIFE

Favorite course: Morey Appell's Mental Hygiene and Behavior Problems at Brooklyn College, CUNY. I learned about non-directive teaching and experiential learning. And the Drug Dependence Institute at Yale University. I became reasonably competent in group processing.
Least favorite course: The Principalship at Fairfield University

TEACHING LIFE

Favorite topic to teach: Raising Sexually Healthy Young People

INSPIRATIONS

Sex educator: Phil Sarrel, Bill Stayton, Dick Cross, Peggy Brick, Konnie McCaffree, Debra Haffner, Mary Lee Tatum, and Bill Taverner
Book: *Male Sexuality* by Bernie Zilbergeld

NATIONAL SEX ED CONFERENCE

Title of presentation: *Designing and Presenting a Workshop for Parents on "Raising Our Children to Become Sexually Healthy Young People"*
Presentation description: Parents do more sex education than we do as professional sex educators. This presentation is designed to help colleagues design and deliver a program for

parents that will encourage and empower them to become more active and preemptive so they can better help their children grow up to be sexually healthy people.

How I Got Into Sex...Ed

I chose to be an educator, but sex education chose me. I was always destined to be a teacher; it was "the family business." After all, one grandfather, both parents, two aunts, and one uncle — and subsequently my wife, sister, son, and daughter-in-law — were/are all teachers. We always had a strong sense of "mission" to help people learn. But I never set out to become a sex educator.

My teaching career started as a NYC junior high school Social Studies teacher in 1961, and then, with an MS in Counseling, I became a junior high and later, a senior high school Guidance Counselor in CT. Shortly after I received my PhD in Educational Psychology (1971), my school system (Westport, CT) decided that it needed to address some tough issues that had not previously been addressed, and I was asked to become the Director of Human Relations. I was given responsibility for developing and implementing programs in Drug Education, Family Life, and Sex Education and Human Relations Education. Although my heart was in the right place — I was committed to improving the social and emotional learning of young people — the truth was that I knew virtually nothing about any of this content!

The Drug Dependence Institute at Yale University helped me learn that content was the least important factor in human behavior. What I did learn was the critical importance of *process* in interpersonal relations, and this has certainly been the most critical aspect of what I have focused on in my 40+ years as a sex educator.

When our school system began the process of developing a

sex education program, it was immediately clear that the problem was no just pedagogical — it was substantially political. Unless we could master the political issues around sex education, we would never get a chance to implement the pedagogy! We moved slowly, holding a variety of community meetings on sex education until it was clear that we received overwhelming community support. We then formed a committee composed of community leaders, clergy, physical and mental health practitioners, school faculty, parents — and students — to develop secondary school sex education programs. I consulted with the most prominent programs extant and spent important time with SIECUS personnel in NYC. When we finally finished, our program was cited by the (then) U.S. Dept. of Health Education, and Welfare (HEW) as one of the dozen or so exemplary programs in the nation.

One of the hallmarks of the program was that while the gender of the teachers of English, math, etc., was not all that important, in teaching about gender itself we needed to have a male/female teaching team — and our Board of Education agreed. I became the male half of the high school teaching team, and I have enjoyed doing so for the 15 or so years, until I retired from the school system in order to devote myself full time to private practice as a psychologist.

I am still arguably the least well-versed sex educator in terms of biological content. But this was never a particular concern of mine, because my primary goal in my classes was to help facilitate the ability of students to communicate about sexual issues. In this elective course, students sat on the carpeted floor in a circle. Distinguishing characteristics of the class included a focus on small-group discussion and value clarification, with an emphasis on the importance of each individual's right to his/her own perspective. The entire thrust of our program was consistent with Dr. Mary Calderone's (one of the SIECUS founders) belief that "How people behave toward each other in all matters — including the sexual — is the most important thing in the world." Sex and sexual behavior is one way in which people relate to each other. However, it is the way in which we relate to each other in other ways that makes this important. In some ways, it is like shouting: "**SEX!** Now that I have your attention, let's talk about you and how you relate to yourself, the world, and to other people."

I retired from my high school teaching position in the early 1990s. Currently, my emphasis is on helping parents become more effective sex educators of their own children.

Jessica L. Shields
CHES

Shrewsbury, NJ

PROFESSIONAL LIFE
Current workplace: Planned Parenthood of Central and Greater Northern NJ, Shrewsbury, NJ
First workplace: Planned Parenthood of Central and Greater Northern NJ, Shrewsbury, NJ
Favorite workplace: Planned Parenthood of Central and Greater Northern NJ, Shrewsbury, NJ

EDUCATIONAL LIFE
Favorite course: Sociology of Death & Grief
Least favorite course: Nursing I (I learned during my first clinical rotation that I HATED needles and blood.)

TEACHING LIFE
Favorite topic to teach: Myths & Facts about Sexuality. I love the energy I get when I talk about this. In addition, I feel I am always learning something new from my participants during a myths & facts session.
Most challenging topic to teach: Contraceptive methods. I love to teach it, but often it is very didactic, so I find it challenging to think of new ways to get the information across.

INSPIRATIONS
Sex educator: My whole team. I work with some of the most creative, caring, intelligent people that I know. They inspire me to do my best every day.
Book: *Unhooked: How Young Women Pursue Sex, Delay Love, and Lose at Both* by Laura Sessions Stepp

NATIONAL SEX ED CONFERENCE
Title of presentation: *Bringing Sexy Back to Education: Incorporating Positive Messages to Reduce the Stigma and Risk of STI Transmission*

Presentation description: Often, educational strategies used to talk about safer sex and STI transmission inadvertently include scare tactics, thus making those living with an STI feel alienated. It further perpetuates the myth that "this will never happen to me." Therefore, this session will explore common safer sex activities from the positive perspective.

How I Got Into Sex...Ed

I guess you can say that I "got into sex ed" in high school. When I was a junior, I was selected to be a peer educator. Peer helping was a very prestigious club at my high school. It was a club only open to juniors and seniors (but only juniors could apply). There were many applicants and only a few were selected, and I was fortunate enough to be among them. Being in this club meant I got to go into the Phys. Ed. classes on a monthly basis and speak to the underclassmen. I got to talk about issues that affect the daily lives of high school students, such as acceptance and self-esteem. It also meant that I got to talk about things like HIV and pregnancy prevention. In addition, I was "available" if any student wanted to talk with a peer about something that was troubling them. At the time, I didn't realize that this was laying the foundation for my becoming a sexual health educator.

I knew I wanted to help people. I wanted a career where I could make a difference, a career where I could help people be healthy and happy. But finding the right major was challenging. I tried public relations, history, and even nursing. Since I had changed my major many times, by the time I was a nursing major, I had fulfilled all of my free electives. But I still had to find classes that would enable me to be a full-time student and enrich my nursing studies. My advisor suggested I take a few public health classes.

I took my first public health class and fell in love with the ideology. I loved the idea that helping people be "healthy" was more than "treating" a disease. Instead, health was composed of many different factors, systems, and theories; so there were many different ways to help people be healthy. My career could go in many different directions. I could help people by developing programs, conducting research, doing health counseling, or creating marketing materials. There were many ways this background could prepare me for the real world. Eventually, I earned a degree in health education. But to do so, I had to complete a very extensive internship.

I was accepted as an intern at the Bergen County (NJ) Department of Health. As an intern, I conducted health programs at libraries, worked on grants, developed health education materials, and attended health fairs in the community. I was at a health fair representing the Bergen County Department of Health, Office of Health Promotion, at Bergen County Technical High School in Teterboro, NJ, when I met Melissa Keyes DiGioia. Planned Parenthood of Central and Greater Northern New Jersey (at the time it was Planned Parenthood of Greater Northern NJ) had sent Melissa to represent them at the health fair. I knew my internship was ending and the department could only offer me per diem work. I needed a job.

Planned Parenthood had always been an organization I respected, supported, and valued. I always wondered how people got their jobs there and what it was like to work for the organization. I saw Melissa sitting at the Planned Parenthood table. I took a deep breath, gained some courage, walked over, and started talking to her about Planned Parenthood. Melissa agreed to eat lunch with me. At lunch, I was able to talk to her about the various jobs at Planned Parenthood, particularly within the education department, and the things I would like in a career. During this brief lunch, I learned that Planned Parenthood was hiring a health educator. Melissa gave me the job information, and when I got home, I immediately submitted my resume.

About two months later, Planned Parenthood called and wanted to know if I was still interested in the position. I did a brief phone interview with Sue Montfort. I guess my answers were acceptable (I don't even remember what questions were asked; all I remember is being ecstatic that I was talking to someone from Planned Parenthood about a potential position), because I made it to the next step, the group interview. The group interview required that I present a sexual health lesson. During my studies, I had learned about the significance of the Human Papilloma Virus. So, for my presentation, I prepared an HPV game. When it was my turn to present, I was soooo nervous. Before I could even start the game or do anything in the lesson, I fell off of my chair. I was humiliated! But I brushed it off and kept going, trying to pretend like nothing happened.

The ride home from my interview was about 35 minutes. That entire car ride, all I could think about was that fall, my hidden embarrassment (or not so hidden, due to the redness of my face), and the basic lesson you learn about acing an interview: "Just don't fall." So, naturally, I figured I didn't get the job. When I got home, I had a message on my voice mail from Bill Taverner, the director of education at the time. I returned Bill's call; he asked if I could meet with him the next day. Of course, I agreed.

I thought Bill was concerned that I was going to sue Planned Parenthood for falling off my chair. I assumed he wanted to meet so that I could sign some sort of form saying I wasn't going to sue Planned Parenthood. When I got to the meeting, not only was it with Bill, but a Human Resources Representative was there as well. Next thing I knew, they were asking me stereotypical interview questions. As it turns out, this was a third interview! At the end of the meeting, I was offered the job of Sexual Health Educator, and I immediately said yes. I became the newest member of the education team at Planned Parenthood of Central and Greater Northern NJ.

Eleanor R. Smith
LCSW, MA, PhD
Risking Connection trainer, Streetwise to Sex-wise facilitator,
Counsel for Young Men and Boys facilitator,
North American Family Institute (NAFI),
Normative Approach trainer

Thomaston, CT

PROFESSIONAL LIFE
Current workplace: NAFI Thomaston Group Home, Thomaston, CT (NAFI CT is based in Farmington, CT.)
First workplace: SUNY Albany undergraduate college (teaching Human Sexuality course), Albany, NY
Favorite workplace: Green Oaks Hospital (running Sexuality group for women's inpatient unit), Dallas, TX

EDUCATIONAL LIFE
Favorite course: Sexual Diversity (part of graduate social work coursework)
Least favorite course: Counseling Substance Abuse Clients about Sexuality

TEACHING LIFE
Favorite topic to teach: Myths about female sexual experiences
Most challenging topic to teach: Reproductive biology to developmentally disabled students

INSPIRATIONS
Sex educator: Adam Carolla and my 4th-grade teacher, Lois Forbush
Book: *Sex Tips for Straight Women from a Gay Man* by Dan Anderson and Maggie Berman

NATIONAL SEX ED CONFERENCE
Title of presentation: *Sex Education in Group Homes: Considerations for the Developmentally Disabled*

Presentation description: NAFI CT's recent implementation of sex education in therapeutic group homes, through running "Streetwise to Sex-wise" groups, will be presented. The focus will be on reviewing how this experience developed, and what modifications of the curriculum were made for students with developmental intellectual disabilities. The goal will be to help others envision how to bring similar insights to their own educational and clinical programs.

How I Got Into Sex...Ed

My entry into the field begins with my attendance at Baltimore Friends School. Since, as the name implies, it's a Quaker School, it might not be a surprise that they began teaching pretty comprehensive sex education in the 4th grade, starting in 1969. (Sidwell Friends School in Washington, DC, where the Obama daughters and Chelsea Clinton attended, had begun a curriculum just the year before, for 3rd-graders. This was a couple of decades before C. Everett Koop recommended beginning sex ed in the 3rd grade!) Baltimore Friends proposed the idea to their teachers, and the only one who stepped forward to say she was comfortable teaching this subject was a 4th-grade teacher, Lois Forbush, who happened to be my teacher for the 1972–1973 school year. We spent the whole spring semester learning about human reproduction, complete with a life-sized model with removable body parts named "Oscar." Mrs. Forbush described hearing from one parent how her child responded at the dinner table one night when asked, "How was school today?" The child's reply: "We put the penis on Oscar." My former beloved teacher also noted to me a few years ago that, in her 40 years of teaching this topic, she never received a complaint from a parent. (Of course, this was a Quaker school, so the parents already had some idea of the type of education their child would be receiving.)

The fact that my parents chose this school for their children hints at the progressive culture of my family. My parents were open to answering all of my questions honestly, and never conveyed shame or embarrassment. But they also didn't have much of an obligation to bring up the subject of sex on their own, since I attended the same school from nursery (starting at age 2) through high school. As my father once remarked to me, "We didn't have to worry about teaching you any of that stuff, 'cause Friends School taught you all of it."

One amusing memory of that 4th-grade experience is how I learned about sexual intercourse. We had spent most of the second semester learning about the reproductive system. (I remember when the teacher wrote "menstruation" on the blackboard, and thinking what a long, strange word that was.) So by late spring, we knew that somehow the sperm fertilized the egg, but we hadn't yet been taught how that happened. I was sick the day that we were, and my best friend talked to me later, saying, "So you wanna know how the sperm gets to the egg? We learned that today." When I assented, she said, "The man sticks his penis in the woman's vagina." I remember thinking, no, she must have gotten it wrong, as that just sounded too weird. She then assured me it was the truth.

In 8th grade we had another round. This course was called "Health" and was taught by a gym teacher, and did not encourage open discussion, which struck my 13-year-old mind as pathetic. (So this may have been my one experience with the more traditional stereotype people have of "sex ed in schools." Fortunately, it was almost irrelevant compared to all the other classes offered at the Friends School.) In 12th grade, we had another opportunity: a weekly class called "Sexuality." It was a lot of open and deep discussion, including one of the teachers passing around different-sized diaphragms one day for us to see and feel. She even offered personal advice on her experiences with birth control, including that adding more spermicidal jelly, whether you are going to end up needing it or not, only "wastes" a few cents. But that few cents could pay for your success at avoiding an unplanned pregnancy. That advice rang through my head during college and my subsequent adult years.

I remember a moment in 6th grade when I saw two friends talking, and I suddenly got a feeling that one of them wasn't "being fully real" — that she felt insecure and was attempting to cover it up. I was immediately enthralled by this idea, not only because I found the ability to experience this inherently enjoyable, but also because it validated the awareness I had of myself —— that I, too, had feelings of insecurity that were not fully revealed in normal social conversation. (I later realized that Piaget would have been happy to hear of my experience at this age. I was likely just entering into normal formal operational thought, which includes the ability to feel strong empathy for the first time, as one becomes capable of more abstract thought.) This experience was later cemented in my desire to become a therapist. I wanted to help people, and as I thought about what causes relationships and systems to become problematic, I concluded that it was the individual's own unresolved feelings, extrapolated out into a larger world, which ultimately caused all unnecessary human suffering. (I still agree with 13-year-old me's revelation.)

By my second year of college, I had experienced another revelation; within those anxious feelings that were influencing everyone's quality of life, one category stood out to me as the source of the most preoccupation and yet the most reluctance to talk openly: sexual relationships. And I noted that others did not seem as comfortable as I did in discussing sexuality. (I, of course, also learned that painfully few others had the primary and secondary school experiences I did, and many had endured repressive and shaming socialization on the topic.) It was then I knew that this would be my career focus and likely my lifelong mission — to promote discussion and education on the topic of sexuality.

By my first foray into graduate school, I also knew I wanted to study it. Not surprisingly, I ended up joining Donn Byrne's research group at SUNY Albany. He was already world famous for his study of interpersonal attraction, and then adolescent birth control behavior. In 1985, largely in response to the Reagan administration's Meese Commission, his research group had turned to looking at predictors of acquaintance rape, and whether watching pornography played a predictive role. As the data continued to roll in on the power of personality and attitudes as relevant predictors of experiences with sexual coercion, my own research on this topic became a further inspiration to promote knowledge of the subject. And during those four years in Albany, I had the opportunity to teach the undergraduate "Human Sexuality" course a few times.

After leaving with a nonclinical PhD, but still having a dream of becoming a clinician someday, I was fortunate to obtain a few entry-level clinical positions in psychiatric hospitals. In the third one of these, they invited me to try "running groups" and soon asked if I would facilitate one for their adolescent clients on the topic of sexuality. On this I stumbled a bit, having no curriculum or guidelines for the frame and limits of the discussion. But the adult unit version of this group, which I then led with women on the inpatient unit, was a huge hit. One compliment I received from a woman at the time of her discharge was that, as a result of my group, she and her husband talked about sex for the first time ever in their 14 years of marriage, and she couldn't thank me enough for how freeing and helpful it was. The idea that simply encouraging people to talk openly was powerfully therapeutic continued to fuel my sense of mission.

Over the next several years I continued to present at

conferences on what I'd learned in the clinical setting, particularly focusing on the myths and perceptual distortions that seemed to be perpetuated. And I finally went back to school and got the clinical degree that suited me best, an MSW. And I did this in the context of a dual master's degree program, which involved also pursuing an M.Div. What became clear in the pastoral classes was that my knowledge of and comfort with sexuality topics were valuable and coveted there, too. I was asked to teach one session of our Pastoral Counseling class, and then to submit a curriculum that I thought necessary for training pastors about sexuality.

Finally, in my current role as a clinician for adolescent boys, the *Streetwise to Sex-wise* curriculum was an obvious desirable choice to use in leading sexuality education groups for these young men, which the state very much wanted us to do. (The wider culture had finally caught up to my progressive Quaker-influenced socialization.) Also worth mentioning is that I am called upon as a Risking Connection trainer (Connecticut's required trauma-informed treatment model) to be the authority on the "sexual feelings" section of the "Countertransference" lesson. The repeated ongoing support I get from colleagues regarding my willingness to talk frankly and firmly with employees about acknowledging and responding appropriately to sexual feelings reminds me that being a sexuality educator is right where I belong.

Judith Steinhart
EdD

New York, NY

PROFESSIONAL LIFE
Current workplace: New York, NY
First workplace: Volunteer and Board Member of Planned Parenthood
Favorite workplace: My favorite jobs are wherever I am currently working. Now I am teaching in a public high school in the Bronx, where I am learning a lot from the students. I also consult, and I love the variety of the work I do.

EDUCATIONAL LIFE
Favorite course: Human Sexuality at State University of New York at Stony Brook, taught by Robert O. Hawkins, PhD

TEACHING LIFE
Favorite topic to teach: All of them! I especially love using role-plays in specific situations. And I love mentoring new people in the field.
Most challenging topic to teach: Abortion

INSPIRATIONS
Sex educator: Peggy Brick, without a doubt. Sol Gordon, Michael Carrera, Andrew Walters, Mariotta Gary-Smith, Trina Scott, Joycelyn Elders, and all my colleagues
Book: *The Kinsey Volumes I and II* and *Lesbian Woman* by Del Martin and Phyllis Lyon

NATIONAL SEX ED CONFERENCE
Title of presentation: *Join the Barnraising Blast! Ideas for Entering the Field, Stepping Up Your Game, Becoming Your Best!*
Presentation description: Bring one goal and one obstacle to our Barnraising Blast, and end your isolation. Leave with new colleagues and possibilities for reaching your goal. Find go-to

places for lesson plans, games for a change, Facebook pages, reasons for teaching about trans people, why YOU need to be presenting at conferences, ways to include people of color at sex ed conferences, and introductions to current and future stars, i.e., YOU!

How I Got Into Sex...Ed

In 2nd grade, we had a book fair at school. I picked out the book, *What Girls Want to Know about Boys*, and we were supposed to show our choices to our moms, who were there with us. I was both curious and ashamed, but my mother was accepting at that moment and said, "Is this the book you want? That's all right," and she bought it for me. Of course, there was no parallel book, *What Girls Want to Know about Girls,* but at least this was a start.

Later, I found the paperback, Evelyn Duvall's *The Facts of Life and Love for Teenagers*. I wasn't a teenager yet, but I read it cover to cover, reading about crushes, twins, and how to say no: A girl was supposed to shake her curls and say, "Why this is Tuesday, isn't it?" or say that she's hungry for a hamburger. Neither response made much sense to me, but I continued to read.

Right before junior high school, a neighbor my age left to "visit/take care of/stay with her aunt in Ohio," which was code for having gotten pregnant. The reason she got pregnant was because "she went for rides in cars with boys," which was code for having sex.

In high school, I had a friend who, at age 16, told me that he'd been in love five times over the course of his life, and two of those were women. Hearing that made me even more interested in his life, as you might imagine. I knew about same-sex relationships and effeminate men and butch women, but this was someone I knew, someone my age.

During my first year of college, Rita, a hippie from Syracuse who was in a different friendship network from mine, asked me a shocking question, with not a little panic in her voice and affect: "Jude, do you know where a woman can get an abortion?" Me? Why was she asking me? I had no idea where to go. I knew someone who went to Puerto Rico, and I knew a student who went to Pennsylvania, but I knew of nothing nearby and safe, and furthermore, why on earth was she asking me??? Abortion was illegal then, although the law was about to change. It was also the beginning of the women's movement, and I had no connection to it, although women were always my friends.

Only in retrospect did I realize that I was seen as askable, safe, and a source of reliable information. My roommates that year saw me as not "open," but loose. I sought, needed, and craved to be informed, though I had little experience. Furthermore, it took me until May of my freshman year to learn that each of them was far more experienced than I, having slept with their boyfriends since they were 14 and 15 years old.

Then a 9th-grade boy changed my life, and career path. When I first student taught, a 9th-grade boy asked me if I knew of a place that would sell rubbers (and not the kind you wear on your feet) to young boys. Again I was shocked, which I hoped I managed to hide. I also knew that at that time, it was illegal for anyone under 18 years old to buy condoms.

I stalled by asking him about what was going on. He told me that this weekend was his church retreat! I then realized how much respect I had for this boy who wanted to be prepared and responsible. So I told him I would find out.

At that time, I knew that Planned Parenthood took care of women, so I called the nearest clinic. I told them my story and asked, "I know you are committed to the reproductive healthcare of women, but what can you do for this young man?" After a long pause, she responded with, "No one has ever asked that before. Let me check." This was long before the introduction of any male involvement programs.

Then she returned to the phone and said, "We can help him. Tell him to come here tomorrow and to ask for Lucille." I was appreciative, both for the information and for Planned Parenthood's willingness to help.

The next day I gave him the information, and he was delighted. I was sure he had to take about three different busses to get there, but he was highly motivated. It was the first time I realized that educators don't just teach subject matter, they teach human beings.

When I started teaching English after graduation, I was isolated, lonely, and living in a new town. I realized that I could volunteer at Planned Parenthood, so I found the nearest one and offered my time. Gradually, I got involved with the women's movement, joined a consciousness-raising (CR) group, learned to lead CR groups, and supported the gay rights movement. At the same time, I also took a course in Human Sexuality as part of my master's degree at Stony Brook. This course provided a new path for my life and career. I knew I wanted to do what the professor, Robert O. Hawkins, PhD, did for hundreds of students each year. With kindness, humor, information, and resources, he helped others open their eyes and their hearts.

Now it is 40 years later, and in many circumstances, in several different cities, with diverse groups, and in many roles, I have been doing just that.

Bill Taverner

MA

AASECT Certified Sexuality Educator

Easton, PA

PROFESSIONAL LIFE

Current workplace: I am the executive director of The Center for Sex Education, which is the national education division of Planned Parenthood of Greater Northern and Central New Jersey. I am also the editor-in-chief of the *American Journal of Sexuality Education,* which is published by Taylor and Francis, which, interestingly, is located in Abington, England.

First workplace: I ran my first sex ed class as a resident assistant while I was an undergraduate student at the State University of New York at Albany. I taught a very small group of students about contraception at an evening event, and I got my lesson plan from the first edition of Carolyn Cooperman and Peggy Brick's *Positive Images,* a resource for which I would later serve as co-author and co-editor.

Favorite workplace: For the past 16 years, I have been fortunate to have my dream job running The Center for Sex Education (formerly the CFLE).

EDUCATIONAL LIFE

Favorite course: In graduate school, I took a cross-cultural course in human sexuality and had the opportunity to spend three weeks in Copenhagen, Denmark. Sixteen classmates and I had the learning adventure of a lifetime. It was in Copenhagen where I met and befriended Dr. Robert T. (Bob) Francoeur, who would become one of my mentors. Bob was one of three professors who helped us explore the world of sexuality beyond our limited spheres. My classmates included a few individuals who would go on to have remarkable careers in human sexuality, including sex therapist Dr. Laura Berman.

Least favorite course: In high school, I struggled with physics and chemistry, subjects for which my children inexplicably appear to have a natural gift. I barely scraped by in biology, so it is amusing to reflect on the fact that I actually taught in the biology department at Fairleigh Dickinson University for nine years!

TEACHING LIFE

Favorite topic to teach: I enjoy training day care and preschool teachers in how to answer young children's questions about sex. I also love teaching older adults. And everyone in between!

Most challenging topic to teach: Once I received a request to teach about self-esteem, and I was flummoxed. I don't think this is a topic that can be taught by itself. Self-esteem is a natural byproduct of empowering sexuality education that addresses many different topics.

INSPIRATIONS

Sex educator: As a co-editor for *How I Got Into Sex...Ed,* I have the advantage of seeing the names of sexuality educators who inspire others. So, it feels cliché to type Peggy Brick's name after seeing it over and over! But, really, she is who taught me how to be a skilled sexuality educator. Before I met Peggy, I was a lecturer. I learned from watching Peggy, writing with Peggy, and from absorbing myself in the manuals she and others developed for the CFLE. I learned a lot from Sue Montfort, too. Peggy and Sue have such different (and complementary) writing and presentation styles. When they collaborated on *Unequal Partners: Teaching about Power and Consent in Adult–Teen and Other Relationships,* I felt they had created a masterpiece.

The other sex educator who inspires me is my friend Bob Francoeur, who died in 2012. Bob's boundless sexual knowledge, strong editorial skills, and international connections resulted in the *International Encyclopedia of Sexuality,* which he and co-editor Raymond J. Noonan would donate to the Kinsey Institute so that people could download the entire massive work for free. (Check it out at *www.kinseyinstitute.org/ccies.*) I think some of the projects I have taken on take a cue from Bob's editorial and collaborative style.

Book: When I received an advance copy of Marty Klein's

America's War on Sex, I could not put it down. I was traveling a lot then, and his manuscript accompanied me everywhere I went. Ira Reiss's *An Insider's View on Sexual Science Since Kinsey* similarly mesmerized me. I think what these books have in common is the ability to give the reader a broader sociocultural context for the work that we do.

Parents sometimes ask me what books they should get for their kids. If the children are young, I always recommend Robie Harris's *It's Not the Stork* (my favorite); if they are a little older, I recommend *It's Perfectly Normal* (also by Harris). If they are heading off to college, I recommend Paul Joannides's *Guide to Getting It On.*

NATIONAL SEX ED CONFERENCE
Title of presentation: *Behind the Music*
Presentation description: I presented *Behind the Music,* which was an adaptation of a music literacy lesson plan I wrote for *Unequal Partners.* The idea is to have students critically examine the music they listen to and rewrite the lyrics, infusing them with messages about the core qualities of a healthy relationship: honesty, equality, respect, and responsibility.

How I Got Into Sex...Ed

The earliest I can remember learning anything sex-related was when my 1st-grade teacher, Mrs. Sweeney, had her students observing live chicks as they hatched. The year must have been 1974, and I remember knowing that there was something controversial about it because we needed permission slips to participate. It was true that we needed permission slips for *everything,* but this was the only time that I can recall some parents denying permission. So, while we observed the scintillating world of chick hatchery (cue the porn music), a few students needed to go into a different room and do something else. I couldn't quite understand why a parent would say no to this. I still don't understand.

Fast forward several years when I found myself in a 7th-grade guidance class, where I was developing quite a bit of skill at making paper airplanes. One day, the teacher declared he was going to teach us *everything* we needed to know about sex. With hormones raging, I couldn't wait to begin! He said he would start with female anatomy, which was fine with me because I had lots of questions. In the next class, he unveiled a six-foot tall, color-coded diagram labeled "female anatomy" on the chalkboard. It looked absolutely nothing like the pictures of female anatomy my buddies and I had seen in the abandoned copies of *Playboy* we had found hidden deep in the weeds near our baseball field. There was nothing familiar in the board illustration, but we were told to copy it and memorize it. It was clear we weren't going to have our questions answered, and so I went back to making paper airplanes.

At my all-boy's Catholic high school in Staten Island, New York, there was one memorable sex ed lesson that I can recall in 9th grade. After the Lord's Prayer, Father Frank seamlessly transitioned to "Now I know a lot of you guys like to masturbate..." Having captured our undivided attention...we were wondering how on earth Father Frank *knew*...he went on, "There are two things you need to know about that. One, it's not something you talk about at cocktail parties. And two, it's something you'll eventually grow out of." That was it. That was all he had to say about sex, and we went on to other matters — suicide, drugs, etc. I remember Father Frank with much affection. While I think he was wrong (actually I have found myself talking about masturbation at a number of cocktail parties!), I think his heart was in the right place. His ultimate message was "Stop worrying!" I am not sure that is a message commonly received in Catholic sex ed today.

In 12th-grade health, we had to memorize a VD chart, which contained such information as the names of venereal diseases, their biological compositions, the Latin roots of their names, and other distinguishing characteristics. It was utterly useless. Let's be honest. Few people really care about how one sexually transmitted infection is distinguished from another. They want to avoid *all of them*. I had a big "Aha!" moment when I would eventually read "Sexually Transmitted Infections — A Summary" in *Positive Encounters: Talking One-to-One with Teens about Contraceptive and Safer Sex Decisions"* by Amy Vogelaar. This resource was replete with information that really mattered: "How can I tell if I have an STI?"; "What should I do if I think I might have an STI?"; "What can happen if I don't get tested and treated?" There is a lot to know in the world of sex ed, and it takes a great teacher to discern and apply information in meaningful ways. Vogelaar? Helpful. Our 12th-grade health teacher? Unhelpful. Great football coach, though.

I had no other formal learning in sex ed until college. At the State University of New York at Albany, I decided to take what I thought would be a breeze of a course, "Human Sexuality," which was offered in the school of psychology. On the first day of class, the professor issued a 100-question pre-test to help discern how much we knew about sex. I scored 50%. Was I discouraged? Nope, I was intrigued with how little I knew about a subject that all guys were supposed to master. I fell in love with learning in that class, and when the class ended, I needed more. There was only one other sexuality course, offered by the school of education. I took that course, and also scoured the other course descriptions, looking for the words "sex" and "sexuality." I found myself in such classes as "Abnormal Psychology," where the professor had an expertise in paraphilias (uncommon sexual attractions) and doing undergraduate research. My first research study was a qualitative examination of men's responses to their partner's abortion.[15] The process of putting that small study together taught me a lot about the political nature of reproductive health. I had posted approved flyers all over campus that read: "Looking for Men Whose Partners Have Had an Abortion to Participate in Research Study." Many of these flyers were torn down. Since the flyers had no clear organizational affiliation, I believe people holding both "pro-choice" and "pro-life" ideologies objected, and assumed the study was being carried out by the "other side."

I took other courses, and made them relevant to my interest in sexuality whenever I could. In "Sociology of Aging," I gave a class presentation about sexuality and aging that questioned common assumptions about the asexuality of older adults. The Consortium on Sexuality and Aging would've been proud, but my classmates squirmed.

When I finished college, I was at a loss as to what to do with this boundless interest in sexuality. I couldn't find any jobs in the want ads. So, I took my textbook with its list of sexological organizations and hopped on the Staten Island Ferry, off to find SIECUS. The text said that SIECUS was located just off Washington Square Park, and I asked the doorman to let me in. He refused. Convinced that he thought I was an "anti," I did my best to explain how sex-positive I was. He still refused, and so I sat in Washington Square Park until his shift was over, when I would try my luck with the next doorman. Of course, I failed to gain entry again, mainly because my textbook was outdated and SIECUS had moved to midtown.

I headed back to Albany to hang out with old friends, and ran into my human sexuality professor, Carol Stenger, at a downtown bar. As we exchanged pleasantries, I learned that she was enrolling in a graduate program in human sexuality at New York University. Thrilled to know that such a program existed, I went home and enrolled myself. Carol and I were classmates!

Meanwhile, I continued to try to find a job in sex ed, and interviewed with Peggy Brick, my predecessor at the CFLE in 1991. Peggy candidly told me I was too inexperienced for the job, and so I did all that I could to secure more credentials. In addition to my studies, I began teaching sexuality classes at the group home I managed. I also became an intern, teaching sexuality for adults with intellectual disabilities. Then I took a job at Phoenix House, running sex ed programs for people in recovery from substance abuse. Every year, I would send Peggy a letter with an update on my new accomplishments, because working at the CFLE was really my dream job. I must have always caught her at the wrong time — or maybe she thought I was a stalker — but I finally got her attention seven years after that first interview when I sent her a copy of my first book, *Taking Sides: Clashing Views in Controversial Issues in Human Sexuality,* which included an essay she wrote. All I wanted was a position as a sexuality educator. But Peggy called me to say she was retiring and invited me to interview for her job!

Anthony Thompson

Brooklyn, NY

PROFESSIONAL LIFE

Current workplace: SUNY Downstate Medical Center, Adolescent Education Program, Brooklyn, NY

First workplace: Albany Medical Center Hospital, Psychiatric Unit, Albany, NY

Favorite workplace: SUNY Downstate Medical Center's Adolescent Education Program

EDUCATIONAL LIFE

Favorite course: Human Sexuality and Sex Education for Health Professionals

Least favorite course: Chemistry and Biostatistics

TEACHING LIFE

Favorite topic to teach: Sexual health education

Most challenging topic to teach: Social issues outside of sex education

INSPIRATIONS

Sex educator: Michelle Greene, DrPH, Brooklyn College Health and Nutrition Department

Book: *Sexuality Today*, 9th Edition, by Gary F. Kelly

NATIONAL SEX ED CONFERENCE

Title of presentation: *Peer Power: Lowering the Risk for Teen Pregnancy, HIV/AIDS, and STDs in African-American, Caribbean, and Latino-American Teens through Evidence-Based Learning*

Presentation description: The Adolescent Education Program of the State University of New York Downstate Medical Center has developed a comprehensive peer leadership program to train adolescents of various ethnic backgrounds to become HIV and pregnancy prevention peer leaders. The goal of the program is to lower the HIV infection and pregnancy rates among adolescents in at-risk populations in Brooklyn. Peer

Leaders participate in a rigorous summer training program consisting of a 76-hour curriculum that includes information on pregnancy prevention, HIV/AIDS, sexual health, and evidence-based learning techniques. Peer Leaders teach other at-risk youth through the utilization of real-life stories and the curricula *Sisters Informing Healing Living and Empowering* and *Be Proud Be Responsible.* Come to this workshop to learn about this comprehensive peer leadership program.

How I Got Into Sex...Ed

Teaching sex education wasn't something I set out do. It simply was a field of study that I somehow found myself doing. My first encounter with teaching health was as an HIV case manager. During this experience, I discovered that teaching others about how to take care of themselves and improve their health came naturally to me. Knowing that HIV is primarily transmitted through sexual means, along with my newfound passion for teaching, I realized that I would enjoy doing this kind of work.

My first introduction to HIV and AIDS was when I lost two close family members to the disease before I graduated from high school. This was a devastating and frightening experience for me. My aunt contracted the disease from her boyfriend, who was an intravenous drug user, and my uncle became infected from one of his partners. I have also lost two close friends to this disease, during my mid- to late 20s. I quickly saw how HIV/AIDS was ravaging the gay and lesbian community. After these events, I felt a spark of desire to educate young LGBTQ about this disease, which was plaguing this community. Also at that time, I came to realize that I was a member of a high-risk population, which led to a burning desire to gain as much knowledge about HIV/AIDS as possible so that I could educate others about this sexually transmitted disease.

Sexual development for me was a major stressor as I struggled with my sexuality. This stressor was compounded by the lack of sexuality education I received in junior and high school. Despite having a health education class, sexual health was barely covered. As a result, I believe that some of the challenges I encountered with my own sexuality during my early and mid-20s could have been averted if I had been equipped with knowledge about human sexuality. As a result of working in the New York City public school system, it appears to me that there is less sexual health education today than there was in the 1980s, when I was in high school. I am baffled and frustrated by the fact that the New York City Department of Education does not allow health educators to conduct condom demonstrations in classes, let alone distribute them to the student population. I truly believe that this needs to change because current research shows that HIV, STD, and pregnancy rates are continuing to rise among high school students.

My introduction to working in adolescent health education was working as a Street Outreach Specialist for SUNY Downstate's Teens Helping Each Other (THEO) program. A major part of my job responsibilities was to teach sexual health education in New York City public schools. I quickly learned that teenagers needed to be educated about how to maintain sexual health. I also became aware that New York City public schools were not providing adequate sex education, and meanwhile, the STD and HIV infection rates in adolescents were on the rise. I discovered that I enjoyed teaching sex education because it prepares students for their future, in which they will become sexually active. Besides, I was providing tools for students who were currently engaging in sex, and that really seemed to grab their attention.

I have spent the last nine years providing sexual health education in the public school system, and it appears that the administration is heavily focused on preparing students for comprehensive state exams and their college careers. However, there seems to be a lack of understanding that educating them about sexual health should be an integral part of their curriculums as well. Not all high school students may choose to go to college, but nearly all will become sexually active. All students need to know that a healthy lifestyle is necessary to complete college and pursue a career.

My nine years of experience working with young people through the Teens Helping Each Other program has inspired me more than ever to continue my education and pursue a degree in public health nursing. This has been a newfound personal goal of mine, and working at THEO has prompted me to consider becoming a school health nurse educator, focusing on young African-American gay teens. I am particularly passionate about working with this group of young people because they need more support to reduce social and sexual stigma, which, in turn, may curb the infection rates within this population.

Kelsey Van Nice

New York, NY

PROFESSIONAL LIFE
Current workplace: SIECUS, New York, NY
First workplace: AmeriCorps VISTA; Missoula Adolescent Pregnancy, Parenting, and Prevention Services; Missoula, MT
Favorite workplace: DC Doulas for Choice Collective, Washington, DC

EDUCATIONAL LIFE
Favorite course: Contemporary Issues in Human Sexuality
Least favorite course: Statistics!

TEACHING LIFE
Favorite topic to teach: Community Organizing 101

INSPIRATIONS
Sex educator: Kurt Conklin
Book: *Feminist Porn Book* by Tristan Taormino

NATIONAL SEX ED CONFERENCE
Title of presentation: *The Beltway Bubble: Why What Happens in DC Matters to You and What You Can Do to Shape It*
Presentation description: Many of the state and local policy controversies surrounding sex education are happening at the federal level. This session will provide the landscape of political and policy discussions happening in Congress and within the current administration to encourage participants to engage in the federal, state, and local policy process. Learning how federal policy impacts the programs at the community level, participants will be provided an opportunity to learn how to "educate" and "advocate" for issues surrounding sex education.

How I Got Into Sex...Ed

Growing up in Montana, I was raised by a community of

welcoming, kind, and easygoing folks. They were also somewhat predictable. So when I got to college and proclaimed my desire to become a sex therapist, no one really knew what to do with that.

I had always been an open person, someone who wanted to talk about things that made others squirm uncomfortably. So when I, unprompted by any earthshattering life event, decided I wanted to support people with their sexual quandaries, it didn't feel entirely unrealistic to me. But when people would ask my mother about where I was headed in life, she would say something along the lines of "Oh, Kelsey wants to be a…counselor."

Fast forward four years, and I graduated college with a degree in Sociology. I wanted to work in the field of human sexuality, but had changed my mind about sex therapy because I realized what I really wanted to do was less "counseling" and more "education." I had attempted to tailor my college career to include as much emphasis in human sexuality as possible, although I found opportunities for such growth and guidance in my picturesque Montana university town to be limited. I wrote papers on STD rates and same-sex parenting, created an internship with a local high school special education teacher to teach sex ed to her class, and went through the Institutional Review Board (IRB) process to collect information on the sexual experiences, beliefs, and behaviors of my peers on campus. I reached out to national organizations for advice, and took advantage of a semester as an exchange student on the East Coast to meet with real people doing the work I wanted to do. I was motivated and enthusiastic, but often felt alone and directionless, lacking mentorship to help guide me, and without the support of the community of people already in the field.

It was because I put myself out there and made connections

that I got my first paid gig as the coordinator of a local teen pregnancy coalition through the AmeriCorps VISTA program. Still living in Montana, this position connected me to the handful of people in the state doing work in the field of sexuality. I expanded my skillset and knowledge base immensely during that year, and ended up being selected to attend a reproductive health/environmental health summit in Washington, DC, at the end of my year of service. I remember that experience as if it were yesterday. I spent time with other young folks from around the world who cared about the issues I cared about, and used the same language I did. I learned from professionals in the field, my first real experience with those who make a living in the sexual and reproductive health and rights world. They encouraged me to join them. Never once did they make me feel like I would be invading their world — in fact, they made me feel like I would be a welcome addition. I actually cried a little on the final day of the summit, knowing that I had finally found "my people."

Coming back to Montana after my incredibly affirming trip to our nation's capital, I began to think about my immediate next steps. I decided that I needed to leave the comfort of my home state to pursue the career I had always wanted—so I moved to New York City. I worked at coffee shops and applied for jobs in the field. I had limited experience, so I hoped that my eagerness and passion would come through enough in interviews so someone would take a chance on me.

Eventually, someone did. Someone I met at the summit in Washington, DC, a year earlier. Someone who saw my potential and believed in me. Someone who worked for an organization I could only dream of one day being lucky enough to work for—SIECUS.

But that's not the end of my story. Everything hasn't been perfect since taking the leap and coming to the East Coast and landing my job with SIECUS. I have weathered layoffs, moves, and other hard transitions. But the important thing is that I haven't given up hope, I haven't stopped chasing my dreams, and I haven't lost the motivation to create the career I want for myself. By taking risks, making connections, and believing in my abilities, I intentionally work each day to better myself and this field.

Because I am only five years out of college, I am a new face to sexuality education. And although it can be somewhat intimidating to be the young kid in the room, I have felt nothing but genuine appreciation and encouragement from those who started working in the field long before me. The unfettered support I've gotten during the beginning of my career has been far more than I could have ever hoped for, and is something that I believe sets our field apart. I am committed to continuing that tradition when I someday transition into a role as a mentor to a fresh, young sexuality educator.

So for now, life is good. I am working for an organization I believe in with all my heart, and I have found a new community of welcoming, kind, and easygoing folks — this time on the East Coast.

Al Vernacchio

BA in Theology, M.Ed. in Human Sexuality

Wynnewood, PA

PROFESSIONAL LIFE

Current workplace: Friends' Central School, Wynnewood, PA

First workplace: St. Joseph's Prep School, Philadelphia, PA

Favorite workplace: I have been a volunteer with ActionAIDS, Philadelphia's largest AIDS-Service organization, for more than 15 years. I give a presentation on the biological and medical aspects of HIV at their Volunteer Orientations, and I bring high school students to volunteer there during school service days. I worked at ActionAIDS from 1994 to 1998 as the Coordinator of Training and Volunteers. Upon leaving that job, I became a volunteer with the agency and have been one ever since.

EDUCATIONAL LIFE

Favorite course: Education Methodology with Dr. Konnie McCaffree. I use what I learned in that course every day in my own classroom. The texts I used and the notes I took in that class are some of my most important sex-ed resources.

Least favorite course: How could a course in human sexuality ever be bad?!

TEACHING LIFE

Favorite topic to teach: This is like asking a parent which child is their favorite. I love being a sexuality educator, especially with adolescents, and I love my time in the classroom with them, no matter what the topic.

Most challenging topic to teach: When it comes to the topic of sexual violence/sexual assault, I prefer to bring in people who are specifically trained in that area. I think this is one place where a sexuality educator, even a trained and well-meaning one, should defer to people who have specific expertise in teaching about this topic.

<u>**INSPIRATIONS**</u>

Sex educator: How can any sexuality educator not be inspiring??

Book: It's a tie between Heather Corinna's *S.E.X.: The All-You-Need-to-Know Progressive Sexuality Guide to Get You through High School and College* and Paul Joannides's *Guide to Getting It On.* Both are revolutionary texts — honest, open, and comprehensive. Every high school student should have a copy of Heather Corinna's book, and every college dorm room should come equipped with a copy of Paul Joannides's book.

<u>**NATIONAL SEX ED CONFERENCE**</u>

Title of presentation: *For Goodness Sex: Reframing Sexuality Education*

Presentation description: Over the years I have presented workshops on the "pizza" model of sexual activity, pre-conference sessions on an integrated approach to teaching sexual orientation, and most recently, I gave the closing keynote address titled: *For Goodness Sex: Reframing Sexuality Education.*

How I Got Into Sex...Ed

I was born into a very traditional, blue-collar, Italian-American, Roman Catholic family in South Philadelphia. The message I got growing up was that God loved everyone, of course, but God *especially* loved "good" boys and girls. No one ever defined what being "good" meant, but it was clearly tied to following rules, being polite and smart, staying relatively quiet, and, most of all, not bothering adults. I mastered the art of being a good boy early in life; heck, I was the poster child for being a good boy. Being a faithful Catholic was absolutely essential to being a good boy, and I was gunning to be the *best* good, Catholic boy ever! If you asked me what I wanted to be when I grew up, my 4th-grade self would have answered "the Pope" without hesitation.

There was only one thing that stood in my way. I couldn't name it back then, but it had something to do with that exhilarating and terrifying butterflies-in-the-stomach feeling I got when looking at other boys. I couldn't ask adults what these feelings were about — good boys didn't bother adults — so I tried to figure it out on my own. Books and the church had the answers to everything, so that's where I looked. The available scholarly books in my house were the Bible, the dictionary, and a one-volume encyclopedia that was published in the 1960s. It was in those books I found the answer, contained in one simple but very *bad* word — homosexual.

So there I stood, as an 11- or 12-year-old boy, faced with two absolutely true but seemingly contradictory facts: I was a good Catholic boy, and I was a homosexual. From that point onward, my goal became to find out if it was possible to integrate those two seemingly contradictory but absolutely true facts. If I couldn't do that, I was in trouble — big trouble!

Books and church had defined the problem, and they were also the only place I knew to look for answers. So, starting in high school (my all-boys Catholic high school, of course) I threw myself into a surreptitious quest for information. Using the library card catalog (this was the pre-Internet, even pre-computer, world) I memorized all the Dewey decimal numbers that had to do with homosexuality. I would breeze by those library shelves, quickly pull off a book at random, and hide in a completely different section of the library to read it. It was easier to read books on church history and sexual morality openly, although I was always ready to flip to a different page if anyone approached to see exactly what I was reading.

After high school, I was accepted to a local Catholic college where studying theology seemed to be a natural step in my quest for information and integration. I was the *only* theology major in my class. I took as many classes on sexual morality as I could find, and every paper I wrote was about the Church's position on sexuality. In my more daring moments, I wrote about homosexuality in particular. The school library was much bigger and had many more books both on sexuality in general and on homosexuality in particular. During those days, I felt slightly less self-conscious about deliberately browsing those shelves, but I still took the books to another corner of the library to read them.

My years of wrestling with my sexual orientation while studying church history and sexual morality had shown me that being gay and being a person of faith was not an either/or proposition. I could be (quietly) gay and participate fully in the life of my church. When I graduated in 1986, I was a mostly in-the-closet young gay man with a bachelor's degree in Theology and a burning desire to be a high school religion teacher. I had no idea anyone *could* be a human sexuality teacher. Religion was the only "in" I had found to that subject area.

I took a job teaching religious studies and English at the same all-boys Catholic high school I attended as an adolescent. The 9th-grade religion course I taught was a study of the Old Testament, with a two-week human sexuality unit awkwardly tacked on at the end of the year. This was my first experience teaching human sexuality in the classroom, and it was transformative! I was having conversations with my students about issues that mattered deeply to them and was doing it under the umbrella of teaching about a loving God who gave humanity the choice to use our sexuality and our bodies to further the Divine work. Over the seven years I taught at the school, I slowly turned that two-week mini-course into a required full-semester course, so the first place I taught sex ed full time was in an all-boys Catholic school!

In the late 1980s, while still maintaining my full-time teaching job, I began a graduate program in moral theology at another local Catholic university. It was sometime during my first semester there that I heard about a graduate program in Human Sexuality at the University of Pennsylvania. I had studied sexuality through the lens of theology for years, but this Penn program offered the chance to study human sexuality itself. I decided to apply to the program, but I was both intrigued and nervous. I had never studied at a "secular" university. Would they be respectful of my dual interests in theology and sexuality? This called for a true leap of faith, and I took it.

I was accepted into the Penn Graduate School of Education Human Sexuality Program in 1990, and, to quote scripture, "something like scales fell from [my] eyes." I discovered a world of scholars and scholarship I had never known. I met professors who would become mentors and even friends. I met students who would become friends, colleagues, and even family. Dr. Ken George taught me how to be a proud gay man, and Dr. Konnie McCaffree taught me how to be a rationale-based, student-centered sexuality educator. And far from demeaning me for being a person of faith, I found my whole self embraced, nurtured, challenged, and supported by the Penn program and its faculty and students. When I graduated with my master's degree in 1993, I felt more alive, more skilled, and more deeply committed to sexuality education than I ever imagined I could be.

I was laid off from my teaching job in 1993, and soon found myself working as the Coordinator of Training and Volunteers at ActionAIDS, Philadelphia's largest AIDS-service organization. For the first time, I lived my life as an out and proud gay man, I used my Penn training to create dynamic HIV/AIDS education programming, and I met warm, dedicated, and fiercely passionate people, both staff and clients, who were on the front lines of creating a better life for people living with HIV/AIDS. At ActionAIDS I learned how to be an activist as well as an educator.

After four years at ActionAIDS, I was ready to go back to the classroom full time, but I knew it had to be at a school where I could fully be myself and bring all my gifts and talents to my work. I found a perfect fit at Friends' Central, a Quaker school where the spiritually-based, values-driven, whole-person-focused philosophy does education exactly the way I want to do it. Although they originally hired me as a full-time English teacher, I asked if I there might be room for me to use my degree in sexuality education as well, and they were enthusiastic about the possibilities. Over the years, I have become the upper-school sexuality educator and have had the opportunity, with the school's blessing, to expand my work beyond the school onto the national stage.

As news of the sexual abuse scandal in the Catholic Church became public, and as the Church's protests against same-sex marriage became more mean-spirited and vitriolic, I made the very painful decision to walk away from Catholicism and seek a new spiritual home. I now worship with The Religious Society of Friends, the Quakers. Today I am proud to be a sexuality educator, a person of deep and abiding religious faith, a teacher of adolescents, an out and proud gay man, and, I think, still a "good" boy.

Leslie Walker-Hirsch

IMEd, FAAIDD

Santa Fe, NM

PROFESSIONAL LIFE

Current workplace: Private practice and consultancy in Santa Fe, NM. At DBA Moonstone, I specialize in teaching students with intellectual and developmental disabilities and their teachers and families to understand the interface between responsible sexuality and their disability.

First workplace: Commerce High School, English teacher at Vocational Technical High School, Yonkers, NY

Favorite workplace: Alternatives, Inc., Narragansett, RI; University of New Mexico, Albuquerque, NM

EDUCATIONAL LIFE

Favorite course: Introduction to Intellectual Disabilities at Rhode Island College, Providence, RI. Students were asked to design a behavior change program with motivators and personal supports. I actually stopped smoking that way (at last!) and became a big fan of using positive reinforcement to change personal behavior.

Least favorite course: Intermediate Algebra at William Howard Taft High School, Bronx, NY. I had to go to summer school to boost up my Regents grade!

TEACHING LIFE

Favorite topic to teach: Favorite topic to teach: Relationship Skill Building using CIRCLES® Curriculum Series[16]. I enjoy watching the students "get it" as they develop their individual works of art. I love to demonstrate the CIRCLES® paradigm to parent groups and hear them say, "I think that would help my son (or daughter) to get along better in school!"

Most challenging topic to teach: Most challenging topic to teach: It is not usually the actual subject matter of any particular topic that is difficult, but HOW to communicate that content to students within the confines of school or parental limits that are imposed upon the subject of sex simply because the students have intellectual impairments. They may have difficulty understanding content without concrete materials such as photos or videos and may need practice at home across a period of time to learn new behaviors. This means that family members must participate in the ongoing support at home!

INSPIRATIONS

Sex educator: Winifred Kempton. Not only was Win Kempton an inspiration, but she became a friend as well. Both of our husbands were dentists, and that gave them something to talk about while we women would share "war stories," give and get advice about how to intercede in different situations, and try to solve the mysteries associated with teaching teens and adults with intellectual and developmental disabilities! She taught me how to be inclusive of both my supporters AND my detractors!

Marklyn Champagne. Marklyn and I have been both dear friends and collaborators for more than 35 years in developing the many iterations of the CIRCLES® Curriculum Series. Although we have different strengths, I appreciate how Marklyn's perceptions add to our projects and to my personal life as well.

Book: I just finished reading *The Goldfinch* by Donna Tartt and was touched by how the losses that the character endures leaves their mark upon his personality, his sense of self, and his safety in relationships.

NATIONAL SEX ED CONFERENCE

Title of presentation: *The Facts of Life...and More: Meaningful Sexuality Education for Students with Intellectual Disabilities*

Presentation description: "So often the sexuality education needs of people with intellectual disabilities never become known to mainstream health educators. The greatest challenge is in how this important information is communicated to these two different populations," Walker-Hirsch tells us. "It will no longer be satisfactory to simply JUST SAY NO when romantic opportunities arise."

How I Got Into Sex...Ed

The Accidental Sex Educator
(of People with Intellectual Disabilities)

Becoming a sexuality educator for teens and adults with intellectual disabilities is NOT one of those careers that you train for early on! You do not come home one day and tell your mom or dad, "Hey, do you know what I want to be when I grow up? I want to be a sexuality educator for people who have intellectual and/or developmental disabilities!!"

This is the story of how becoming a reluctant sex educator happened for me.

Once upon a time, I was in graduate school at Rhode Island College in Providence, RI, getting a master's degree in Special Education and Administration so I could become a resource room teacher in the public schools. Straight from college, I had already spent four years as an English teacher at an inner-city vocational/technical high school in Yonkers, NY. But it was a very long time before I began graduate school.

As with so many of us, it was necessary for me to work my way through grad school with a paying job. I looked for work in a related field that was available close enough to home so I could to pick up my young son at daycare before it closed.

In the newspaper, I had already been following the Consent Decree to close Ladd Center, the one and only institution for people with intellectual disabilities (the condition formerly known as mental retardation) in Rhode Island. When I spotted the tiny want ad for an administrative assistant at a new agency, Alternatives, Inc., I applied immediately. This agency was a not-for-profit that was providing community residences to adults with intellectual disabilities who had been held captive for their whole lives in the hellhole that was Ladd Center.

I was thinking that my work at Alternatives would help prepare me to become a resource room teacher! Well, that work did set some wheels into motion, but not the ones I expected to be rolling. My administrative work included a lot of paper shuffling as well as interfacing with an array of community groups, state and federal offices, and neighborhood homeowners.

When a man with intellectual disabilities (ID) from this residential program was accused of sexually touching a young girl at a neighborhood playground, it did not take long for him to be arrested and for the agency headquarters to be called. We knew that this man was NOT a sex offender, but his attempt at helpful behavior with the child was misinterpreted by the family as offensive, sexually. This male resident had never lived in a community setting before and, needless to say, had not had any social/sexual education or training that would inform his socialization with children.

Prejudice against people who looked different or spoke oddly or walked in a strange way was rampant in 1978. Even more prejudice and ignorance existed at that time than exist today. There were many false "urban legends" regarding the sexuality of people with ID that ran from being nonsexual to being uncontrollably sexual.

Community citizens had no experience with this population because people with intellectual and developmental disabilities had been segregated from typical family and community life while housed in Ladd Center and other horrific institutions of cruelty and neglect throughout the country. A big meeting was called to try to intervene in the awful situation created by the resident's arrest. Everyone involved was there. It was not a friendly, informal meeting. Both fear and anger abounded. When it was suggested that "these people" belonged in prison, a new danger was introduced.

People with intellectual disabilities who ended up in prison did not fare very well; they were frequently the objects of abuse by fellow inmates and workers. They were often unable to adapt to prison life or understand the etiquette of prison society and social expectation or quickly develop survival skills for self-protection.

Knowing the importance of keeping the resident out of the penal system, a suggestion was put forth that our agency would provide sexuality education, not only to this man, but also to all of the agency residents to prevent this kind of social error from happening again. In exchange, the charges would be set aside and the situation reevaluated after several months of sexuality education and training. The proposal was accepted, and we returned to the office with a great sigh of relief.

Because I had interfaced with so many people and organizations involved with intellectual disabilities, it became my first order of business to phone everyone I knew and to HIRE someone to run the promised sexuality education program. I spent the next two weeks trying to hire someone to undertake this assignment. It became clear that time was passing and we were no closer to finding a sexuality educator for nine adults with rather mild developmental delays who were finally living in a community setting for the first time in their lives.

Since there was no on else, and since I was in the midst of my master's degree in Special Education and Administration, the task of providing this education fell to me. Despite my own naiveté, I realized that I could not undertake this alone. I called a registered nurse named Marklyn Champagne, who had had some experience working with those with intellectual disabilities.

After a two-hour phone conversation with Marklyn about the project, the beginning of a marvelous adventure and a friendship had taken place. I did not know it at the time, but my life would be changed forever, for the better!

Marklyn and I limped along in an unknown area of education, because we recognized that sexuality education was a critical life skill for the people we served if they were to experience acceptance and inclusion in cities and towns across the country. Sexuality education would aid in making people with ID/DD less likely to be victimized and would set the stage for developing good friendships and loving relationships. We had been tapped to undertake our lifelong work as sexuality educators.

The struggle to become the best sex educators we could eventually led to the creation of the Circles Concept and the CIRCLES® Curriculum Series.

Susie Wilson

Princeton, NJ

PROFESSIONAL LIFE
Current workplace: Senior Advisor (part-time), Answer
First workplace: Time Inc., Time Advertising Department, which led me to my job as a reporter for *Life* magazine
Favorite workplace: Network for Family Life Education (now Answer), Rutgers University (23 years), home of *Sex, Etc.,* a magazine and website for teens, by teens

EDUCATIONAL LIFE
Favorite course: Constitutional Law (college level)
Least favorite course: Geometry (high school)

TEACHING LIFE
Favorite topic to teach: Birth of a baby and other age-appropriate family life topics to young children in grades K-3
Most challenging topic to teach: HIV/AIDS to fearful New Jersey health education teachers at the start of the pandemic

INSPIRATIONS
Sex educator: Peggy Brick
Book: *However long the night* by Aimee Molloy, which tells the beautiful story of how the women of Senegal in West Africa, with the help of one American woman, Molly Melching, decide to end the practice of female genital cutting throughout the villages in this country. Its lesson for me: Listen to those whom you want to teach; they will clear a pathway to learning.

How I Got Into Sex...Ed[17]

"Sex, Etc." — two words in brilliant-red capital letters leap out from a piece of stained glass that hangs above the window in my alcove office. You'd have to be blind not to see them. I received the stained glass as a gift on October 23, 2003, at a conference held by the Network for Family Life Education (now known as Answer), the national comprehensive sexuality education organization that I led for 23 years.

More than 400 sexuality educators and advocates had gathered to celebrate the 20th anniversary of the passage of the New Jersey State Board of Education's requirement for family life education for all public school students. It may have been the largest gathering of sexuality educators in U.S. history, and the buzz of excitement in the room was palpable.

This gift is precious to me: It symbolizes my more than 30 years of work in the state and national sexuality education movement, which began when I became a member of the State Board of Education and helped create and pass the family life education policy. I continued this work when I became the executive coordinator of the Network for Family Life Education, where we helped to implement the policy in local school districts and protected it from opponents — primarily religious and conservative groups that didn't think sexuality education could help students lead safe, responsible, and healthy lives. At the Network, I also helped to create what I feel was my major contribution to the national sexuality education movement, the *Sex, Etc.* magazine and website written by teens, for teens, on sexual health.

Beginnings

I would never have dreamed that the most important work of my life outside my family would be sexuality education. My own sexuality education at home and school was woefully weak, and I didn't have the expertise to help my own children receive a much better one. When I began working in the field, I certainly didn't know how to help young people or realize the full importance of sexuality education for them. In fact, I would never have become engaged with the subject if Governor Brendan T. Byrne hadn't appointed me to a six-year term on the New Jersey State Board of Education, which set policies for the state's public schools in approximately 600 districts. The State Senate confirmed my appointment on July 11, 1977.

The Fateful Question

About a year into my term, the state's commissioner of health, Dr. Joanne Finley, presented her annual report on child and adolescent health to the board. Dr. Finley, who had led a Planned Parenthood affiliate and held a master's degree in public health from Yale, didn't mince words that January afternoon in 1979. She said that the state's teens had rising rates of unplanned pregnancy, abortion, and sexually transmitted infections (STIs), and that ignorance was at the root of these health problems. She asked the board to take concrete action to improve the state's public school sex education programs. At the time the programs were scarce, if they existed at all, and caused intense controversies at local school board meetings, which prevented their further development.

"Schools are a promising avenue for conveying vital information to children and adolescents about sexuality," Dr. Finley said. "Please do not shrink from your responsibility to provide a thorough and efficient education for New Jersey's students. So many will benefit if you are willing to bite this bullet."

She sat back in her seat, and there was silence throughout the room. Her obvious concern for the students, whom I had sworn in my oath of office to protect, struck a chord with me, and I wanted to know exactly what she thought our next steps should be. I didn't feel a bit afraid as I leaned forward and said, "Dr. Finley, at what age do you think students need to know how their bodies work?" It was an awkwardly phrased question that indicated my unfamiliarity with sexuality education, but I wasn't afraid to ask it.

"By age 10," she promptly answered. She meant that by 5th grade, all students should know about human reproduction and how to protect themselves from unplanned pregnancy and STIs. She thought that accurate, age-appropriate information was a necessary first step for children in the early grades.

After my question, the silence returned; no other board member waded into the sticky wicket of sexuality education. Dr. Finley and her staff gathered up their papers and left the room, and Paul Ricci, the board president, promptly appointed a five-person subcommittee to suggest improvements for the state's sexuality education policy. He leaned in my direction.

"I would like Susan Wilson to chair the subcommittee," he said.

I am sure he handed this role off to me because I was the only person who had asked Dr. Finley a question. Years later, when I spoke to young people at conferences, I would say, "Be careful what questions you ask. The answers can change your life. The answer to a particular question about sexuality education that I asked at a public meeting reshaped the direction of my working life, changing it positively for me — and I hope for the good of others."

Shaping a Statewide Policy

My subcommittee requested a report on sex education from the State Department of Education, which found that many school districts were unwilling or unable to adopt programs in previous decades due to local controversies; the committee recommended that the board pass a policy *requiring* family life education for all elementary and secondary schools. Our policy required K–12 family life education cover specific topics, including human reproduction, child abuse, incest, and sexually transmitted infections by the end of 8th grade, and a review of all of the above plus preparation for marriage and family planning by the end of 12th grade. Parents had the right to remove their children from the program and inspect and review the curriculum. We consciously chose the words, "family life," rather than "sex education," in order to lessen the potential political controversy the policy might generate.

The board anticipated a battle over the requirement, but the reliable and respected Eagleton Poll at Rutgers University found that 78% of state residents favored sex education, and a majority favored requiring it for all public school students. I was confident that we would prevail and schools would implement the program, making New Jersey the second state in the nation to create such a requirement for public schools.

Public Extravaganzas
The board passed our subcommittee's policy by a vote of 7 to 1. The word "requiring" soon shook the rafters and caused the storm clouds to gather. Despite the policy's assurances that parents could remove their children from parts of the program that conflicted with their moral or religious views, our opponents were adamantly opposed to it. Clergy, parents, and groups like the League of American Families and Right to Life argued that sex education should not be taught outside of the family and the "mandate," as they insisted on calling it, would cause children and teens to engage in sexual activity. (Opponents used the word "mandate" because it conjured up the heavy hand of the government curtailing people's rights to make their own decisions. They wanted to persuade the public to oppose the "mandate" because it was a state government requirement that came without funds to aid local districts with its implementation.)

The board was required by law to hear public comment on any substantive policy under discussion, and the challenges came with a suddenness and virulence that surprised most board members and the New Jersey political establishment. It is one thing to read about controversies in the newspaper and quite another to hear the distortions and invectives hurled by opponents at close range in a committee room. As public servants, we had to exhibit self-control and patience, allow citizens to make their points during hearings, and give equal weight to each argument — pro or con. Yet whenever a member of the public appeared in support of the policy during those tense hearings, it came as a small wave of relief.

Sometimes it was hard to keep a straight face when opponents charged that teaching students about contraceptive use "would enable them to prey on younger children" and sex education would "include such unwanted subjects as abortion, masturbation, homosexuality, bestiality, frigidity, and impotence." I couldn't believe that someone actually thought that public servants would create a policy with the ulterior motive of hurting children. It dawned on me that some opponents sincerely held the views they were espousing. I realized it was going to take a lot of time, effort, and patience for them to be able to understand where the board and I were coming from.

True Child Advocacy
In April 1980, the State Board held another extensive public hearing at which more than 120 proponents and opponents of the requirement testified for nine hours. I was mulling over the effect the opposition might have on the policy when I put in a telephone call to Paul Ricci the Sunday before the meeting. His wife, Margaret, answered and said that Paul was on his tractor. "When Paul has concerns, he climbs aboard his tractor and goes off to plough the fields," she said. Her reassuring tone made me smile.

Paul called back several hours later, and I said, "Paul, these education organizations always say that they're working on behalf of the state's children, but here they are with family life, retreating behind the idea that the board has exceeded its statutory responsibility. What do you think of that?"

Again, my naiveté almost got the better of me. Why would I think organizations that trumpeted how much they cared for children would stand tall on sexuality education? They cared more about posturing before the public than about how our sexuality education policy could help students. Paul reassured me that the policy was worth fighting for, because it was on behalf of the students. His words helped move me past a discouraging moment.

He showed the same common sense at one of the large public hearings. A woman named Catherine Denk, who was with New Jersey Concerned Parents, interrupted the session several times by shouting at board members about the outrageous effects the policy would have on children. The state police were called, and finally, to attract even more attention, she sat down in the middle of the auditorium floor, hoping that Paul would sign a complaint against her so then photos of her being carried out by burly policemen would be all over the news, eliciting sympathy for her cause.

Paul immediately understood what our opponent wanted and called a recess for tempers to cool. The room emptied, and Denk sat alone on the floor surrounded only by her allies, air slowly escaping from her balloon. When the hearing resumed, she departed, sensing no support for her dramatics. Paul taught me how to be an honest child advocate and a calm leader in a crisis.

The Lion's Den
The State Legislature was soon drawn into the struggle. In May 1980, acceding to demands for action from New Jersey Concerned Parents, the Senate Education Committee held a one-day hearing on the policy. Normally someone from the State Department of Education would testify on an incendiary

issue, yet no one in the department stepped up to the plate. All eyes turned to me, and I didn't have a choice. I was going to have to testify on behalf of the board since I had chaired the subcommittee. The time had come for me to become the board's public face.

I felt surprisingly calm and unafraid. I knew sexuality education was worth fighting for, because so many people had told me that it prevented them from making life-changing mistakes. I knew that if I didn't become a leader and give the policy the support it deserved, the State Board might lose the battle and its ability to improve students' lives.

Prior to the hearing, I had one less serious and very female concern that I raised with Kathy Waldron, the young woman who served as the staff liaison between the board and State Department of Education: "What does one wear to testify at a senate hearing?" I asked.

"If you have a [nun's] habit in your closet, I suggest you wear it," she replied, "I think you'd look great in it."

I laughed out loud at her joke, which helped me to relax, and decided to wear a light gray pant suit.

Learning to Compromise
The Senate Education Committee asked us to make certain changes in our policy, and we knew that if we didn't make some compromises in this late-stage battle, we might very well lose the war. The governor's office had asked Paul and me to meet with his legal counsel, Dan O'Hern, to again explain why the board supported this policy so strongly. We went to O'Hern's office and calmly went over the process we had engaged in to find out why local school boards couldn't implement sex education programs on their own because of their controversial nature, and how this hampered students'

need for honest, accurate information.

"I see the purpose and reasons why you have created this policy," said O'Hern, who was later appointed to the New Jersey Supreme Court. Back on the street, I told Paul that I thought we had won that round — and I was right. The governor's office signaled to the Democrats in the legislature that they should not vote to overturn the policy.

I learned a great deal about the legislative process from my work on the policy. I told anyone who would listen that "opponents of family life education never sleep," and I knew if they lost one round, they would find another way to block the policy, which they did in 1981, when New Jersey Concerned Parents brought a suit (*Mary K. Smith et al. vs. P. Paul Ricci et al.*) in New Jersey Superior Court to prevent implementation of the policy.

The Supreme Court moved to take the case directly. Deputy Attorney General Mary Ann Burgess argued the board's views, and on May 25, 1982, the court handed down its decision, 7–0, unanimously rejecting the appellant's points and finding no constitutional problems with our policy.

The decision made the front page of *The New York Times,* and I was thrilled to read the article, because it showed that the board had exercised its powers wisely and correctly, and young people would receive sexuality education that would benefit them greatly. *The Times* quoted me in the last paragraphs of the story: "Susan Wilson, a board member who supported the requirement, said the court's decision parallels the sentiments of the overwhelming majority of parents. She added that the program would 'help young people lead responsible and healthy lives and prepare them to assume family roles.'"

I knew what complete satisfaction and deep happiness felt like when I read those words on the front page of one of America's great newspapers. The opponents appealed to the U.S. Supreme Court, which refused to consider the case for "want of a substantive federal question."

Meeting in Another Governor's Office

I would continue to fight for the family life education policy and the programs that rolled out from it but not from my perch as a member and vice president of the State Board of Education. (I had been elected vice president in 1981.) Republican Thomas Kean was elected governor in 1982, the year my six-year term ended, and my reappointment was on his desk. The rumor was that I would not be reappointed to another term because of my leadership on the sex education policy issue, which his party had opposed. Governor Kean also did not believe in "education mandates." What mattered much more to me than reappointment was the status of the policy, which was scheduled for full implementation in 1983.

I needed a one-on-one meeting with Governor Kean, and was able to have one arranged at his State House office. He greeted me cordially, and after some chitchat, I said, "Governor Kean, I know you'll be deciding whether or not to reappoint me to the State Board soon. I have liked serving on the board and felt useful there, but the family life education policy is more important to me than another six-year term. Its implementation will mean a lot more to the young people in New Jersey than my reappointment. I'm not asking that you reappoint me; I'm asking you to allow the policy to go forward in local districts, as is happening as we speak."

My speech was long, but I meant every word. The governor didn't respond or ask me any questions about my strong feelings for the policy. He is a courteous man, and after some more general discussion, he thanked me for coming and said he would think about what I had said. I walked out of the State House wondering if I would ever return there again.

Governor Kean did not reappoint me to the State Board; he replaced me with Dr. Gustavo A. Mellander, the president of Passaic County Community College. However, he allowed the state's implementation of the policy to proceed. I felt I had won a critical battle, but the children and young people of New Jersey and their parents were the true winners.

Jean Workman

MA

Durham, NC

PROFESSIONAL LIFE
Current workplace: Children's Aid Society-Carrera Adolescent Pregnancy Prevention Program, Durham, NC
First workplace: Triad Health Project, Greensboro, NC
Favorite workplace: Triad Health Project, Greensboro, NC

EDUCATIONAL LIFE
Favorite course: Health Education across the Lifespan
Least favorite course: Physiology

TEACHING LIFE
Favorite topic to teach: Contraception
Most challenging topic to teach: There are three topics that are considered taboo in the state of NC: homosexuality, abortion, and masturbation. Therefore, all three are topics I have rarely addressed in the classroom due to the limitations that have been placed by policy makers on assertively discussing with students. I have always answered questions with no judgment and medical accuracy, but rarely have the topics been a part of an existing curriculum that I have taught.

INSPIRATIONS
Sex educator: My co-worker Lindsay Fram; she is the most assertive and dynamic educator I have ever met.
Book: *How Girls Thrive* by JoAnn Deak. This is not really a sex education book per se, but the concept of building competence, confidence, and connectedness in young women inspired my philosophy of how I interact with young people in the classroom and inspired much of the vision for the *ABOVE THE WAIST* curriculum Lindsay Fram and I have recently developed. And *Yes Means Yes!: Visions of Female Sexual Power and a World Without Rape* by Jaclyn Friedman and Jessica Valenti changed the way I think about enthusiastic consent and taking shame out of all sexual messaging.

Title of presentation: *ABOVE THE WAIST: Family Life & Sexuality Education Beginning with the Brain*

Presentation description: Dr. Michael Carrera will provide an overview of the past, present, and future growth of the Children's Aid Society-Carrera Adolescent Pregnancy Prevention Program within the context of his half-century of work within the sexuality field. This workshop will center on our holistic, *ABOVE THE WAIST* approach to Family Life & Sexuality Education (FLSE) rooted in the CAS-Carrera philosophy, and it models creative, student-centered engagement strategies. The newly developed *ABOVE THE WAIST* curriculum joins the growing number of resources in the field of sexuality education that work toward creative solutions to reducing adolescent pregnancy. It focuses on cutting-edge research in the field of adolescent brain development to support healthy sexual decision-making during adolescence and throughout adulthood. Each lesson begins with the brain and promotes dynamic teaching strategies that build unforgettable student-centered learning experiences reenergize the spirit for positively engaging youth.

How I Got Into Sex...Ed

Finding My Assertive Voice

Brittany was a "goth girl" with jet-black hair, black fingernails, and black attire. She had a chip on her shoulder the size of a boulder. On the first day of group, I asked the girls to share one of their coolest qualities. When I got to her, she belligerently stated she had none. I knew her type well. I asked her if I could share a quality that I had noticed, and with rolled eyes she said sure. I said, "Brittany, you dare to be different in a room full of girls who all look the same. You stand out, you own your look, and you have the assertive voice to match." She sat up a little straighter that day and came each week to the group, participating like a leader should. On the last day of class, she gave me a hand-made card. It read: "I didn't want to come to this class, but you made it fun, and for the first time in my life you made me feel special. Thank you for what you do."

I had the unfortunate experience of an abusive relationship for the first three years of college. I saw the red flags early on, but wanted to believe he would change and go back to being what he was when we first started dating. He was controlling, manipulative, jealous, insecure, and downright mean. The verbal and emotional abuse was at times intolerable, but his apologies were sincere and sweet. I stuck it out. My college life, along with my grades, suffered as a result.

By the third year, I was growing tired of having to build his self-esteem due to his multitude of insecurities. It took three times to break up with him. The third time was the final straw, when his verbal and emotional abuse turned violent and he hit me in my parent's driveway during an argument.

I came home that semester with my tail between my legs. My mother greeted me in the driveway with open arms, so relieved I had finally given up on that abusive relationship, but disappointed that I had no real game plan for what would come next. I told her I had dropped out of college because I didn't get into nursing school. Over the next few days, she kept asking me what I was going to do. Finally, I drove back to campus to register for the fall semester, declaring Community Health Education as major number three. Health Education through the field of sexuality education changed my life.

I have often said that I did not choose sex education, it chose me. I remember my mother asking me, "What do you plan to do with this health education degree when you graduate in May?" I had no idea. It was during my last semester while participating in my course internship with a local AIDS Service Organization, Triad Health Project, that I found my calling. I worked in the prevention education department and had the task of teaching what we call AIDS 101 to anyone who would listen. My first presentation was with a church youth group. I practiced that presentation until I had it memorized and sat with that group of youth like I was one of them. I realized that night that I was good at something — teaching. But it was more than just teaching, it was teaching about sexuality. I made the audience laugh, and I could see the light bulbs turning on in their brains. It was truly a magical experience, and it was the first time I felt competent and confident. I had found my assertive voice.

That same year I met Randall. He was a client at Triad Health Project and was paired with me when I spoke to youth and parents about HIV. He had AIDS and had recently been released from the hospital after a bout with Cytomegalovirus and Pneumocysitis Carinii Pneumonia (PCP). His vision was altered due to the Cytomegalovirus, and he had temporarily lost his voice due to PCP. On our first speaking engagement together, he told parents that he was losing his vision because he had seen all he needed to see, but God had given back his voice because he had not yet said all that needed to be said regarding the prevention of HIV. He inspired me and gave me a meaningful vision as to how I should approach sexuality education.

I got into sexuality education to help the Brittanys of the world find and use their assertive voices. I got into sexuality education to build the competence, confidence, and connectedness young people need in order to become successful adults, so they can walk away from the relationships that raise the red flags. I teach sexuality education because navigating adolescence is not always an easy journey. I teach sexuality education because I want young people to learn how to communicate their wants, needs, and desires — to enthusiastically say yes to amazing relationships that are healthy and fulfilling. I teach sexuality education to inspire young people to view their bodies as powerful, extraordinary, and worth protecting! I continue in this field because there is so much more that needs to be said. My passion and assertive voice for sexuality education inspires others to positively view it as a necessary and vital resource for all young people.

Mara Yacobi
MSW

Allendale, NJ

PROFESSIONAL LIFE
Current workplace: Youth Development Specialist, JLoveandValues — Bringing Jewish Values to Sexuality Education, NJ
First workplace: Planned Parenthood Hudson Peconic, Rockland County, NY
Favorite workplace: Physicians for Human Rights – Tel Aviv, Israel

EDUCATIONAL LIFE
Favorite course: Multimedia Communications
Least favorite course: Statistics

TEACHING LIFE
Favorite topic to teach: Puberty
Most challenging topic to teach: Sexuality and Gender Issues

INSPIRATIONS
Sex educator: Dr. Ruth, of course!
Book: *Does God Belong in the Bedroom?* by Rabbi Michael Gold

NATIONAL SEX ED CONFERENCE
Title of presentation: *5 Engaging Ways to Connect Text, Values, and Scripture to Your Sexuality Education Presentation*
Presentation description: Sexuality educators Mara Yacobi, from the Jewish faith tradition, and Amy Johnson, from the Christian faith tradition (United Church of Christ), will present practical ideas for how to incorporate text, values, and scripture into your sexuality education lessons.

How I Got Into Sex…Ed

In the spring of 2003, during my second year as a sexuality educator with Planned Parenthood, I was invited to do the annual STI and contraception workshop for a diverse public high school. In the middle of my presentation, a sophomore raised her hand to ask the question that so many teens had asked countless times: "So how do you know when you are ready to have sex?" I gave her the standard answer I had given many times before:

> *"This is a very important decision. It requires you to carefully consider your relationship, the emotional and physical risks to you and your partner, as well as your personal values. Think about what your family and your religious views are about sex, and be sure to make an informed decision."*

Of course, my response was more detailed, but I never felt like I was fully answering this loaded question. There were too many shades of gray, too many unanswered issues I could not explore, and there was never enough time. In a public school setting, I was there to present the facts and help the students process the universal values in all healthy relationships. Filled with angst and frustration, I had an idea. What if I could offer my community sexuality education with a twist of Jewish values? That's when the dream for my business, JLoveandValues, was born.

I pursued a career in the field of sexuality education for many reasons, but first and foremost, it was my strong interest in reproductive health that led me down this path. As a result of a variety of life experiences, prevention education and risk reduction became just as important to me.

In college, I obtained my degree in sociology with a concentration in health. There I learned about the important work being done by Planned Parenthood, and my heart became set on working for the organization after I graduated. First, however, I found myself living in Israel where I worked for Physicians for Human Rights for two years. In 2001, upon returning to the United States, my dream of working as a sexuality educator at Planned Parenthood came true. This began a passionate career, but it had been long in the works.

I understood at a young age the importance of openly discussing sexuality precisely because it was not discussed with me throughout my formative years. Having attended a Jewish nursery school, an Orthodox Yeshiva, and later a Conservative Jewish Day School, I became acutely aware of the traditional roles expected of Jewish boys and girls and the standards for modesty — from how to dress to what topics were forbidden.

Learning about our bodies, puberty (except for the very basics), healthy relationships, or HIV/AIDS (even during the height of the epidemic) was off limits. Worse yet, there was no discussion of sexual abuse or sexual peer pressure, nor any ideas on how to get help or information. In fact, there was no use of the word "sex" whatsoever. In 6th grade, I missed the half-hour puberty lecture ("the talk") during our regularly scheduled recess in which we were to learn everything we would need to know about the changes that undoubtedly had already started to happen. My close friend saved a pamphlet for me.

I instinctively knew that there was much more I needed to know. However, it wouldn't be until a few years later, when at the age of 15, I was hospitalized for a massive dermoid cyst on my ovary, that I began to do my own research. In learning what I needed to know about my condition, I discovered that research on reproductive health fascinated me. From medical documents to journal articles, I was completely hooked.

Then, at age 16, the friend who had saved me the pamphlet became pregnant. We had been so much alike that I was utterly shocked to hear this news — how could this happen to one of us?! Over time, I came to realize that we just weren't armed with the information we needed to prevent pregnancy. This had a profound effect on me and on my eventual career choice. Years later, another close friend from middle school confided in me that she had been sexually abused during adolescence. Again, she hadn't been given the information she needed to prevent such a tragedy — or at least the knowledge she needed to seek help.

While these experiences were certainly life-altering, the question, "Who am I?" also played a significant role in my choice of profession. As a 10th-grader, my English teacher instructed us to ask about our roots and share our families' stories with the class. This question led me to discover the truth of what it meant to be an Eastern European Jew whose grandparents were Holocaust survivors.

As a result of this assignment, my 67-year-old grandmother told me her story for the first time. I learned about her hometown, the ghetto from which she fled, the night her father was killed, the time she slid across the ground to prevent capture, and what it was like to live in a fetal position in a potato hole for six weeks. I also developed a new relationship with my late grandfather as I read his diaries in which he shared horrific and often grotesque memories of the war. My grandparents' experiences became my legacy — an unbelievable testimony I would share at every opportunity to make sure that no one would ever forget. This legacy strengthened my identity and provided me with a positive foundation from which to make good choices. I felt more empowered and secure.

I presented my discoveries to my English class, and then to a history class. I was also invited to share my family story with other schools and community groups, and in this way, I discovered that I enjoyed speaking before groups and educating them on topics of importance. At that point, public speaking became one of my passions — the larger the audience, the better.

Being secure in who I was eventually drove my passion to help teens discover and explore their own identities and to know themselves intimately, so that they, too, could make good choices. Knowing the answer to "Who am I?" empowers teens to contemplate their actions, stay true to their personal values, and seek help from people they trust, as needed.

Part of knowing oneself also includes understanding one's sexuality and the many related topics. I believe when teens have a strong sense of who they are and the values they believe in, they are more likely to make informed and healthy choices. The essence of sexuality is that it represents one's identity and one's ability to have positive loving relationships.

After nearly five years with Planned Parenthood, I resigned my position in order to obtain my master's degree in social work. I also worked in a clinical setting as a degree requirement. On graduation day, I gave birth to my first child. I was determined to find a balance between caring for my son and continuing in the field I love — sexuality education. I truly enjoyed the dynamics of teaching young people to embrace their sexuality with positive regard, helping them learn about their bodies without shame, and challenging their critical-thinking skills as they relate to their values, relationships, and health.

I reflected on the dream I had during that spring workshop and on the question I could not fully answer. I knew the time had come for me to start teaching sexuality with an emphasis on Jewish values. I decided I would strive to provide Jewish teens with an opportunity to make informed choices from a personal and religious framework.

Today I am proud to tell the world I began my career as a sexuality educator at Planned Parenthood. I am honored to have learned from the best educators, mentors, and colleagues. I am pleased to bring those teachings with me to JLoveandValues. Using my background combined with my Jewish tradition and studies, I feel fulfilled and grateful when I can fully answer the question by sharing the following:

> *Your body is a sacred gift from G-d. In Judaism, sex is not just a physical act, but a holy act that requires your mind and heart to be completely present with your partner. In fact, the biblical word for sex is yada — to know someone in the fullest sense of the word. You must ask yourself, "Do I really know this person? Have we revealed everything we need to share with one another?" I encourage you to wait until you can answer yes to these questions with confidence, knowing that you are in a long-term committed relationship based on mutual pleasure, modesty, and dignity. We must remember that one of the most important things Judaism teaches us is personal responsibility for our own actions and for our actions toward others. My greatest hope is that you have the most fulfilling sexual relationship with a partner with whom you share the greatest and most pleasurable intimate moments.*

The subject of sexuality and teaching sex ed can be quite controversial. Fortunately, I am honored to work within a community that has embraced this essential information with an understanding that we are all sexual beings, from birth to death. I am passionate about providing teens with critical-thinking tools to make healthy choices for the rest of their lives. I believe I could not have made a better career choice, and I am grateful for the life experiences that led me on this path.

Acronyms

Our field is filled with acronyms, isn't it? Some of them come up over and over again in these essays. Rather than spell out every organizational name dozens of times, we thought we'd make a handy cheat sheet right here.

AASECT – American Association of Sexuality Educators, Counselors, and Therapists

ASET – Advanced Sexuality Educators and Trainers

CFLE – The Center for Family Life Education (changed to The Center for Sex Education in 2014)

NCFR – National Council on Family Relations

OWL – Our Whole Lives

SAR – Sexual Attitude Reassessment

SIECUS – Sexuality Information and Education Council of the United States

SSSS – The Society for the Scientific Study of Sexuality

Endnotes

[1] [Carole Adamsbaum] In those days, both SIECUS and AASECT used "Sex" in their names. It wasn't until much later that they changed this to the current preferred terminology, "Sexuality."

[2] [Jeffrey W. Anthony] "GRID" was an early term for what we now know as AIDS. It stood for "Gay-Related Immune Deficiency."

[3] [Al Craven] Being "seconded" means assigned to a job for a designated period of time, while retaining one's primary employment.

[4] [Sam Killermann] The "grown-ass man" here was my health and sex ed teacher, referring to (unfortunately) himself.

[5] [Sam Killermann] *Dabbling in Improv* is the name of my forthcoming *50 Shades* fan-fic-style memoir (I use the word *memoir* in the same way James Frey used it in his book, *One Million Little Pieces,* which is to say, very loosely.)

[6] [Sam Killermann] "Giant Sexual Exploits Elephant" is not a brilliant idea for a children's toy, or so the lawyers keep telling me.

[7] [Sam Killermann] Not to be confused with all those people who don't have genders or sexualities.

[8] [Wayne V. Pawlowski] See "In Memoriam: Terry Beresford, Abortion Pioneer" at www.rhrealitycheck.org/article/2014/04/30 /memoriam-terry-beresford-abortion-pioneer.

[9] [Mark Schoen] www.Transthemovie.com.

[10] [Mark Schoen] Beloit International Film Festival, Power in Film Award, "TRANS" (2014); Long Island Gay and Lesbian Film Festival, Transgender Award, "TRANS" (2013); Council on Social Work Education Film Festival, Audience Choice Award, "TRANS" (2013); Julien Dubuque International Film

Festival, Audience Choice Award "TRANS" (2013); Julien Dubuque International Festival, Cultural Catalyst Award, "TRANS" (2013); Fresno Reel Pride Film Festival, Best Documentary, "TRANS" (2012); AASECT (American Association of Sex Educators Counselors and Therapists) Audiovisual Award, "TRANS" (2012); Louisville LGBT Film Festival, Best Documentary, "TRANS" (2012); QFEST, Philadelphia, PA, Best Documentary, "TRANS" (2012); 27th Torino GLBT Film Festival in Turin, Italy, Best Documentary, "TRANS" (2012).

[11] [Mark Schoen] *Using Sexually Explicit Media to Educate,* Mark Schoen, PhD. www.sexsmartfilms.com/news_explicit Education (2009).

[12] [Mark Schoen] *The Language of Love,* "A modern advanced film about sexual education and behavior, based on the clinical research made by famous American and Swedish doctors. The film centers around a panel: Inge and Sten Hegeler, Maj-Brith Bergstroem-Walan and Sture Cullhed. All are well known, reputable experts who have devoted their scientific studies to the various fields of sexual life. The film deals with all kinds of problems connected with the sexual relationship of people. Every question is discussed by the panel, while the film illustrates the discussions, i.e., the difference between male and female sexual organs and their functions, positions, and authentic coition is explained, while a split-screen system is used, enabling us to see the various reactions in different parts of the body. In connection with this as well as in other parts of the film, diagrams and animations are used to simplify the understanding of the complicated reactions that occur when a person is experiencing sexual stimulus. The panel also discusses the role of sex in society, the question of prejudices and taboos, sex in clothes, sex in art, etc., etc." Written by Stefan Nylen, red@defekt.cinemacabre.se (1969).

[13] [Mark Schoen] This film, and many of the films mentioned in this essay, are available at SexSmartFilms.com.

[14] [Mark Schoen] *Bellybuttons Are Navels,* Mark Schoen, Illustrated by M. J. Quay, Introduction by Mary Steichen Calderone, 1980.

[15] [Bill Taverner] Taverner, W. J. (1990). "Men's Responses to their Partner's Abortions," unpublished manuscript. Please indulge me while I cite myself. I don't think anyone other than my college professor, Carol Stenger, has ever actually read this.

[16] [Leslie Walker-Hirsch] Circles® and the Circles Paradigm© and related content are registered trademarked and copyrighted materials of the James Stanfield Company, Inc. Used by permission only, All Rights Reserved.

[17] [Susie Wilson] This excerpt is part of a chapter in the recently published book, *Still Running: A Memoir,* by Susie Wilson, available without cost from the author at susie.wilson@comcast.net.

Notes

_____

_____

_____

_____

_____

_____

_____

_____

_____

_____

_____

_____

_____

_____

_____

Notes

_____

_____

_____

_____

_____

_____

_____

_____

_____

_____

_____

_____

_____

_____

_____

_____

Notes

_____

_____

_____

_____

_____

_____

_____

_____

_____

_____

_____

_____

_____

_____

Notes

_____

_____

_____

_____

_____

_____

_____

_____

_____

_____

_____

_____

_____

_____

Notes

_____

_____

_____

_____

_____

_____

_____

_____

_____

_____

_____

_____

_____

_____

www.SexEdStore.com

Notes

_____

_____

_____

_____

_____

_____

_____

_____

_____

_____

_____

_____

_____

_____

Notes

_____

_____

_____

_____

_____

_____

_____

_____

_____

_____

_____

_____

_____

_____

Notes

HAVE ONE OF OUR
SEX ED
TRAINERS AT YOUR NEXT EVENT!

The Center for Sex Education's nationally known trainers present **workshops** and deliver **keynote addresses** that help professionals teach about safer sex and other sexual health topics.

Attendees leave our programs empowered with the skills and confidence to teach sex ed. (Plus ready-to-use lessons!)

Our trainers have many years of experience providing sexuality education in an array of settings, and are widely respected as leaders in the field.

To arrange a speaker at your next event, please contact
(973) 387-5161 or email
Info@SexEdStore.org

CAROLE ADAMSBAUM

JEFFREY W. ANTHONY

LAUREN BARINEAU

BRANDY BARNETT

RACHEL BILLOWITZ

PEGGY BRICK

STEVE BROWN

BARBARA BUNTING

MICHAEL CARRERA

JENNY CARUSO

REBECCA CHALKER

KAREN B. K. CHAN

JULIE CHAYA

DEBRA CHRISTOPHER

BARBARA HUSCHER COHEN

HEATHER CORINNA

AL CRAVEN

MELANIE DAVIS

KIRSTEN DEFUR

MELISSA KEYES DIGIOIA

SHANNA M. DUSABLON DRONE

CATHERINE DUKES

JOYCELYN ELDERS

JOANNA GATTUSO

ASHLEY GAUNT

CHARLIE GLICKMAN

AMY JO GODDARD

EVA S. GOLDFARB

THE REV. DEBRA W. HAFFNER

LYNN HAMMOND

JOYCE HUNTER

JACQUELINE JAFFE O'DUOR

PAUL JOANNIDES

AMY JOHNSON

SAM KILLERMANN

DARREL LANG

ERIN LIVENSPARGER

LUCA MAURER

KONNIE MCCAFFREE

CONNIE NEWMAN

BRANDYE NOBILING

SU NOTTINGHAM

JOAN O'LEARY

WAYNE V. PAWLOWSKI

MARY JO PODGURSKI

KAREN RAYNE

REBECCA ROBERTS

LAURENCIA HUTTON ROGERS

TIMAREE SCHMIT

MARK SCHOEN

ELIZABETH SCHROEDER

ROBERT SELVERSTONE

JESSICA L. SHIELDS

ELEANOR R. SMITH

JUDITH STEINHART

BILL TAVERNER

ANTHONY THOMPSON

KELSEY VAN NICE

AL VERNACCHIO

LESLIE WALKER-HIRSCH

SUSIE WILSON

JEAN WORKMAN

MARA YACOBI